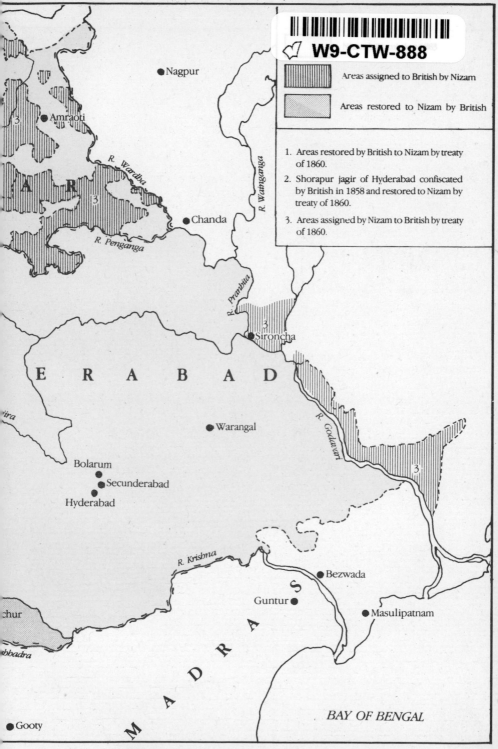

Nagpur

Amraoti

3

3

R. Wardha

A   R   A

R

Chanda

R. Pengangа

R. Wainganga

R. Pranhita

Sironcha

3

BAR

E   R   A   B   A   D

Warangal

Bolarum

Secunderabad

Hyderabad

R. Godavari

3

R. Krishna

Bezwada

Guntur

Masulipatnam

M   A   D   R   A   S

chur

bbadra

Gooty

BAY OF BENGAL

The Nizam's Dominions

W9-CTW-888

Areas assigned to British by Nizam

Areas restored to Nizam by British

1. Areas restored by British to Nizam by treaty of 1860.

2. Shorapur jagir of Hyderabad confiscated by British in 1858 and restored to Nizam by treaty of 1860.

3. Areas assigned by Nizam to British by treaty of 1860.

HYDERABAD AND BRITISH PARAMOUNTCY

1858–1883

Sir Salar Jung I

HYDERABAD AND BRITISH PARAMOUNTCY
1858–1883

BHARATI RAY

DELHI
OXFORD UNIVERSITY PRESS
BOMBAY CALCUTTA MADRAS
1988

Oxford University Press, Walton Street, Oxford OX2 6DP

New York   Toronto
Delhi   Bombay   Calcutta   Madras   Karachi
Petaling Jaya   Singapore   Hong Kong   Tokyo
Nairobi   Dar es Salaam
Melbourne   Auckland

and associates in
Beirut   Berlin   Ibadan   Nicosia

SBN 19 562231 6

Typeset and printed in India
at Crescent Printing Works Private Limited, New Delhi 110001
and published by S. K. Mookerjee, Oxford University Press
Y.M.C.A. Library Building, Jai Singh Road, New Delhi 110001

In memory of
my father
and
to my mother

Contents

Illustrations

The illustrations listed above are reproduced with the permission of the following:

[1] Andhra Pradesh State Archives   [2] Din Dayal Collection
[3] The National Library, Calcutta   [4] © The British Library
[5] Permission applied for

Preface

This book is a revised version of my doctoral dissertation entitled 'British Policy Towards Hyderabad, 1858–1883', submitted to Calcutta University. It seeks to analyse the specific policy that the British followed towards Hyderabad, the premier princely state in India for twenty-five years, the motives that actuated and the forces that dictated that policy, the agents who executed it and the pattern of the execution. The impact on Hyderabad and the interaction of the British and Hyderabadi strategies have naturally come within the scope of the study, although to a limited extent.

The policy of the British towards the princely states constitutes one of the most important segments of their imperial strategy in India. The manner in which they allowed these states to survive as distinct political entities and controlled them through the special form of indirect rule, known as paramountcy, offers a fascinating field of investigation to historians and political scientists alike. And yet, while modern Indian historiography has focussed considerable attention on British India, the history of the Indian states, which formed one-third of the subcontinent, is largely unwritten. Only a few serious studies have been made so far on princely India. The first generation of writers, of whom the most well known was Sir William Lee-Warner (*The Native States of India*, 1894), followed by Sir Charles Tupper (*Our Indian Protectorate*, 1893), represented the imperialist standpoint and adopted a legalistic approach. Clearly, their object was to assert, formalize and justify the superimposition of paramountcy—that vague yet all-embracing concept—which the British wielded or claimed to wield over the Indian states. It was, of course, convenient for the paramount power to keep paramountcy undefined. Its spokesman, Lee-Warner, who was a member of the Indian Civil Service, wrote in an atypical Canningite fashion, 'There is a paramount power in the British Crown, but perhaps its extent is wisely left undefined. There is a subordination in the Native states, but perhaps it is better understood and not explained.' Lee-Warner thus played a seminal role in the evolution of the theory and concept of paramountcy and his interpretation was officially upheld and developed through many years.

In the first half of the twentieth century a second series of writings appeared. This school, the chief exponents of which were K. M. Panikkar and K. R. R. Sastry, highlighted the princes' point of view in the context of their relations with the paramount power. They sought to establish the princes' right to autonomy and to the continuance of a distinct existence. The dominant theme of all these works was the origin of paramountcy, the extent of its jurisdiction as well as the legal theories concerning it; they did not touch upon the intricacies of the system by which paramountcy operated or its impact and import. The problems as they saw them were, in the main, the relation of the Rajas with the Raj. On the other side of the fence was Edward Thompson who argued that the princes had been 'picked up' and 'set' in their 'positions' by the paramount power.

In the course of the past few years another set of well-researched, scholarly studies has emerged; a series of new questions are being asked and new and more sophisticated interpretations evolved. Why did the British choose and follow the policy they did? What did they hope to gain in political and economic terms? Historical scholarship has now established the princes as bulwarks of British rule in India; on the 'unsteady base of foreign soil' the Raj needed collaborators and the princes were chosen as its principal local allies. The Raj's policy towards the princes has been placed in this perspective, while a penetrating look is being directed to the society and politics within the states, the contradictions implicit in the internal system, etc. Most of the recent works are really concerned with the downfall of the states. While Urmila Phadnis, *Towards the Integration of the Indian States, 1919-1947* (1968) offers a thesis on the development of events and forces that led to the states' seemingly dramatic merger with India, Barbara Ramusack in a scholarly monograph, *The Princes in the Twilight of Empire* (1978), investigates the complex phenomenon of the dissolution of a patron-client relationship with special reference to North Indian states. L. I. and S. H. Rudolph probe why and how indirect rule did not prepare the Rajput states for independence, and Ian Copland, *The British Raj and the Indian Princes* (1982), focusses attention on the Western Indian states. Perhaps the most significant contribution in the field is a collection of articles, *People, Princes and Paramount Power* (1978), edited by Robin Jeffrey. It contains papers dealing with different aspects of British and princely politics, and studies of individual states which examine 'the social bases of princely rule'.

The dominant theme of all these studies, however, is princely India of the twentieth century. Few of these studies seek to define adequately the special qualities of paramountcy and the specific characteristics of its operation as they were reflected in particular state-arenas in the nineteenth century, the period on which I have done my work. Besides, the main thrust of the current researches on Indian states is about why and how the people and the princes responded the way they did to the paramount power's role, and whether and how far the changes in the states were really responses to the British intrusion. ·The focus is on the extent to which British imperial attitudes were reflexes of the natural internal tensions of the areas they ruled. But this perspective leaves in the shadows other major factors of imperialism, viz., its own logic of expansion, its need for maintaining the already superimposed system, the multiple interest groups at home and their mutual interactions. Moreover, the nature of the pressures exerted on the Indian states by the imperial power is clearly a dimension that needs careful and intensive investigation. It is this, the character and intensity of these pressures, the objects of the Raj, and its system of operation in a given state-arena that commanded my interest. This study is not *per se* an intensive review of Nizam–British relations; it does not intend to look closely at the society and polity of Hyderabad, still less to interpret Hyderabad's policy in terms of its own political, social and economic compulsions. This is a study of the facts and policy of paramountcy, confined to a definite arena, for a fixed period of time.

I chose Hyderabad, a twenty-one gun state, as the field of my investigation and decided to focus on the post-1857 period. Of the authorities on Hyderabad, Syed Hossain Bilgrami and C. Willmott, *Historical and Descriptive Sketch of His Highness the Nizam's Dominion* (1883-4) and Moulavi Cherag Ali, *Hyderabad (Deccan) Under Sir Salar Jung* (1886), give a long and detailed account of the internal history and administration of the state during this period, while Karen Leonard in several excellent articles investigates the multiple relationships existing between the ruler, the Minister, the nobility, the bureaucracy and various other groups of people in the state, the changing social compositions of the groups and the Mulki–Non-Mulki conflict. With regard to the relations of the British with Hyderabad, we have Briggs' masterly book, *The Nizam* (1861) and H.Fraser's *Our*

Faithful Ally, the Nizam (1865) both of which narrate the story sub-stantively up to 1857. More recently, Sarojini Regani has produced a well-documented study on the subject for the period from 1724 to 1857. I decided to begin the story where Regani and Briggs leave it. V. K. Bawa's doctoral dissertation, 'Hyderabad in Transition under Salar Jang I, 1853–1883; An Indian State under British Influence' (Tulane University, 1967), gives good coverage to the period, but does not take into account private papers, apart from those of Salar Jung. My investigations, on the other hand, have concentrated very extensively on private papers in India and abroad.

The importance of Hyderabad, the largest princely state, lay in its central geographical position, which is of supreme importance since the first instinct of the British was to look at the state strategically; its rich soil, a lucrative field for large capital investment and for the supply of raw materials for industry; and the Nizam's status as the greatest Muslim prince in India. The first to embrace the subsidiary alliance, although never annexed or conquered by the British, it maintained a semi-independent existence in name, while in practice, like others of its kind, it was under the full sway of British paramountcy. This study commences with 1858 and the subsequent changes that gave a definite shape to British imperial attitudes in the following decades when paramountcy became formalized. In 1869 a minor succeeded as the Nizam and the British used the occasion to push their claims and establish new rights and precedents. The fact that throughout the period from 1858 to 1883 Hyderabad was ad-ministered by its greatest Minister and effective ruler, Salar Jung, who in one sense was a principal collaborator of the British power and at the same time its chief adversary, added a further dimension to the study. The history of Hyderabad from 1858 to 1883 reveals how British paramountcy, already superimposed on the state, assumed wider significance, how it was resisted by Salar Jung, how that resistance was ultimately overcome by the British and what the consequences were of that final triumph.

Given this context, I asked a few basic questions. If princely rule was upheld in the interests of the Raj, what specific role, if any, was assigned to Hyderabad in its power-structure? I was also curious to discover how the British treated a faithful ally, who had stood by them during the crisis of 1857. Did they show him any specially favourable consideration? Further, I wanted to find out how the system of indirect rule actually worked and to map out the system of alliances that the

British evolved within the domestic situation of the state. It is now known that British intervention worked at several levels and that in the Indian states, just as in British India, they ruled through collaborators within the internal system. Since the princes, however loyal, could not be fully trusted—they knew themselves to be the rightful rulers—the British had to build up an internal system of checks and balances. The best way obviously was to forge an alliance with the Minister and to use him as an agent of modernization of the state along British lines. As Copland rightly observes, the British believed that the Ministers represented a constitutional counterweight to royal autocracy, an impression which the princely state Ministers did their best to foster. How did the British try to utilize the traditional rivalry between the ruler and the Minister? How did they devise a pattern that kept them conveniently divided? And what happened if their political arithmetic went wrong and the carefully maintained balance threatened to snap when the Minister proved not-so-tractable and as determined as the prince to free the state from the bonds of overpowering, overweening paramountcy?

In Hyderabad, the pro-British Salar Jung, along with his non-Mulki, English-educated bureaucracy imported from British India, had striven successfully for the physical modernization of the state. He had co-operated with the Resident in multiple ways, but he, too, slowly started to challenge British authority, to break through the cordon of diplomatic isolation and to resent the politico-economic exploitation of the state. There was a certain dichotomy in Salar Jung's character and policy. While on the one hand he adopted British administrative ideas, on the other, he was determined to maintain the Mughal court-culture; he did not displace the old nobility, but surrounded himself with Englishmen and English-educated men; he yielded with apparent grace to various unfair demands of the Government of India, but at the same time he was keen to preserve and enhance Hyderabad's autonomy. He had probably calculated that, given the situation he was in, this was the best way of upholding Hyderabad's interests. He could not foresee that this policy was doomed to failure for factors he could not control as well as from its implicit contradictions. But how did the British react when they realized that it was the interest of the state, and not their interest, that was uppermost in the Minister's mind? They immediately turned from him and allied themselves with the retrograde party, the conservative nobility, which opposed the Minister as well as modernization. If they were awkward allies, no matter. They could be jettisoned when the time came (which did come all too soon). Imperial and pragmatic considerations, and no ideology or zest for modernization, after all, dictated British action in each state and in each case. By siding with the forces of modernization if possible, by supporting reactionary elements when necessary, British paramountcy was steadly sustained.

A related issue that comes up here is the role of the Resident in the state. It is usually held that the Resident, the man-on-the-spot, familiar with local conditions, played an important part in the formulation of specific policies towards a princely state. But Hyderabad was too important to be left to the local officer. Interestingly, all the Residents at Hyderabad apart from Meade, namely, Davidson, Yule, Bayley, and even Saunders (initially) and Temple (partly), were sympathetic to Hyderabad and had a great regard for Salar Jung. But in almost every case their advice—except that of Bayley, Ripon's chief adviser on Hyderabad—was overruled by the Governor-General. It is also significant that Calcutta's jealous regard of its rights notwithstanding, the India Office frequently intervened to play a decisive role in making the Hyderabad policy. But then, the Home Government, too, was not a free agent. It had its own politics and its own pressure-groups. What were those? How did they affect the formulation of British policy towards Hyderabad? What were the calculations that shaped the process of decision-making? The pressure-tactics of the cotton magnates and investors in Britain reveal themselves with stark reality in the British handling of Hyderabadi issues—in particular on the twin questions of Berar and the railways. Because of the crucial importance of these two issues, I have added two separate chapters on them.

It is tempting to apply Gallagher and Robinson's model relating to the 'formal' and 'informal' empire of Britain in the nineteenth century ('The Imperialism of Free Trade', *Economic History Review*, vol. 63, 1953) in the context of direct and indirect British rule in India. If there was a fundamental continuity in British expansion in the world throughout the nineteenth century, in the form of either a 'formal' or an 'informal' empire, it is equally true that there was a basic logic underlying British rule in India, direct or indirect. Although the states were not annexed by the British, they were nevertheless controlled, used or exploited by them. Nor is it true that they did not witness the techniques of colonial exploitation, like the planned promotion of products required for British industry, manipulation of tariffs to help British exports, or railway construction at high and guaranteed rates of interest for the benefit of the Empire and British capitalists.

What was the response in Hyderabad to this systematic exploitation? Was there any emergence of popular protest? The immense complexities of the forces at play in the state could well be the subject of another study, but one must ask whether Hyderabad benefited in any way from the system of indirect rule. Did the changes that occurred have any roots in society? Does Hyderabad owe her modernization solely to the paramount power? These and other related issues came up before me. In trying to explore them I have tried to look at the rough outlines of British policy regarding the princely states and then examine their application in the specific state-arena of Hyderabad.

None of the studies of Hyderabad, to my surprise, makes any use of the private correspondence between the Secretaries of State and the Governors-General and between the latter and their agents, the Residents. It was there that I looked for a deeper comprehension of the motives that actuated policy-making and the forces that propelled them. This work is based primarily on these private papers. I have consulted the Canning Papers preserved in the Leeds Archives, which reveal the story of how a loyal prince and an even more loyal Minister were treated after 1857. The Wood Papers and the Gladstone Papers in the India Office Library and the Ripon Papers and Elgin Papers in the British Museum were used by me concerning their policy towards Hyderabad. At the India Office Library, I also went through the very valuable series of manuscripts known as the Temple Collection. The letters between Salar Jung and Richard Temple and Temple's day-to-day political diary offer an insight into the role of a Resident in a princely state. The papers of Claude Clerk, which I discovered in the same Library, give a good idea of contemporary Hyderabadi politics and the jockeying for power that went on in a princely state. Microfilm copies of the papers of Argyll, Dalhousie, Curzon, Lawrence, Lytton, Northbrook, Mayo and Salisbury, available at the National Archives of India, are a mine of information about British policy and the interplay of multiple forces in London and Calcutta as well as a tripartite tussle between London, Calcutta and Hyderabad on vital issues like Berar and the railways. The Salar Jung papers at the State Archives, Andhra Pradesh, throw light on the other side of the story. I have also used relevant unpublished official records and a number of published works to fill in the details of the working of the system of indirect rule.

I have great pleasure in recording my gratitude to those who helped me in the pursuit of my study. I am deeply indebted to my research supervisor, Professor Amales Tripathi, for his guidance. Sincere thanks are due to the staff of the British Museum and Library and the India Office Library, London, the Central Library, Leeds, the National Archives of India, New Delhi, the Andhra Pradesh State Archives, Hyderabad, and the National Library, Calcutta, for their cordial cooperation. I would like to acknowledge specially my debt to the Earl of Harewood for his gracious courtesy in allowing me to use and publish materials from the Canning Papers which are his property; to the British Library for permitting me to publish a letter from Sir Salar Jung to Sir Richard Temple; to Hemlata Jain for her consent to the reproduction of several photographs from Raja Din Dayal Collection; to the editor of *The Indian Economic and Social History Review* for letting me use my published article; to Pritish Nandy for his personal interest and help; to Professor Sabyasachi Bhattacharya for his suggestions; to the anonymous referee of the OUP for his comments; to Professor Parthasarathi Gupta, Dr Narayani Gupta and Professor Sarojini Regani for their assistance; to Dr V. K. Bawa for letting me have a look at his unpublished thesis; to Rosemary Beaumont for the trouble she took to assist me in England; to Chandra Uttam and Ida Selwyn for their cooperation and, finally, to the members of my family for their support.

Bharati Ray

Abbreviations

Actg.	Acting
Addl.	Additional
Adm.	Administration
App.	Appendix
A.R. & C	Agriculture, Revenue and Commerce
Asst.	Assistant
Co.	Company
Chap.	Chapter
Com.	Commerce
Consult.	Consultation
Court	Court of Directors
Dept.	Department
D.O.	Demi-official
Desp.	Despatch
Dy.	Deputy
E.I.Co.	East India Company
E.I.R.	East Indian Railway
Encl.	Enclosure, enclosed with
F.	*Fasli*
Fin.	Finance, financial
For.	Foreign
G.I.P.	Great Indian Peninsular Railway
.Genl.	General
G.G.	Governor–General
G.G. in C.	Governor–General in Council
Gov.	Governor
Govt.	Government
H.	*Hijri*
H.S.	*Halli Sicca*
IB	India Board
IO	India Office
LB	Letter Book
Mily.	Military

N.D.	Not dated
No.	Number
Offg.	Officiating
Pol.	Political
P.P.	Parliamentary Papers
Progs.	Proceedings
Pvt.	Private
P.W.D.	Public Works Department
Res.	British Resident at Hyderabad
Rev.	Revenue
Rly.	Railway
Sec.	Secret
Secy.	Secretary. Unless otherwise mentioned, For. Secy., Home Secy., P.W.D. Secy., and Mily Secy., mean Secretary to the Government of India in the Foreign Department, Home Department, Public Works Department and Military Department respectively.
Sup.	Supplementary
Supdt.	Superintendent
S.S.	Secretary of State (for India)
Tel.	Telegram
Vol.	Volume

Prologue

If you were to visit the city of Hyderabad today, the minarets of the Charminar and the treasures of the Salar Jung museum would recall the vision of a state with all the trappings of a medieval kingdom. The very name, Nizam, the title of the former rulers of Hyderabad, evokes the picture of a resplendent Mughal prince, of untold riches and priceless jewels. This picture, of course, is more romantic than realistic. Regardless of the Nizam's family jewels, his Government was often hard pressed for money. The last of the Nizams, Mir Osman Ali Khan,[1] died about two decades ago, yet the aura of his name still lingers in the memory of the people of Hyderabad. His state, now part of the Republic of India, has been distributed between the states of Maharashtra and Andhra Pradesh.[2] His one-time capital still remains a capital city, for the state of Andhra Pradesh, and bears the memory of its captivating past as the nerve centre of the Nizam's dominion.

The state of Hyderabad in the nineteenth century occupied a very central and strategic position on the map of the Indian peninsula. It spread over an area of 97,728 square miles (comprising Berar or the Berars, i.e., East and West Berar),[3] and formed, as it were, the very core of the Deccan. Flung almost completely across the Indian peninsula, it could, in an emergency, isolate the south of India from the north. The state possessed natural boundaries on three sides and covered the centre of the Deccan from the river Tapti in the north to the Tungabhadra in the south. On the west it was bounded by the Maratha territories and in the east it extended just beyond the rivers Wardha and Godavari. The northern and western parts of the state were well known for their fertile black soil. The southern and eastern parts yielded rich rice crops. In fact, the entire state was well covered with rivers, and so bore abundant produce, the principal crops being jowar, bajra, wheat, rice, sesamum, linseed, pulses and cotton.

The state of Hyderabad had originally been built upon the ruins of the Kutubshahi kingdom of Golconda, one of the five Sultanates into which the Bahmani kingdom had been split. Golconda was annexed by Emperor Aurangzeb in 1687. Since then, the country had become a part of the Mughal Empire and remained so until the dissolution of the Empire. The first Nizam, Asaf Jah I, of Turkoman descent, was appointed by Emperor Furrukhsiyar as viceroy of the six Deccan provinces and the *faujdar* of the Carnatic in 1713. He was given the title of Nizam-ul-Mulk Bahadur Fateh Jung, a title which thereafter became the hereditary title of the family, finally to be abolished in 1970.

The Nizam-ul-Mulk came to the Deccan when it was in a state of complete confusion. With rare tact and courage he restored order and re-established imperial authority in the provinces within a comparatively short time. He was made the Chief Minister or *Wazir* of Delhi in 1722—during Emperor Muhammad Shah's rule—but, disgusted with the factions at the imperial court, he resigned his position and marched towards the Deccan. The troops that the offended Emperor sent after him were defeated, but Muhammad Shah, showing great diplomatic foresight, accepted the defeat with grace. He allowed the Nizam to continue as the viceroy in the Deccan and, in order to conciliate him, conferred on him the title of Asaf Jah, another hereditary title. The Nizam on his part sent a letter of submission to the Emperor expressing sentiments of obedience and loyalty. Henceforward the Nizam ruled Hyderabad as a *de facto* independent ruler and made the city of Hyderabad the capital of his dominion. Thus began the autonomous rule of a provincial dynasty, the Asaf Jahi or Asuphea dynasty, in the Deccan at about the same time that another provincial dynasty, founded by Murshid Quli Khan, established itself in the eastern part of India, Bengal. Outwardly, however, Asaf Jah never threw off his allegiance to the Emperor and remained loyal to him throughout his rule. The coins of the state were struck, and the *khutba* read, in the Emperor's name. When Nadir Shah, king of Persia, invaded India in 1739, the Nizam rendered valuable services to his sovereign and negotiated the peace settlement with Nadir Shah. It is said that before his departure Nadir Shah offered this obviously capable man the throne of Delhi. The Nizam, to his credit, did not succumb to the temptation and said, 'I and my ancestors have, from ancient times, been in the service of the King of Delhi. Such an impropriety of conduct on my part will make me notorious as one untrue to salt.'[4]

Thanks to his overlordship in the Carnatic, the first Nizam himself came into direct contact with the French and English trading companies,[5] then fighting with each other for commercial supremacy in the Coromondal coast. He was astute enough not to be seriously involved in the war between the foreign traders, or to allow them to exert any influence on the internal affairs of his state. His successors, unfortunately, were less discreet. Immediately after his death, they started wars of succession among themselves, and each candidate invoked the help of either the English or the French. Consequently, they became embroiled in the Anglo-French wars in South India and, worse still, gave the foreigners an opportunity first to interfere in, and later to establish control over, their state.

The initial success in Hyderabad lay with the French under the able leadership of Bussy until Nizam Salabat Jung, Asaf Jah I's third son, decided to change sides, a decision obviously influenced by a series of brilliant British victories in the Carnatic and Bengal. He concluded a treaty with the British in 1759 and conferred on them as a free gift the two *sarkars* of Masulipatam and Nizamapatam, which gave them a firm foothold in the Carnatic.[6] Nizam Ali, the fourth and youngest son of Asaf Jah I, who usurped the government in 1761 made no change in his brother's policy. On the other hand, by two treaties, concluded respectively in 1766 and 1768, he handed over the Northern Sarkars to the East India Company. For its part, the Company promised to help the Nizam with a body of troops whenever he required it, and when he did not, to pay him an annual *peshkush* of Rs 9 lakhs for the Northern Sarkars.[7]

The Company's promise of help did not work in practice as the Nizam might have hoped. On more than one occasion, Nizam Ali drifted into war, or seemed about to drift into war with the Marathas, his traditional rivals. In the first instance, Governor-General Cornwallis, who needed the assistance of both the Nizam and the Marathas to fight Tipu Sultan, managed to bring about a triple alliance between the Marathas, the Nizam and the East India Company.[8] Though the Nizam gained some territory by the treaty of Seringapatam following Tipu's defeat in 1792, the alliance with the Marathas was too fragile to last. The Nizam's second appeal for help from the Company against the Marathas was treated as unsympathetically as the first. Cornwallis' successor, Sir John Shore, had no desire to intervene in the hostilities amongst the Indian states.[9]

The Marathas attacked and defeated the Nizam at Kharda in 1795. The Nizam was forced to conclude a humiliating treaty with them, by which he had to cede territories yielding an annual revenue of Rs 30 lakhs. Nizam Ali was thoroughly alienated by what he considered abandonment by the British and, making up his mind to depend henceforward on the French rather than the British, he handed over the training of his troops to French officers. The most important of them was Francois Raymond who disciplined and trained an army of 14,000 men and was soon assigned territories yielding Rs 16 lakhs a year for the maintenance of these troops.[10] This posed a grave threat to the British in the Deccan, and they needed a man who could restore to them their former power. They found him in Marquess Wellessley, who came out to India as Governor-General in April 1798.

With the introduction of Wellesley to the Indian scene, Hyderabad–British relations changed dramatically. The initiative and the decision-making authority seemed to be completely taken over by the British. Wellesley, a hard-core imperialist, came to India with the ambition of furthering British expansion and obliterating French influence in the country. To do this properly, it was necessary to crush Tipu, the most formidable foe of the British in the south, whom he regarded as a friend of the French. Wellesley thus concluded a treaty with the Nizam in September 1798. It made the British troops at Hyderabad permanent and increased their numbers, and disbanded all French troops in the service of the Nizam.[11] This was the first of Wellesley's subsidiary treaties with Indian states. With it, the East India Company's military frontier was shifted to the territorial frontier of its ally, with absolutely no cost to itself.

Tipu was finally defeated and killed at the battle of Seringapatam by the allied forces of the Nizam and the Company. With his death the whole of Mysore was made available to the East India Company. The astute Wellesley did not care to divide the country equally among the allies. Such a solution would have placed in the hands of the Nizam many of the strong fortresses on the northern frontier of Mysore and would have therefore weakened the British frontier in that quarter. By the Partition Treaty of 1799, the Nizam and the East India Company each took a chunk of territory from Mysore and the rest was placed under a Hindu Raja who was brought into a subsidiary alliance with the East India Company. The Nizam was not allowed to be a party in this alliance. If the Nizam was disappointed, he was also helpless. Wellesley was 'prepared' to carry out the new treaty with 'British arms alone'.[12]

With the removal of Tipu, the East India Company found itself thinking about the Marathas who had observed with growing jealousy the increasing power of the British. The Maratha threat brought the Nizam and the British closer to each other, and consequently a treaty was signed between them in 1800. The treaty increased the size of the subsidiary force in Hyderabad. It also required the Nizam to provide for its payment, and this he did through the cession to the Company of all the territories he had acquired by the treaties of 1792 and 1799 with Mysore. In times of war the Nizam agreed to spare the subsidiary force and help the East India Company with 6,000 infantry and 9,000 horses from his own troops. The Nizam was forbidden to negotiate with foreign powers without consulting the East India Company, but the Company recognized the Nizam's absolute rights over his children, subjects and servants.[13]

In the history of Nizam–British relations the importance of this treaty cannot be exaggerated. The territorial gains the British made put the resources for the support of the subsidiary army completely under their control, and defined their frontiers along the Krishna and Tungabhadra rivers. The treaty, so advantageous to the British, deprived the Nizam of territory, reputation and power. He lost his share of the spoils from the Mysore wars. His sovereignty was curtailed as his power to deal with foreign states was gone, while the Company was left free to make peace or war in any part of India without consulting him. Hyderabad, once an equal ally, became essentially a protected state.

Nor did Wellesley ignore trade. To him belongs the credit of officially settling the commercial relations between the East India Company and the Nizam's Government. By the treaty of 1802, concluded between the Company and the Nizam, it was decided that the produce and manufacture of one state would enter the other on paying a duty of 5 per cent on the prime cost. All locally imposed *radharry* or transit duties which had so far impeded the free flow of trade were abolished.[14] The way was opened for the penetration of British manufactured goods into the Hyderabad market.

By the time Wellesley left India in 1805, the pattern of the Company's Indian Empire had clearly emerged. The British were supreme in Bengal; the Mughal Emperor Shah Alam II had come under their protection. The Peshwa, Bhonsla and Sindhia had all accepted subsidiary alliances, the French had been totally disbanded, and Mysore was a protected state. The East India Company prepared to tighten its hold over Hyderabad still further. The state was already under the Company's control in all its external affairs; it would now be dominated internally by the Company as well. The East India Company decided to established its sway over the state through the Resident.[15]

The Resident had neither any legislative nor executive authority; nevertheless, his wishes were obeyed as representing those of the Governor-General. As the Nizam's co-operation could not be fully depended upon, it was considered good policy to place the administration of the state under the control of an exclusively pro-British Minister.[16] But this step embittered Anglo-Nizam relations and also introduced a kind of dual government with divided and undefined responsibility.

In 1804 the Resident persuaded Sikandar Jah, Nizam Ali's successor, to appoint the pro-British Mir Alam the Dewan. On Mir Alam's death, the Nizam chose Munir-ul-Mulk as the Dewan, but was forced by the Resident to appoint Raja Chandu Lal, a puppet of the British, as *Peshkar*. It was arranged that the actual administration would remain in the hands of the *Peshkar* and Munir-ul-Mulk would not interfere with his administration. The Nizam, divested of all power, ceased to take any interest in the administration. Chandu Lal was well aware that his position in office depended solely on his subservience to the Resident's wishes. He ruled Hyderabad without any check from the titular head, neither in the people's nor in the ruler's interest, but in the interest of the British. His greatest service to his real masters was the extension of active support to Russell, who came as Resident in 1811, in the organization and maintenance of the Russell Brigade, which formed the basis upon which the Hyderabad Contingent was subsequently organized.

According to the treaty of 1800, the Nizam was to help the East India Company with troops in times of war. Russell, finding the Nizam's army not quite up to the British standards, reformed two battalions which were known as the Russell Brigade. They were armed and equipped like the East India Company's troops, and functioned like a part of the Company's army. They were never engaged in the Nizam's service but were paid for by the Resident at the Nizam's cost. To acquire the money for this payment Chandu Lal became involved in disreputable financial transactions with Messrs Palmer & Company,[17] and together they managed to 'lend' the Nizam a sum of Rs 60 lakhs at the exorbitant rate of interest of 33½ per cent a year. The swindle continued until the upright Metcalfe succeeded Russell as Resident and stopped the plunder.[18] When Fraser came as Resident in 1838 Chandu Lal fell out completely with him. Embarassed by immense financial difficulties, he tendered his resignation in September 1843, leaving Hyderabad in a state of disorder and bankruptcy.

Meanwhile, Sikander Jah had been succeeded on the throne by his elder son Nasir-ud-Daula, and Siraj-ul-Mulk was made Dewan in 1846. The new Dewan's main concern was the acquisition of money for the upkeep of the Hyderabad Contingent. Under the care of Chandu Lal and the British Residents, it had grown into a formidable body. It consisted of five regiments of cavalry, eight regiments of infantry and five companies of artillery, a medical department, and arsenals at the principal military stations.[19] Each part of the Nizam's dominion was within a few days' march from one or other of the army's cantonments, which kept the whole state under the control of a troop that was virtually the East India Company's own.

Everything connected with this outrageously expensive force was managed on a princely scale. Since the Resident sanctioned appointments, managed the army and sent the bills to the Nizam, there was no effort at all to reduce the expenditure. 'The poor Nizzy pays for all' was a proverb in those days.[20] But the Nizam had no means to pay and his dues were constantly in arrears. To meet these demands the Nizam farmed out districts, pawned state jewels and borrowed money from the Company's Government. To that Government, therefore, the Nizam gradually became more and more indebted. His debts amounted to Rs 37 lakhs in 1847, the year before Lord Dalhousie came to India as Governor-General.

Dalhousie appeared not to care about certain fundamental requirements of social and political morality. He represented a particularly aggressive form of his Government's policy of annexation and imperialism. He saw the depth of Hyderabad's misfortune, but chose to ignore Resident Fraser's recommendation to save the state from financial catastrophe. It was not his 'mission', after all, to 'regenerate' misgoverned Indian states.[21] He therefore watched the Nizam dismiss his capable Minister Siraj-ul-Mulk and increase his debt with the East India Company. Then the Governor-General, his hands freed from the Punjab wars, instructed the Resident to inform the Nizam that his whole debt was to be paid off by 31 December 1850. That, of course, could not be done. Dalhousie immediately proposed that the Company take a part of the Nizam's territory in settlement of the debt and asked the Resident to suggest suitable districts.[22] Fraser pointed out that Berar and the Raichur Doab were by far the most fertile parts of the Nizam's domain, but he mentioned that it would not be fair to the

Nizam to occupy them. Dalhousie saw no need to go by Fraser's opinion and called upon the Nizam to deliver to the Resident the specified districts.[23] The cornered Nizam re-appointed Siraj-ul-Mulk as Dewan, but could pay off only a part of his debt.[24] The debt soon rose to Rs 50 lakhs. Dalhousie chose this moment to strike,[25] bullied Fraser out of office and appointed the subservient Colonel Low in his place.

The Governor-General sent the draft of a treaty to Low with instructions to negotiate with the Nizam. The negotiations would concern settlement of his debt and, as a security for future payment to the Contingent, permanent (or failing that, temporary) cession of Berar and the Raichur districts.[26] Becuase of the Nizam's extreme dislike for the word 'in perpetuity', Low urged a temporary cession only. In an interview with the Nizam he pressed the Nizam to sign the treaty. 'If you say no', Low warned the Nizam, 'I shall regret it for your own sake.'[27] The Nizam was extremely unwilling to conclude the treaty but a note from the Assistant Resident to the Minister informed him that British troops were going to be moved into Hyderabad.[28] In the face of this thinly veiled threat of military action, the Nizam eventually agreed to sign on the dotted line.[29]

The treaty of 1853 between the Nizam and the East India Company laid down that the subsidiary troops would consist of eight battalions of sepoys and two regiments of cavalry with the requisite guns and artillery. It would be employed only to render important services, like the protection of the Nizam and his heirs, and not on minor jobs. The East India Company was to maintain under its own control an auxiliary force, styled the Hyderabad Contingent, in times of peace as well as war. It was to consist of 5,000 infantry and 2,000 cavalry with four field batteries of artillery. It would help the Nizam to put down rebels only when the 'reality of their offence' had been ascertained by the British Resident. To provide regular payment to these troops and to pay the 6 per cent interest on the debt of Rs 50 lakhs due to the East India Company by the Nizam, as well as to meet certain other commitments,[30] the Nizam assigned Berar, Raichur Doab and the districts on the border of Sholapur and Ahmednagar,[31] yielding an annual revenue of about Rs 50 lakhs, to the management of the Resident. An account of the revenue from and the expenditure on these territories was to be submitted to the Nizam every year and any surplus revenue after meeting the obligations was to be surrendered to him.[32]

The Court of Directors approved of the treaty and Sir Charles Wood, the President of the Board of Control, declared that he was 'very glad'. He had earlier advised Dalhousie to administer the Nizam's territories for the Nizam until his affairs had been 'brought round'. This was not to be a free service. 'Pay yourself for the charge', Wood had said. The terms of the treaty of 1853 had been decided by Dalhousie without Wood's knowledge or without much consideration for his advice, but Wood approved of the treaty. 'The only point in your treaty which I doubt about', he wrote to Dalhousie, 'is the accountability to him [the Nizam] and paying over any surplus.' Wood preferred the simple way. 'Take the revenue, maintain the Contingent, and let us have no accounts.' Nevertheless, he admitted that Dalhousie 'did the best that was possible' and congratulated him on his achievement.[33] 'Nagpore and the frontiers of the Nizam's territories which we occupy give us I think pretty nearly an uninterrupted line from Calcutta to Bombay.'[34] Dalhousie was pleased with his success. Low had indeed 'exceeded' his 'expectations'. 'I consider', he wrote to Low, 'the successful completion of this settlement with the Nizam as a feather in my cap.'[35]

During the transactions and negotiations that culminated in the cession of these districts to the Company, it was neither the settlement of the Nizam's debt nor the security for the payment to the Contingent that was uppermost in Dalhousie's mind. The real interest involved in the case was the British need for cotton. The cotton-textile industry of Lancashire, now Britain's premier industry, depended almost solely on the United States for its supply of raw material. To end this excessive dependence, Lancashire looked upon India as a second source of supply.[36] Berar, ideally suited for cotton culture, was taken to satisfy the cotton magnates, just as Nagpur was. In his famous Review, Dalhousie boasted that he had secured 'the finest cotton tracts' in India and thus opened up a channel of supply 'to make good a felt deficiency in the staple of one great branch of its [Britain's] manufacturing industry'.[37] Once taken, Berar was not meant to be returned, although the Nizam had been hoodwinked by the promise that the cession was merely for a time. Dalhousie wrote frankly to Low, 'Whatever may be the future surplus of revenue, these districts *will never be returned to the Nizam's Government*[38] and we must therefore plan an arrangement on a footing of permanency.'[39] That is why he had no scruples about adding the revenue of Berar to the annual income of British India.[40]

Clearly, Dalhousie did not even have the force of law, not to say the

spirit of equity, to support his demand for Berar. The Contingent, the
root cause of the trouble, was not based on any treaty. The treaty of
1800 merely provided that the Nizam's army should go to the aid of the
East India Company in times of war. 'If he [the Nizam] were to take his
stand upon the Treaty', Dalhousie privately wrote to Fraser, 'I could
not argue that either the letter or the spirit of it bound the Nizam to
maintain 9,000 troops of a peculiar and costly nature, in peace, because it bound him to give 15,000 of his troops on the occurrence of
war.'[41] Thus, to pay for an army nurtured by the British and deliberately imposed on him, the Nizam was intimidated into concluding a
humiliating treaty. 'I should lose my honour', he once told Low in a
private interview, 'by parting with my territory.' Nor could his faithful
Minister, Siraj-ul-Mulk, sustain the shock. He died on 27 May, six days
after the conclusion of the treaty.

At the suggestion of the Resident, the Nizam appointed Siraj-ul-
Mulk's nephew, Salar Jung,[42] as the new Dewan. He could have made
no better choice. This brilliant young man, destined to become the
greatest Minister that Hyderabad ever produced, was at that time only
twenty-four years of age. Well educated, highly cultured, and belonging to a family which had produced Dewans for Hyderabad for half a
century, he had already proved his worth as the *talukdar* of Khammam. As soon as he became the Dewan he devoted himself whole-
heartedly to the welfare and improvement of his state.

In 1857 Nizam Nasir-ud-Daula died and was succeeded by his son
Afzal-ul-Daula. In the same year the Great Revolt broke out.[43] Starting
as a sepoy rebellion, it soon assumed dangerous proportions and
spread among the civilian population and the dispossessed princes
and landlords in northern and central India. This was a golden opportunity for the Nizam to avenge himself for the humiliation brought
upon his father by the treaty of 1853. 'If the Nizam goes, all goes', so
telegraphed the worried Governor of Bombay to the Resident at
Hyderabad.[44] The Nizam, however, under the counsel of Salar Jung,
chose to remain faithful to the British. Salar Jung's policy during the
rising appears to have been the product of enlightened self-interest.
He must have foreseen that the British had a good chance of victory
and, in that event, he hoped to get back Berar as a reward for
Hyderabad's loyalty in the moment of crisis.

His task was not easy. Contrary to the popular notion that the
Deccan was peaceful during the Revolt, it seethed with discontent. The
people of Hyderabad hated the *feringhee* infidels. They were un-

happy over the loss of Berar as well as over the constant British interference in their administration.[45] Emissaries of Tantia Topi, *maulavis* and fakirs, and the sepoys disbanded from the Company's army, constantly urged them to take up arms against the British. The contemporary press too reported symptoms of disturbances in Hyderabad. The *Englishman* was worried about the people's 'disposition to rise' in revolt[46] and the *Bombay Telegraph and Courier* frankly asserted that the state of Hyderabad was 'a source of constant alarm' to the British in India.[47] Colonel Davidson, the Resident at Hyderabad, also reported that Hyderabad was 'a hot bed of disaffection' and that the quiet in the Nizam's dominion was 'a false tranquillity'. Any attempt on his part to arrest the anti-British element in the durbar would, he was afraid, lead to a general outbreaK.[48] In these trying circumstances, the Nizam and Salar Jung, although themselves threatened by agitators, firmly kept Hyderabad in check. Salar Jung ordered the arrest of fakirs preaching sedition and of mutineers seeking rufuge in Hyderabad. A seditious gathering at the Mecca Mosque was dispersed.

On 17 July the Residency itself was attacked. About fifteen minutes before the incident Salar Jung informed Davidson that five hundred Rohillas, headed by Maulavi Alauddin and Torabiz Khan, were marching to the Residency, and requested him to defend the Residency until the Minister could send the Nizam's troops. The Resident succeeded in defeating the rebels.[49] None the less, the fact that the agitators were permitted to proceed to the Residency and that many of them, including the two leaders, escaped proved that the Nizam's troops were not devoted to the British causes.[50] Nor was Venkatappa Naik, the Raja of Shorapur,[51] any more loyal, despite the fact that he had long been under the guardianship of an Englishman, Captain Meadows Taylor. A tributary of the Nizam, this young princeling decided to join the rebels. He was, however, defeated and captured by the joint forces of the Company and the Nizam.[52] In despair, he committed suicide and his principality was then immediately confiscated by the East India Company.

By 1858 the storm of the Great Revolt had blown over, although discontent smouldered in different parts of British India as well as in Hyderabad. The rising initiated a new era in the history of India and British policy changed and assumed new dimensions after 1858.

CHAPTER I

The Nizam's 'Reward'

'We have just got a telegram announcing fall of Delhi on 20th September. Thank God!'[1] wrote an elated Ross Mangles, Chairman of the East India Company, to Canning in October 1857. The British had recaptured Delhi from the rebels and the suppression of revolts in other areas could only be a matter of time. The relief Mangles expressed was only natural. The Revolt of 1857 had profoundly shaken the British people. The suddenness of the outbreak had caught them completely unawares and the realization of the vulnerability of British power in India had come as a rude shock.[2] Even Prime Minister Palmerston, who was usually indifferent to Indian affairs, was particularly disturbed over the news, more so because the fear of an 'eventual' Russian attack upon the sub-continent always lurked in his mind.[3]

The daunting task of dealing with the revolt fell on the shoulders of Charles John Canning. Son of a more famous Prime Minister, Canning had started his career as a Peelite and later joined the Whig cabinet of Palmerston in 1855. He came to India as Governor-General in 1856, to succeed his friend Dalhousie and to face the resentment created by Dalhousie's ruthless policy of annexation and his much hated Doctrine of Lapse. Canning was not an outstandingly brilliant man, but he was a good planner and a capable diplomat. He was soon able to restore order and proclaim peace on 8 July, 1858.[4] Extremists among the British at that time criticized his policy of moderation and diplomacy, but he was warmly congratulated by the more sober elements of his country. 'You were praised by every man whose opinion is worth having', wrote Palmerston in a flattering note.[5]

When the revolt was suppressed, and the terrible excitement of the struggle was over, the Government began a thorough reappraisal of the policy followed by the East India Company in India. It was decided that power be transferred from the hands of a trading company to the Crown and that the Company's policy vis-à-vis the princely states be reoriented.[6] The revolt had demonstrated that the sepoys on whom the Company had depended for support in India were not as loyal as had been believed. The princes whom they had regarded with suspicion, however, were clearly their chief strength. The Nizam, Sindhia, Holkar and the Punjab chiefs could be depended upon to help the British in similar emergencies if ever they should arise in future. Prudence and a sense of gratitude induced the British Government to reward the princes who had stood by them during their most difficult time.

Vernon Smith, President of the Board of Control, was not quite sure about how to reward the princes who had 'behaved well'.[7] Ross Mangles recommended merely 'some special mark of distinction from the Queen' and believed that rewards for services rendered should be prompt.[8] But Canning judged rightly that 'an order invented for the purpose is never much appreciated'. He also preferred not to reward anyone upon the first show of goodwill, and would not do anything 'that could look like a desire to buy them' until the ordeal had fairly passed.[9] It was also desirable, in the process of rewarding the princes, to further British interests in India. Canning felt that some accession of territory would generally be the most acceptable reward to the smaller chiefs and the one most easily given. To the greater chiefs—such as Sindhia and Holkar—his recommendation was some relaxation or alteration, which these chiefs would welcome, in their treaties with the British. In the process, the British would also derive some advantage. 'Many of the treaties are inconvenient to ourselves', Canning explained to Vernon Smith, 'and they have been framed at different times, with great inconsistencies. ...There is something to amend in almost all of them.[10]

While discussions were going on between the Governor-General and the Court and Board at home, Palmerston's Government fell, almost without warning, in February 1858. The Earl of Derby formed his second cabinet and Stanley took over as the President of the Board of Control. The following August, on the passing of the Act of 1858, he became the first Secretary of State for India. Stanley was probably the most generous of the men controlling the fortunes of India at the time. Land, he believed, was 'the fittest recompense' for those princes who had supported the British. 'I hope you will not be sparing of rewards, especially in land,' he wrote to Canning, 'to those native allies who have really stood by us. It is full time to show that we can recompense as well as punish.' This generosity was partly born of a shrewd policy. The princes who had stood by the British, Stanley explained to Canning, should be dealt with generously, if only to induce others to act likewise.[11]

Finally, the chiefs of small states received jagirs, houses and additional decorative titles. Of the greater states, Sindhia's territory was enlarged, although he was not given Dhar.[12] Holkar, about whose loyalty there existed some doubt, was rewarded by a slight revision of territory, though he was none too pleased with it.[13] The question of a reward for the Nizam, however, presented problems.

The Nizam had undoubtedly been a faithful ally during the Great Revolt. Vernon Smith declared before the Commons that the conduct of the Nizam and his Minister Salar Jung had prevented Indian troops in the presidencies of Madras and Bombay from revolting simultaneously with those of Bengal.[14] That some recognition of the Nizam's valuable services was called for, was, therefore, widely agreed on. Stanley, Vernon Smith's successor, wanted the Government to show its gratitude by some substantial mark of favour. Stanley had already suggested land as the best reward and expressed concern over Canning's delay in taking a decision on the subject.[15] Canning's initial reaction to the idea of giving land to princes like Sindhia or the Nizam was lukewarm; he preferred to fall back upon money-payments or the remission of contributions to the Contingents. 'Our own Revenue arrangements and customs line', he wrote to Stanley, 'and the impolicy and unfairness of making over to either of them any District which has been long under our Government, are points which must be taken into account, as also the preserving of a convenient frontier for ourselves, and of a due proportion between the rewards allotted to each.' Nevertheless, he made a strong case in favour of restoring the Assigned Districts to the Nizam as the only reward worth giving him. If this was denied, he commented, there would be nothing left but to reward the Nizam with what he called 'a shipload of truppery—gilded carriages, furniture, arms, horses etc.', buttressed by complimentary letters. 'But a restoration of the Assigned Districts—even a partial one—would be by far the most acceptable gift we could offer; and the political effect will be good. We shall show convincingly that we can sometimes relax our grasp upon the good things that come within it.'[16] Stanley had long been inclined to some measures of the kind. 'I don't believe native princes value fine words or decoration half as much as we English do; they know how little they cost; what they want is land.'[17]

Stanley was right, of course. The Nizam *did* want land. In the expectation of such a reward his Minister Salar Jung had supported the British during 1857. Salar Jung was already in correspondence with his friend Colonel J. Oliphant, a former director of the East India

Company, who had been pleading with the Home Government on the Nizam's behalf for the restoration of the Assigned Districts to him. Oliphant informed Salar Jung that the Nizam and his Minister were certainly to be rewarded for their service during 1857 and that this would be a good opportunity to retrieve the Assigned Districts. He further advised the Minister, 'Should there be any hesitation in India to do this, stand out manfully and insist upon it and it must be granted on a reference to this country.' According to him, there was a growing feeling in England that the annexation of the districts had been an arbitrary exercise of power.[18]

Unfortunately for the Nizam and Salar Jung, a change of ministry took place in Great Britain in June 1859. The Derby Ministry gave way to the second Palmerston Government and Sir Charles Wood took over from Stanley as the Secretary of State for India. This Yorkshire baronet (later made a Viscount), whom Granville described as 'the spider',[19] showed great astuteness in securing for himself a key post in the cabinet, and kept that post for seven years. A minister of long standing with previous experience at the head of the India Board, the energetic and masterful Wood enjoyed and asserted an almost unchallenged authority over Indian affairs up to 1866. Though formally a member of the Liberal Party, his imperial instincts were no less strong than Disraeli's, only less glamorous.

The change of ministry augured ill for Hyderabad. Oliphant informed Salar Jung on 17 June that the ministry had been overturned since his last letter and that Stanley was no longer head of the India Office. 'I will not say', Oliphant warned the Hyderabad Minister, 'that I think your chance is improved by the change of Ministers.' Without a favourable recommendation from Canning there was no hope that the Home Government would step in to intervene in the Nizam's favour.[20]

Oliphant proved right. Wood was less sympathetic than Stanley towards the feelings and aspirations of Indians. He would be the last person to restore the Assigned Districts to the Nizam, not to speak of intervening on his behalf with Canning's plans. During his term as President of the India Board Dalhousie had taken Berar. At that time Wood had expressed 'sorrow' that Dalhousie had not been able to 'deal on more comfortable terms.' He had complained bitterly against the two obligations imposed by the treaty of 1853—the payment of the Berar surplus and the submission of the Berar accounts to the Nizam.[21] Here was the opportunity for Wood to get what he had wanted in 1853. While rewarding the Nizam for his loyalty, a new treaty could be made with him and the Government of India could get rid of the inconvenient provisions of the treaty of 1853.

Wood had another scheme in mind, and to explain this it is necessary to digress a little. The opening of navigation in the upper Godavari had become a much-discussed political issue in England. The correspondence on this subject is voluminous. In spite of all the minute details, the problem was really very simple, viz., the interest of Manchester. As stated earlier, Manchestermen attached great importance to the supply of raw cotton from India as a reserve against excessive dependence on American cotton. The Manchester Chamber of Commerce and the Cotton Supply Association (formed in 1857) clamoured for more and more Indian cotton and pressed the Government both in and outside Parliament to procure cotton for them, and for improved communications in India to facilitate its transport.[22] The cotton people looked to Dharwar and Berar in particular, and believed that cotton from these places could easily be transported to the eastern coast of India through the river Godavari. The Godavari, often described as the 'Mississippi of India',[23] flowed for about one hundred miles through the finest cotton fields of India and its course was literally directed along the chief cotton centre of the peninsula to Coringa, a fine port on the eastern coast. The river, however, was not fully navigable, and opening it up to the cotton fields of Berar was not easy. Various impediments, like masses of rocks and a succession of waterfalls, obstructed continuous navigation, but Captain Haig claimed in his report that these impediments could be removed or avoided. If three rock barriers in the river were removed, the river would provide an excellent route into Berar and the Central Provinces, the fine cotton of Berar and Nagpur could be brought down to the eastern coast at a reduced cost and the river itself could be better used for irrigation purposes.[24]

Manchestermen in favour of the project both pressed it upon the Government and found able advocates of their cause in Parliament. The Earl of Shaftesbury neatly summarized the arguments of Manchester. 'If Godavari were opened,' he said, 'we would not have to beg that from America ... what we may have from our own India.'[25] It was further argued that the river when opened would provide a safe, speedy and cheap way of transport not only for cotton, but also for corn, millet, rice and other exportable products, and for troops and military stores as well.

Wood, under pressure from the cotton people, had encouraged the survey of the Godavari as early as 1854, when he headed the India Board.[26] As head of the India Office he took up the scheme with vigour. 'The object is', he wrote, 'to get the Berar cotton, which is very good, down, and salt and manufactured goods up the river.'[27] It was, he believed, the duty of the Government to improve the lines of communication. And a navigable channel into the heart of the Deccan was bound 'to bring the Berar cotton cheaply to the coast and would stop the mouth of our Manchester grumblers'.[28] Although Wood later lost patience with Manchester for depending too much on the Government—'they are a hopeless set' he grumbled in 1861[29]—he nevertheless played up to them. In early 1860 he directed Trevelyan, Governor of Madras, to take the necessary steps for the commencement of the Godavari works and asked Calcutta 'to spare some money' in order to enable Madras to open the river up to the southern part of the Nizam's cotton-fields.[30]

There were, however, some political difficulties regarding the matter. For about two hundred miles the Godavari ran entirely through the territory of the Nizam, and the first of the three river barriers that had to be removed lay in the Nizam's dominions. 'It would be absurd', Wood explained before the Commons, 'to commence work in a territory not belonging to the Indian Government.'[31] He decided, therefore, that the British ought to have at least one side of the river in their possession.[32] Dislodging the state of Hyderabad from one bank of the river was vital for the British for another reason. The Nizam used to levy a 5 per cent duty on all goods in transit on the river. In addition, the border zamindars also levied whatever taxes they pleased.[33] These did not suit the interests of British traders and manufacturers who, in the middle of the nineteenth century, propagated *laissez faire* economics.[34] There was thus little point in improving river navigation before the removal of the duties.

Wood had always been in favour of abolishing all transit duties.[35] 'I mean to do something for the Godavari.' He explained his scheme to Trevelyan: 'We ought to do two things, (i) to acquire possession by exchange or otherwise of the left bank of the Godavari, (ii) make some arrangements to free the navigation from tolls.'[36] Having given the whole matter some consideration, Wood decided that, while rewarding the Nizam for his loyalty, Canning might ask for some concessions as well.[37] Canning needed no persuasion. He quite saw Wood's point, i.e., rewarding the Nizam provided there was a favourable opportunity to make the necessary proposals. Taking his cue from his chief, he decided to combine the 'reward' to the Nizam with a fair measure of 'bargaining', and hoped to make an arrangement which would be 'satisfactory' to Wood.[38]

The occupation of one bank of the Godavari, Canning judged correctly, was not likely to pose too much of a problem, but Wood's wishes regarding Berar would be more difficult to accomplish. Although Canning had earlier advocated its restoration to the Nizam, he quickly changed his mind when Wood came to power. He informed Davidson that he had 'given up the thought of restoring any portion of the Assigned Districts by way of reward to the Nizam. Shorapur he must have. The rest must be eked out by presents and flummery of one sort or another.'[39]

It is not quite clear why Canning made such a *volte-face* on this issue. The only possible explanation seems to be that he had actually never been enthusiastic about the restoration, and had suggested it only to please Stanley. Aware of Wood's views on the subject, he decided to toe the line, with which he was probably more in agreement. Once he had made up his mind not to restore the Berar districts, it did not take him long to decide what he would do with them. First of all, he must get rid of the rendering of accounts, a clause which he himself disliked in the treaty of 1853. 'A more ingenious recipe for keeping up dispute and suspicions with a native government it would be impossible to invent.' 'How could we ever', he grumbled, 'with our eyes open, undertake such an obligation, I do not understand.' The treaty, he complained, gave the Governor-General all the responsibility of governing the country, but made it impossible to do so creditably without a yearly wrangle of the most undignified kind. In his view, money relations with the 'native courts' were thoroughly ill-advised.[40]

The stipulation in the treaty of 1853 providing for the payment of the Berar surplus to the Nizam had created a definite rift between the two Governments. The Nizam always complained that the British had never paid a rupee of the surplus since 1853,[41] but Canning felt that the cost of administration in Berar in the last seven years had risen so high that, in spite of increases in revenue, there had been no surplus to be handed over to the Nizam. While the Nizam expected that the cost of administration would not exceed 12½ per cent of the gross revenue, the Government of India found it impossible to secure efficient administration with so 'little' a sum. Canning did not want to force the Nizam to pay more for the administration of Berar than he would like to do, but at the same time the prospect of being bound by the limits set by the Nizam was hardly an attractive one. Canning's idea was to retain only so much of Berar as would provide for the payments guaranteed by the treaty of 1853 plus 12½ per cent for its administration, which would leave the Government free, once and for all, from all obligations to render accounts and hand over the surplus. The portion of Berar to be retained by the British was to be consolidated by the inclusion of the *surf-i-khas* estates, which had been left to the Nizam by the treaty of 1853. Further, Canning wanted to take the Berar districts from the Resident's control and place them under the Chief Commissioner of Nagpur.[42] This would definitely have been economically advantageous from the British point of view, but the Governor-General failed to see that this would be indistinguishable from annexation, and that the Nizam's consent would be difficult to procure.

Canning's terms for the new treaty with the Nizam were at first clearly described to Davidson in a demi-official letter from Cecil Beadon. The Resident was informed by the Foreign Office that the Government of India was anxious to dispose of the standing arrangements concerning its relations with the Nizam and to define a new one, which should at once show the Nizam the appreciation of his loyalty during the Mutiny and also put an end to the complicated provisions of the existing treaty of 1853.[43] A confidential draft of the terms of the agreement to be proposed to the Nizam accompanied the letter. First, the principal of the Nizam's debt to the Company was to be cancelled. Second, Shorapur was to be given to him. Third, the Berar districts were to be made over to the Government of India, preferably in perpetual sovereignty. If the Nizam objected to this, the districts were to continue to be held in trust by the British so long as Article 3 of the treaty of 1853 remained in force. Fourth, no accounts of the revenue and expenditure of the Assigned Districts were to be rendered to the Nizam's Government. Fifth, the *surf-i-khas* estates in these districts were to be handed over to the Government of India. Sixth, if the revenue of the Assigned Districts was found to be more than that required to meet treaty obligations, a part of the territory would be restored to the Nizam. Seventh, the Nizam's territory on the left bank of the Godavari was to be transferred to the Government of India. Finally, the Nizam was to abolish duties on all goods exported from and imported into Hyderabad by the Godavari in lieu of a monthly payment or a cession of territory.[44]

It is interesting that the first strong and spirited opposition to these terms, proposed by the Foreign Office under Canning's instructions, came from the British Resident himself. Davidson seems to have been quite shocked on receiving the letter and the draft agreement from Calcutta. It was obvious, Davidson pointed out, that the terms offered were not only very unfair to the Nizam, but even harsher than those originally proposed by Lord Dalhousie in 1853 and subsequently rejected by the Nizam. At that time the British had had an excuse 'to apply the screw', for after all the Nizam was supposed to have been under a debt to them. Now they had none, especially as they were talking of rewards. Davidson suggested a few alternatives which would indicate British appreciation of the Nizam's loyalty and, at the same time, give a few advantages to the British. The treaty of 1853 should be continued in its existing form, and Shorapur returned, but the Nizam could be asked to exchange *surf-i-khas* estates and the Godavari districts for land of equivalent value elsewhere.[45]

Acceptance of the terms suggested by the Government of India would undoubtedly mean a sacrifice of the Nizam's vital interests for the benefit of the Government of India. On being informed of the terms, Salar Jung naturally reacted sharply against them. These, he regretted, did not meet the views of his master. The Nizam had told his Minister in the most authoritative manner, 'I require the districts to be restored. It is your business to arrange this.' In a written communication to the Resident the Minister thus expressed the rights and expectations of his master and his Government. They expected the Assigned Districts to be returned to them. If, however, the Indian Government refused to restore the Assigned Districts, it should at least furnish yearly accounts and pay the surplus to His Highness. In the latter case, it would be necessary to fix a certain rate per centum to cover the expenses of management (roughly 12 per cent), and to arrange for the payment of the accumulated surplus of past years (which had not been paid at all), inclusive of the customs duty abolished in the Berar districts. He further hoped that the debt due by the Hyderabad Government would be cancelled and Shorapur restored to the Nizam. Salar Jung also felt that the subject of the cession of the Godavari land was a new one, and that, without knowing the British views on the restoration of Assigned Districts, the Nizam could not be induced to consider the matter. The two questions could be settled jointly.[46]

Canning dismissed Salar Jung's solicitations as well as Davidson's recommendations. Instructions were sent to the Resident to conduct negotiations for a new treaty with the Nizam. The Nizam was to cede the lands on the bank of the Godavari, abolish customs duties on the river, and dispense with the Berar accounts. The Government of India would give him Shorapur, cancel his debts and restore to him the districts of Raichur and Dharaseo. It would keep only East and West Berar, amalgamated by the transfer of the *surf-i-khas* estates and as much adjoining territory as would make up a gross revenue of Rs 32½ lakhs (to provide for treaty obligations and cost of administration at 12½ per cent),[47] less the amount equal to the value of the Godavari districts and the duties levied on the river to be relinquished by the Nizam. Canning would have preferred sovereignty over the Berar districts, but Davidson was convinced that the Nizam would never agree. Canning then had to be satisfied with the trust, provided he was at liberty to manage the districts through any agency that he might think best.[48]

When approached by Davidson with these proposals, Salar Jung agreed to hand over the Godavari districts to the British and to abolish the transit duties on the river. The Berar districts could not, however, be managed by the British in any manner they liked. Their administration, the Minister insisted, must continue to rest in the hands of the Resident, and the surplus revenue go to the Nizam. Any other arrangement would virtually imply the making over of Berar to the British.[49]

Privately, Canning expressed to Wood his great annoyance at the fact that the Nizam was 'still stickling for some sort of future accounts and hesitated to assent to our administering the Berars after our own fashion—by which I mean ... the attaching to Nagpur'. The Governor-General, however, hoped to get the Nizam's consent on both points. He was going to send Davidson a ready-drawn treaty to which the Nizam's assent was to be invited. 'It is everything to strike while the iron is hot, with this man', Canning explained sarcastically, 'for his mind is never the same two days together.'[50]

Over Hyderabad, therefore, Canning adopted a more stubborn attitude then before. He accepted as final and binding the Minister's letter regarding the transfer of the Godavari districts and the abolition of the Godavari customs, but ignoring the Minister's appeal, insisted on placing the Berar districts under the Commissioner of Nagpur for the sake of what he called 'administrative convenience'. He asked the Resident to make a package deal with the Nizam—the restoration of Raichur and Dharaseo, the cancellation of the debt, the withdrawal of the Nizam's claim for the Berar accounts, and the transfer of the *surf-i-khas* estates in Berar to the British. The proposals were either to be accepted or rejected as a whole.[51] While Salar Jung insisted that the transfer of the Godavari districts was connected with these four proposals, Canning clung determinedly to the view that the present proposals were entirely unconnected with the cession of the Godavari districts to which the Nizam had already absolutely agreed. He hoped His Highness would not rescind his commitment.[52]

Davidson seems to have been sympathetic to the Nizam's point of view for which he was severely rebuked by his superior. Canning was most annoyed that Davidson had not carried out his instructions properly.[53] Rather than risk removal from his post, Davidson asked Salar Jung to comply with the Governor-General's views.[54] The Nizam and his Minister were quite powerless to oppose the purposeful Governor-General. Although the Nizam could not help feeling that he had been hood-winked—had the situation been explained to him he would never have consented to surrender the Godavari districts, he said—he accepted all the four proposals submitted by Canning. He only requested that the Berar surplus, if any, be paid to him, and the Berar administration be kept in the hands of the Resident and not transferred to those of the Commissioner of Nagpur. This would, at least, assure public recognition of the fact that the Berar belonged to his state.[55]

Canning expressed his satisfaction at the Nizam's acceptance of his conditions, particularly the one regarding the Berar accounts, and agreed to grant him his two requests. The requests were not granted unconditionally. The Nizam was to understand that the Government of India was to be given the widest latitude over the cost of administration of the Berar districts. Morever, His Highness could not question the administrative charges which were to be defrayed from Berar before any surplus could be earned.[56] Canning explained to Wood why he had agreed to give up his demand to transfer Berar to the Commissioner of Nagpur. 'The Nizam was so sensitive on the point of sovereignty, and showed himself so suspicious of such an arrangement being only a first step towards making the districts red in the map that I did not press it.' Canning also wanted to assure the Nizam that the British wished to treat him with generosity and consideration.[57]

The treaty between the Nizam and the Government of India was finally concluded on 7 December 1860. Shorapur was restored in full sovereignty to the Nizam. His debt of Rs 50 lakhs was cancelled. The Raichur Doab and the Dharaseo districts were restored to him. The

Nizam was to forgo all demands for the Berar accounts of the past, present and future, but the Indian Government was to pay him any surplus that might accrue after defraying the cost of administration, the cost itself being entirely at the discretion of the Government. The Berar districts, together with all *surf-i-khas* estates and such additional adjoining districts which would provide an annual gross revenue of Rs 32 lakhs were to be held by the Government of India for the payment of the Contingent and various other payments provided for by the treaty of 1853. The Nizam gave the British complete control over all his possessions on the left bank of the Godavari and the Wyneganga above the confluence of the two rivers. The navigation of the Godavari and its tributaries as far as they formed the boundary between the Nizam's dominions and the British dominions in India was to be free and no more customs or other duties were to be levied by either of the parties or by their subjects on goods passing up and down the river.[58]

This document, which was sent to Canning for ratification had the Nizam's seal fixed at the top. In the context of the well-understood significance of a document on which the head of a state in India signed or placed his seal at the top, Canning refused to accept it. 'This implies a document addressed to an inferior', he explained to Wood, 'nothing in oriental formalities is more plain than the meaning.' Records at Calcutta showed that the Nizam's seal and signature had always been placed at the bottom of treaties. Both Canning and Wood were annoyed that though Davidson knew this he had permitted the Nizam to deviate from the custom.[59] Two copies of the treaty were finally sent to Davidson on which were marked in pencil the proper places for the Resident's and the Nizam's seals. The Nizam first objected to this, but later decided to acquiesce.[60]

Needless to say, the treaty was approved by Wood, who congratulated Canning and signified Her Majesty's approval of the arrangements with the Nizam. These would give the Madras Government necessary command of the Godavari and 'solve many difficulties and please our cotton people'. His only regret was the re-transfer of the Raichur and Dharaseo districts and the inability to get the Assigned Districts in full sovereignty.[61]

Canning, too, was pleased with the treaty, and took it as a personal diplomatic triumph. He felt that these terms could never have been obtained had the British not pressed for concessions while rewarding the Nizam at the same time. In reply to Wood's objection to the handing over of two out of the four Assigned Districts to the Nizam, he requested the Secretary of State 'to bear in mind that they were only assigned; that we did not possess them as our own; and that we had administered them for less than six years'. However, Canning was a little unhappy that he could not transfer Berar to the Commissioner of Nagpur. For this he laid the blame squarely on Davidson. If Davidson had done his duty, so Canning complained to Wood, the Government of India might have succeeded in administering Berar through the Commissioner of Nagpur. Fortunately, however, the Nizam had agreed to forgo all demands for accouns and not to question the cost of the Berar administration. Although this was not the same as unconditional possession, because the British themselves could not make any extra profit from the districts, Canning told Wood that they could now govern them with a free hand. Under the treaty of 1853, the Nizam's Government was at liberty to express any dissatisfaction at any 'expenditure of administration beyond a certain limited amount', and did, in fact, consider the British expenditure on public works and education unnecessarily large. Henceforward the British were 'clear of the obligation ... to justify our ways of government to native Durbars'.[62]

Indeed, the treaty of 1860 gave the British almost everything they wanted. They had full control over Berar. The Godavari districts had been handed over to them even before the conclusion of the treaty, making possible the unhampered movement of British goods on the river. After the transfer, the new frontier between the two Governments was the Godavari till it reached the confluence of the Wyneganga, the Wyneganga till it reached the confluence of the Pranhita, the Pranhita till its confluence with the Wardha—and afterwards the Wardha. This was a good natural frontier between the Nizam's dominion and the British.[63]

Not surprisingly, the Nizam was very dissatisfied with the treaty. He felt that he had been coerced into agreeing to its terms. In fact, the taint of unjustified compulsion, which had vitiated the treaty of 1853, was not effaced by that of 1860. The Nizam's Government, already in possession of the Parliamentary Blue Book on the treaty of 1853, was acutely conscious of the injustice done to it at that time. Under normal circumstances, it would not have consented to any disadvantageous revision of the treaty;[64] the Nizam yielded only because he was compelled to do so and was forced to express public satisfaction with it.

The new arrangement gave the Nizam nothing that was not his own. The treaty of 1800 had called the Raja of Shorapur a zamindar and the

Nizam's subordinate, so the Nizam's claim to the land was legally more valid than the British claim. He could also refer to the Partition Treaty after the Maratha War of 1818, when the principality had been unreservedly included after a survey of the frontier (1822) within his boundary. The British had confiscated it only after the Raja's rebellion in 1857-8, but it was the Nizam who had an undisputed right to Shorapur.[65]

The other 'reward' that the Nizam received was scarcely a reward. He could not possibly accept the cancellation of the debt as a reward, because he had never considered the debt to be due from him at all. It had arisen because of the Contingent, the history of which was only too well known to him. And he believed that in 1853, as well as after it, the British had no pecuniary claim against him.

The only reward that the Nizam would have appreciated, indeed the only reward he would have accepted as being worthy of the name, was the restoration of Berar, but evidently that was not to be. Raichur and Dharaseo were restored to him purely because the revenue from Berar had increased, and because the *surf-i-khas* and other districts had been acquired by the British. Moreover, even in the restored districts, the British protected their interests, making Salar Jung promise that all land required for the Madras and Great Indian Peninsular railways and the extension of the Madras Irrigation Company would be given to the British, following the return of Raichur.[66]

Happy with his 'bargains', Canning now decided to send as 'rewards' (as he explained to Wood) presents to the value of Rs 1 lakh to the Nizam, and small presents to Salar Jung and his colleagues.[67] He sent these gifts to the Nizam's court, requesting the Nizam to accept these as tokens of his friendship and expressing the desire of his Government for a 'lasting concord' between the two states. In a full durbar, Davidson delivered the gifts from the Governor-General to the Nizam and his officers. The gesture delighted the Nizam and he wanted to reciprocate. But he was given to understand that, while he could certainly send gifts if he wished, the Governor-General could not accept them personally. The Nizam's pride required an exchange of gifts, so the presents, estimated value Rs 1,57,000, were dispatched and duly laid before Canning. Canning lodged them in the Government treasury according to custom. None of the European officers present at the durbar was allowed to accept any gift from the Nizam,[68] an indication of the superior position which the British thought they enjoyed vis-à-vis the Indian states.

Soon after the conclusion of the treaty of 1860 it was found that the boundary demarcation needed readjustment. In the first place, the revenue of East and West Berar fell short of Rs 32 lakhs by Rs 84,964. This deficit could be covered by taking over additional parganas lying to the north of the Penganga river from the Nizam. By this arrangement the Penganga would form the bounday of East Berar to the south. Second, between Maikar and Buldana, there was a strip of country still held by the Nizam's Government, running close to the new military station of Telgaon, which interrupted communication between the taluks of Maikar and Devalghat. The Resident proposed to make the British holdings in the Assigned Districts compact by taking this strip from the Nizam in exchange for certain *mahals* situated within the periphery of the Nizam's lands. The transfer of the districts was completed on 23 October 1861.[69] The districts retained under the new arrangement yielded a revenue of Rs 86,000 in excess of the stipulated amount of Rs 32 lakhs a year. To repair the anomaly and to make the British holdings even more compact, several villages and parganas situated far from the British headquarters were restored to the Nizam.[70] The Assigned Districts now had the Satpura range to the north, the Wardha river to the east and the Penganga to the south. Only in the west and south-west the boundary continued to be irregular and less distinctly defined than was desired by the British.

In the final analysis, the treaty of 1860 was scarcely a reward for an ally who had supported the British during their most disturbed days. It cancelled the Nizam's debts, but, then, he had considered the debts spurious to begin with; it gave him Shorapur which was always legally his, and it gave him Raichur and Dharaseo, but took the *surf-i-khas* districts as well as the Godavari districts. It was the British who gained by strengthening their control over Berar, redefining boundaries to their advantage, securing freedom of navigation along the Godavari and land for their canals and railways. Above all, this carefully calculated 'reward' established their supremacy over Hyderabad and gave their paramountcy in the region a very firm foothold.

CHAPTER II

Paramountcy and Subordinate Co-operation

I

By 1858, the East India Company had established its control over the whole of India. Although technically the Company had not assumed imperial powers or any title, its paramountcy was gradually becoming a reality. The princely states, while still enjoying nominal independence in internal administration, had for all practical purposes come under its domination. But the Company's very successful career of empire-building was abruptly cut short in 1858, when the old East India Company was abolished and the Crown took over the direct administration of the country in its own hands.

The initiative in bringing about this constitutional and organizational change in the Government of India was taken by Prime Minister Palmerston himself, a decision apparently made as a direct result of the Mutiny. Soon after the fall of Delhi to the British army, Palmerston informed Canning, 'My own opinion is that things cannot be left to go on as they have been, and that a vast Territory, and a Population of 150 million cannot continue under the nominal supremacy of a Company of merchants, but must be placed under the direct authority of the Crown.'[1]

This was also the opinion of the leading members of his cabinet. The Marquis of Clanricarde, the Lord Privy Seal, had no doubt that no good could be done to India 'until the Directors were cleared away.'[2] The Duke of Argyll, the Postmaster-General, while asserting that all the charges brought against the Company were not just, still advocated a change. The 'errors' of the Government of India were 'always connected with its structure'. Argyll regretted that Gladstone (now no longer in the cabinet) did not support the move. 'Gladstone', he wrote with some asperity to Canning, 'who said last session that the first day of returning common sense would see an end of the rule of the East India Company, is now disposed to postpone common sense as long as possible. I told Aberdeen the other day that if Gladstone voted for his own opinion, he would support us, as I knew he hated the Company. "Aye that may be", said Aberdeen, "but he hates you worse"—which is quite true.'[3]

It was Palmerston, and not Gladstone, who ran the Government of the day, and he knew his mind. A bill for the better government of India was ready by December 1857. The Company, when informed of the proposed change, made a valiant last-minute effort to preserve its power and to justify its rule in India.[4] In a petition to Parliament drawn up by John Stuart Mill, the Company argued that its responsibility for the Mutiny or its failure to govern India had not been proved conclusively. If it was at fault, so was the Government, since under the existing system Her Majesty's Government had 'the deciding voice', and was 'in the fullest sense accountable' for all that had been done in India. So great a change should not be decided upon without giving proper consideration to the Company's past services, and certainly not in the very midst of the fearful crisis through which India was passing.[5] Canning, too, hoped that the Government would not let Parliament legislate against the Company 'in the midst of the turmoil'.[6]

Unimpressed by these arguments, the resolute Palmerston went ahead with his bill proposing to transfer the Company's Indian administration to the Crown. The bill, however, fell—not because it aroused great criticism (which it did)—but because of the sudden and unexpected fall of Palmerston. Palmerston was replaced by Derby in June 1858. This did not brighten the Company's prospects. Parliament and the public were, as Mangles reported to Canning with a touch of sadness and cynicism, 'quite determined to sweep away— whatever they may determine to substitute—the Corporation which won and preserved India for England'.[7] Derby's first India Bill was rejected, but his second came up before the House on 17 June. Mainly the handiwork of Stanley, the President of the India Board, it was passed with minor amendments to become the Act for the Better Government of India, 1858. It received royal assent on 2 August.

The Act decided that India would henceforth be governed directly by and in the name of the Crown acting through the Secretary of State in Council. The duties of the Council, comprising fifteen members, were essentially advisory. The Secretary of State could, if necessary, overrule their decision in all except financial matters. He also had the right to send secret dispatches to the Governor-General on important matters like war and peace. In India, the Governor-General-in-Council continued to rule at the centre, while the Governor-in-Council or Lieutenant-Governor headed the provincial governments.

When the Bill became an Act, it was universally acknowledged that the change was merely one of 'nomenclature'—a formal rather than substantive change.[8] There is some truth in this, for there was no immediate change in the personnel of the Government of India, and no apparent break in its traditions. And yet the Act had significant psychological and practical implications. The Indian people and Government and the princely states in India came into direct contact with the Crown and its ministers. More importantly (to borrow the words of Bernard Cohn), 'a social order was established with the British Crown seen as the centre of authority, and capable of ordering into a single hierarchy all its subjects, Indian and British.'[9] The impact of this development was to become increasingly apparent in the following years.

In accordance with the last clauses of the India Act the change of government had to be announced to the Indian people through a Royal Proclamation. Stanley, now Secretary of State, instructed Canning to make some 'formal announcement' of the transfer of authority from the Company to the Crown after a Proclamation in the Queen's name reached him from London. Stanley was against a very ostentatious announcement, for there was the danger of such a ceremony being 'misunderstood' by the Indian princes. His idea was to avoid, above all things, raising expectations of larger and indefinite alterations in the system of Government.' This suggestion was in line with Canning's own thinking. He finally decided that the Proclamation would be read in India on 1 November 1858 at Allahabad (in his presence), at the three Presidency capitals, and at other important centres—Lucknow, Lahore, Peshawar, Karachi, and Rangoon on the Irrawaddy. At Calcutta and Allahabad, there were to be illuminations and fireworks, 'the show most congenial to the natives.'[10]

On 1 November, at 5 p.m. at Allahabad the Proclamation was read in a dignified and impressive ceremony which, according to Canning, 'went off well.'[11] By this Proclamation the Queen promised to be bound by the same obligations to the Indian people as to her other subjects and to pay due reverence to the ancient customs and laws of India. To the Indian princes she promised to show respect for their rights and dignity, as well as for their treaties and engagements with the East India Company. She also disclaimed any desire for further territorial extension in India.[12] Translations of the Proclamation were made into seventeen Indian languages and copies of it sent to all the princely states. The Home Government expressed particular satisfaction that the Proclamation had been received at all the principal Indian courts in the proper spirit, and the Queen jubilantly wrote to Canning that it was 'a source of great satisfaction and pride' to feel herself in direct relationship with that enormous Empire which was a bright 'jewel of her Crown.'[13]

The first and most important effect of the change was the establishment and the positive recognition of British paramountcy. During Wellesley's regime the idea of paramountcy had been in a foetal stage, but now it came into being with a reality which the princely states were forced to feel. After 1858, 'paramountcy not only as a historical fact but as a legal principle capable of interpretation and expansion was promulgated as an essential feature of the new system.'[14] Canning, the great upholder of this paramountcy, declared, 'The last vestiges of the Royal House of Delhi ... had been swept away. The last pretender to the representative of the Peishwa has disappeared. The Crown of England stands forth the unquestioned ruler and Paramount Power in all India, and is for the first time brought face to face with its feudatories.'[15] Interestingly, the princes, the erstwhile allies of the East India Company, were now transformed into the feudatories of the Crown. The concept of the Queen, the head of the British Empire, was something very tangible and real, and could inspire the princes with a certain sense of loyalty—a quality strongly emphasized by all her representatives.

The Crown reserved the right to penalize a state as heavily as it thought it should, and even with confiscation, in the event of disloyalty or flagrant breach of engagement. The Crown also emphasized the need for good government by the princes, and asserted its right to rectify any serious abuse of power in an Indian state that might threaten any part of the country with anarchy or disturbance. This condition, apart from ensuring discipline and order in the states, had another major advantage. It could provide an excuse for interfering in the internal administration of any state. No state in India was ever allowed to dispute the right of the British Government or defy its paramountcy.

Canning, who laid down the basic principles of the so-called Canning system' that lasted throughout the century, decided that if the states remained loyal and subservient and reasonably well governed, he would not think of annexing them. He was against further extension of British territory in India anyway, as it would not make the British any stronger unless accompanied by an increase in European troops, and this was out of the question. Canning's object was 'to establish a native aristocracy, which did not exist before.' During the Revolt of 1857 he came to realize that in a vast country like India the

British were 'literally at the mercy of the natives.' Peace was to be kept mainly by the upper classes, that is, the landlords and the princely chiefs, who could be induced to act as upholders of British imperialism in India. It was the interest of these classes to keep the country quiet, so the British could 'seek some extra and willing service from them'.[16] In a bid to win over the princes, Canning totally rejected Dalhousie's Doctrine of Lapse, and decided to grant them the right of adoption in case of failure of a natural heir. In an official dispatch, a masterly one, he made out an outstanding case in favour of adoption, and laid down the basic principles to be followed henceforth regarding succession in the states. In the case of Hindu chiefs, the paramount power should promise to recognize adoption of a successor under Hindu law, on failure of a natural heir. To the Muslim chiefs assurance was to be given that any succession which might be legitimate according to Muslim law would be upheld. The grant of the Adoption Sanad to the princes, Canning argued, would not only be an act of grace, but a sound policy designed to make them friends of the British. In times of peace the states would offer employment to many who found no scope in British India, and in times of danger they would prove to be the mainstay of British power, just as they had been during the Mutiny.[17]

In a number of private letters to friends and the Secretary of State, Canning elucidated further his real motives for granting the right of adoption to the princes. It was not another Mutiny that Canning feared, but a European war, which would try British strength in India far more than any internal convulsion.

A war in which France and Russia shall be against us, would bring on an internal convulsion of the most perilous kind, unless we set our house in order whilst there is yet time. And the surest way of doing this is so to treat our Native fellow subjects and the Native Princes and their subjects, as to give them no inducement to lend themselves to intrigue against us, to convince them that they have nothing to gain, but much to lose by any change in the Paramount Power in India; and to bring them into that temper in which, when the danger comes, we may safely throw the reins on their necks, and trust to their maintaining their fidelity with a minimum of support from an English army. When the danger does come, our English armies will have enough to do outside India.[18]

This was no 'mere speculative romancing'. In the event of a prolonged European war, the British might have to withdraw some of their European regiments from India. The enemies of the British would at once try to 'tempt' the Indian chiefs to come over to their side. To prevent the chiefs from rising, the British would do well to concede to them a few privileges with good grace. Now was the time to build 'the policy of trust and reliance' which the British might 'utilize' in the day of need. 'We must begin by making ourselves believed and trusted,' observed Canning 'before we can hope to bring those with whom we have to deal into that condition of mind in which we may believe and trust them.' The grant of adoption would be a less flashy measure than a great durbar and the bestowal of large rewards, but it would be far more general in its effect and the results would be permanent. Canning, therefore, pleaded with Wood to let him have his way in this matter.[19]

While basically approving Canning's policy of friendship with and reliance on the princes, Wood gave but reluctant approval to the Viceroy's Adoption proposal. The annexationist in Wood regretted not having a wider opening for appropriating some of the localities in the hills favourable for European settlement. But to attach the chiefs permanently to the British was certainly of far more importance than the possession of a few districts fit for European colonization. It was also important to deprive the active and stirring elements in the country of any possible leaders. So those men 'who have some sort of influence which they can use for us or against us' should be on the side of the British.[20] 'We cannot divest ourselves of the character of aliens in blood or religion', Wood was convinced, 'and we stand in need of all we can do, to create and strengthen bonds of union between us and the natives.'[21] Later, while upholding Canning's policy before Elgin, Canning's successor, Wood remarked that it was not at all inconsistent with 'keeping a tight hand over the princes'. 'We are guardians of the peace in India .... We have, therefore, a perfect right to say that they shall not so govern as to endanger the peace of India, or indeed of their own dominions.' In other words, while the chiefs might adopt successors to their hearts' content, they were expected to rule in accordance with the wishes of the paramount power which had the right to interfere in their internal administration in the name of good government.[22]

These, then, were the fundamentals of the policy towards the Indian princes and chiefs in the post-1858 era. Its two salient features were cultivating the friendship and support of the princes, and insistence on their subservience and loyalty to the paramount power. Every chief was to be assured that the paramount power desired to see his government perpetuated (as long as he was faithful to his engagements), and that a feudal aristocracy would be kept alive.[23]

In Hyderabad, more than in any other state in India, the impact of this policy became immediately apparent. The Nizam of Hyderabad, the premier prince of India, was not, according to the treaties with the Company, a vassal or a feudatory of the British. But his own treaty position was materially affected by this general change. He became a clearly subordinate ally, bound to be loyal to the paramount power. The Nizam received the Queen's Proclamation with the utmost humility and special honour—a gesture which pleased Wood.[24] To adjust to his new position, the Nizam prepared a new seal which omitted all allusion to his allegiance to the Mughal ruler of Delhi, hitherto regarded as the Nizam's master. In the old seal were imprinted the words which, translated into English, read thus: 'Subservient to the King who is as powerful as King Suleiman, conqueror of countries, Muhammad Bahadur Shah, the brave Emperor, the holy warrior.'[25] These words were now totally left out. Needless to say, this change was made under the influence of the Resident. Davidson had some difficulty in persuading the Nizam, and had to convince him that the King of Delhi had not only been convicted as a traitor and a rebel but transported beyond the seas.[26] The Nizam's allegiance to him had thus automatically come to an end and was now to be transferred to the new rulers of India.

The Nizam's coinage also showed a similar change. From the day of the first Nizam, the Hyderabad coins bore an inscription relating to the Emperor of Delhi, to whom the Nizam professed allegiance. The Government of India wanted the princely states to do away with such a superscription on their coins. Canning admitted that the Government had 'not in strictness any right to interfere' with the mints of the states, and that their prerogative of coining was one of which all Indian princes were 'very jealous'. Nevertheless, he felt that it would be of great convenience if the value of their coins could be brought on a par with those in British India when the inscription was changed.[27] Since the former was not immediately practicable, Canning merely advocated a change in the superscription. Salar Jung agreed that no purpose would be served by retaining an inscription which referred to a sovereign who no longer existed, and new coins were struck.[28] Upon the obverse of the coin were inscribed the words 'Nizam-ul-Mulk Asaf Jah Bahadur', instead of the name of the Mughal ruler,[29] and the figure 92, signifying Muhammad according to a well-known Arabic device, was impressed upon it.

In 1859, when the Nizam himself proposed a change in the inscription on his coins by substituting the name of the Prophet for the digit 92, .Davidson immediately opposed any such alteration, suspecting that the move was designed to deny the supremacy of the Crown, and to show that the Nizam's sovereignty was derived from Muhammad. On this point the Resident and the Viceroy were at one; Canning refused to sanction the Nizam's proposal and informed him that any change in the coinage designed to defy Her Majesty's supremacy was an unfriendly act.[30] This warning put an end to the Nizam's hesitant and faltering attempt to change his own coinage or to assert his independence in about the only field, still left to him.

It became increasingly obvious that an inexorable force was pushing the Nizam into total subordination to the Crown. In London an important decision was taken on a subject in which both the Queen and Prince Albert took great personal interest—the institution of the Order of the Star of India. As early as May 1859, the Queen informed Canning, her trusted lieutenant, of her desire to institute a high order of chivalry for the chiefs of India. The object was to bind the Indian princes and chiefs of high distinction in a fraternity and attach them 'by a personal tie to their sovereigh.'[31] The Queen's idea fitted in perfectly with Canning's own calculated policy. The Order, Canning proposed, should be created for both the Indian chiefs and English officers. This would serve the double purpose of raising the chiefs' self-respect and creating a desire to govern their states well so that they could associate themselves with high-ranking officials of the British Government. It would also convey the stamp of the Queen's sanction on the principle that her 'chief Indian subjects and feudatories' and the foremost of her English servants in India were equally amongst 'the first members and officers of her Indian Empire.'[32] The princes would thereby be identified with the Crown's Government, which was exactly what Canning wanted. The Queen was pleased with Canning's proposal and asked Wood to go ahead with its execution.[33] After prolonged discussion, the star, the collar, the badge, the riband, the motto were all decided upon in England. The Statute provided for the Queen as sovereign, the Viceroy as Grand Master, with not more than 25 Knights. The Order of the Star appeared in the Gazette, and on 3 July 1861, Wood was able to write to Canning, 'The Earl Canning, G.C.B.,

K.S.I., I suppose I may call you, as the Star is out.'[34] The first formal investiture took place on 1 November 1861, the day of the third anniversary of the Royal Proclamation. The entire process added, 'an important European component to the ritual idiom which the British were establishing in India'. The concept and the 'accoutrements' of the order were all 'English and feudal', and the investiture was in 'the European style'.[35]

The Indian princes received the new Order well, and 'with much eagerness'—all, except the Nizam. Wood had informed Canning as early as January 1861 that he had some doubts as to whether all those who were to receive the Order would accept it willingly. The two persons mentioned in this connection were the Nizam and the Rana of Udaipur. 'It would not do to have the Order even unwillingly received', and so Canning was to find out whether the proposed recipients would accept it in the proper spirit.[36] Despite Wood's warning, Canning went ahead with his pet scheme. He sent a *khureeta* to the Nizam enclosing a grant under Her Majesty's Sign Manual, appointing the Nizam a Knight of the Most Exalted Order of the Star of India. In a durbar on 31 August the Resident presented the *khureeta* to the Nizam and delivered the Queen's grant. At this point the half-anticipated complication arose. The Nizam, while expressing himself highly pleased at the honour bestowed on him, observed that some of the Statutes were not in accordance with the usage and religion of the Muslim princes of India. The wearing of any effigy was opposed to their religion and unbecoming in people's eyes. The wearing of a silk robe, as described in the Statute, was objected to for the same reason. Canning was furious, and Wood worried about the 'difficulties' raised by the Nizam. Davidson strongly advised the Nizam to accept without objection the honour which Her Majesty had conferred on him, for otherwise he might displease her and her Viceroy.[37]

Eventually, the Nizam was persuaded to waive his objection.[38] The pressure exerted on him becomes clear from Canning's private letter to the Queen. Canning reported to the Queen that of all the princes in India, the Nizam alone had been 'the least open to reason'. But he was very ignorant and weak, and surrounded by fanatics whose object was to bring him into 'trouble' with the Governor-General. There had been objections raised by him or on his behalf regarding the new Order, and great pains had been taken to persuade him that some covert attack upon his religion had not been intended. The long discussion with him had come to an end only when it was made known to the Nizam that the Governor-General 'would not listen to any questioning of the Rules of the Order, and that these must be accepted unreservedly', if the honour were to be conferred at all. The Nizam, Canning complained to the Queen, had not been 'judiciously dealt with by Davidson,'[39] and he severely admonished the Resident for the mismanagement of the Order. 'Instead of frightening the Nizam's acceptance, you should have taken the higher ground of vindicating the Queen's favour and mark of honour against being accepted with qualification.'[40]

On 25 November 1861, a full durbar saw the Nizam invested with the insignia of the Star of India. Everything went off admirably. The Nizam's manner was friendly and he assured the Resident that he considered the presentation of the Star a great honour.[41] While the Nizam thus accepted defeat and professed happiness, the people of Hyderabad refused to do so. They distrusted and disapproved of 'honours' bestowed by outsiders and expressed this in Persian placards which appeared in the city condemning the British and their friend, Salar Jung, who was believed to be involved in an intrigue aimed at tarnishing the Nizam's image.[42] Popular feeling ran high against the British and their pretensions.

II

The Royal Proclamation of 1858 decorated the Governor-General with the impressive title of Viceroy. Now officially the representative of Her Majesty, he was in a position of greater authority and respect than his predecessors. The position of his representative, the Resident, rose correspondingly and his powers, although necessarily undefined, became omnicompetent for all practical purposes.

The Resident at Hyderabad was the political officer watching and controlling the conduct of the state, the head of the cantonments of Secunderabad and Bolarum, and the judicial and civil chief of Berar. Not only did the ministers consult him on vital affairs of state, but all important men in the region vied with one another to secure his favour. The chief nobles and their sons, the principal traders and bankers, all sought private interviews with the Resident. The common people, however, were not so easily won over. They showed a distinct distrust of the British and their representative at the Nizam's Court.

An unexpected incident occurred in 1859 which revealed this popular sentiment. On 15 March, Davidson went to attend the Nizam's durbar in order to present a *khureeta* from Lord Canning. After the durbar was over, and while he was walking arm-in-arm with Salar Jung, an Indian fired a shot which wounded one of the Minister's attendants. The Indian rushed at the Resident with a drawn sword, but was seized by the Minister's followers and the incensed Nizam called out his entire retinue of 2,500 armed men to accompany the Resident and his staff to the Residency. The streets through which the Resident passed were lined by the population of the city armed to the teeth. Davidson felt there was a fanatical hatred against all Europeans throughout the country, with even the sight of a white man putting them on fire.[43]

The Government of Hyderabad was very anxious about the manner in which the incident would be viewed by the British Government, and the latter was not disposed to take a light view of the matter. Stanley, the Secretary of State, expressed great concern over the attack on Davidson, and Canning warned the Nizam that the British Government held the person of its representative sacred from all insult or violence. The durbar was responsible for the safety of the Resident, and the Nizam, if he wanted to maintain friendly relations with the British, should take vigorous measures to ensure that.[44]

This incident was not the only indication of popular resentment against the Resident or the power that he represented. A conspiracy to depose the Nizam, attack the Residency and proclaim Nana Saheb as ruler of Hyderabad was soon discovered. This project, which may be regarded as the tail-end of the Great Revolt of 1857, was organized by a Maratha Brahmin, Rao Sahib, who came to Hyderabad from Baroda. When the plot was discovered, about thirty men were arrested, tried and sentenced to imprisonment, but the ring-leader, Rao Sahib, managed to escape. The British Indian authorities were very annoyed by the escape of the chief conspirater and roundly blamed the Hyderabad Government for its inefficiency. The truth is that the rebels enjoyed the sympathy of the masses, including the police. What was more, the *sahukars*, hitherto the chief supporters of Salar Jung's administration, were implicated in it.[45] It was obvious that the British had thoroughly aroused the hatred of the common people, and alienated the mercantile community and the moneyed classes who were afraid that the British banking and treasury system would be imposed on them.

Given this situation, it was necessary for the British to build a strong alliance with a powerful man in the state. Their interest in the politics of Hyderabad was not restricted to the assertion of the power and

prestige of the Resident. They interfered actively in the selection and
maintenance of the Minister of the state as well. The well-established,
time-honoured tradition of the British was to rule Hyderabad through
a friendly and pliable Minister. The only mode of securing an efficient
administration in the state, or so they thought, was to find an able and
powerful Minister, who would govern in the name of his master, but
who would also be willing to modify his views on the advice of the
Resident. Accordingly, they upheld the position of the Minister, Salar
Jung, who was their acknowledged friend and to whom principally
they owed the Nizam's loyalty during the crisis of 1857. Mangles,
Vernon Smith, Stanley, and even Wood had, on more than one occasion, expressed their gratitude to Salar Jung, whose conduct appeared
to 'have been above all praise.' Nizam Afzal-ud-Daula, like all his
ancestors, disliked and was wary of the British. The preponderance of
British influence at his court was entirely due to Salar Jung. He
believed that the well-being of his state would be secured by casting its
lot with the British and by modelling its administration along the lines
of that of British India. There was thus a happy collaboration between
the British and the Minister in the years following the Great Revolt.
The British stood faithfully by the Minister, as the Minister stood
loyally by them.

Nizam Afzal-ud-Daula was often annoyed with his Minister. Apart
from the fact that Salar Jung was a Shia, and he himself a Sunni, he was
jealous of the Minister. According to a banker of Chadarghat this was
because the Nizam thought that he, rightful master, was nothing, while
the Minister was everything, and that the Minister acted on the advice
of the Resident.[46] He found fault with the Minister's habit of resorting
to the British for support and resented the Minister's independent and
insubordinate manner, with frequent threats of resignation if he did
not get his way.

As early as mid-1858, the Secretary of State, Stanley, was told that
Salar Jung was losing the support of the Nizam, that his enemies were
gaining ground at the Nizam's Court, and that the support of the
British Government was essential to keep him in power. Stanley
considered it important not to lose Indian friends for want of backing
them. 'We have not many, I fear', he wrote to Canning, 'and unless I am
much misinformed, he has been one of our best.' Stanley was clearly
well disposed to Salar Jung, and repeatedly requested Canning to send
the Minister some special reward in recognition of his services to the
British.[47] Canning was more reticent, and did not intend to give undue

importance to the Minister of a princely state.[48] Yet he came to the Minister's support whenever the latter faced trouble with his master.

The Nizam's suppressed resentment against Salar Jung was not usually openly expressed, but the public became aware of the growing discord between him and Salar Jung as early as 1860. An inhabitant of the Residency Bazar had been thrown into prison by Muzaffar-ud-Daula, the Nizam's uncle, for refusing to sell him a garden. When the Minister asked for his release, Muzaffar defied the Government and fired for three days on Government troops. Upon turning to the Nizam for support, the Minister failed to obtain the Nizam's consent to punish a prince of the realm like a commoner. The matter was settled by amicable negotiations at which Muzaffar and his mercenaries dictated their own terms. Salar Jung, unhappy at the rejection of his advice, tendered his resignation.[49] There was no likelihood of the resignation being accepted, as it was well known that he was strongly supported by his friend, the Resident, Davidson. The whole tension-fraught incident disturbed the court of Hyderabad and the basic lack of co-operation between the Minister and his master stood clearly revealed.

Once the rift became public, the relationship between Salar Jung and the Nizam deteriorated further. An individual named Yakoob Ali Khan, who had become a frequent medium for the Resident's communications with the Nizam, convinced the Nizam that the Resident was in favour of the Minister's removal, a fact which, incidentally, indicates that Salar Jung had bitter enemies at all levels in the state. This was but natural. Salar Jung's attempt at modernizing Hyderabad administration had struck at vested interests and alienated the old nobility which had the Nizam's ear. In any case, the Nizam, only too willing to believe that Salar Jung had fallen out with Davidson, informed the Resident in a durbar of his intention to dismiss Salar Jung. Davidson immediately objected to the step and advised the Nizam to wait at least till the Viceroy's decision on the issue came. This the Nizam was unwilling to do; he insisted upon his right of instantaneous dismissal of his Minister without consulting the Viceroy. He rightly pointed out that his father had removed many Ministers from office, and there was no reason why he should not do so. 'I tell you', he firmly told Davidson, 'I am displeased with my Minister.' Alarmed at this situation, Davidson wrote an official note to inform the Nizam that the Governor-General would be extremely 'displeased' to hear of his intention. This had the desired effect. When Salar Jung, grieved and indignant at the insulting manner in which he had been treated, offered to resign, the Nizam turned down the offer. Under the protection of the Resident, whose proceedings received the full support of Canning's Government, Salar Jung stayed on as the Minister.[50] The reconciliation between the Nizam and his Minister was ostensibly effected in a durbar, where the Nizam presented the Minister with a *khillut* of jewels of the value of about forty to fifty thousand rupees. To placate him further, Shorapur, Dharaseo and Raichur, given to the Nizam by the treaty of 1860, were placed by the Nizam under Salar Jung's personal control—a step taken at the request of the Governor-General.[51] Salar Jung's triumph was complete, but it was achieved with British aid. It seriously damaged his popularity both with the Nizam and with his people. It must have been evident to everyone that, beneath the facade of cordiality, there lurked in the Nizam's mind the most intense hatred of Salar Jung.

Meanwhile, Canning's term in India was running out. At the end of his usual five-year term, he had stayed on for an entire year at Wood's request. 'For the public service your stay for another year seems to me to be of the highest importance', the Secretary of State wrote to the Governor-General with whom he had worked in perfect harmony.[52] Now was the time for Canning to leave India. Before he left the country, he had one last thing to do, and that was to send the Nizam his favourite brain-child, the Adoption Sanad. The sanad assured the Nizam that on failure of a natural heir, any succession to the Government of Hyderabad, which might be legitimate according to Muslim law, would be upheld, and that nothing would disturb the engagement so long as his House was loyal to the Crown and faithful to the condition of the treaties or engagements with the East India Company.[53]

The Adoption Sanad was placed in the Nizam's hand in a durbar. He made no comment but merely placed it on the cushion beside him[54] in implicit recognition of the power of the British Government over his state and throne. This was not the first time that the British had interfered in the matter of the Nizam's succession, but their ultimate authority regarding the matter had never been officially and formally recognized. Davidson pointed out that the Nizam had been treated as an independent sovereign, and the succession in his family had invariably been regulated by the acknowledged custom of his House and by Muslim law.[55] The sanad announced a new policy. It associated in unequivocal terms the grant of a conditional concession dependent on loyalty and subordination. That the treaties had given the British no such power to regulate succession or to grant a concession to the Nizam was forgotten. The British as the paramount power henceforth assumed the undisputed right to settle all questions of succession in Hyderabad.

The Adoption Sanad was Canning's parting gift to the Nizam. He signed the document on 11 March 1862, on the eve of his retirement from India. Canning left behind him a profound impression on the Indian body politic. He was unquestionably the founder of the system which, with minor modifications, operated for the rest of the century. His two not-too-distinguished successors merely followed in his footsteps and were completely overshadowed by the lingering memory of his dominating personality and political sagacity.

As far as Hyderabad was concerned, Canning had initiated the main strands of the policy to be followed henceforth towards it by the Government of India. With the effective support of the powerful Wood, he had concluded with the state negotiations favourable to the British; he had brought the state closer under their control, and turned the Nizam into a feudatory knight of the new British imperial structure. His rule did not mark the beginning of an era of reform in Hyderabad, nor did it usher in a period of enlightenment or modernization. His policy of alliance with the landed gentry—so vigorously pursued in Awadh—was not applicable to Hyderabad. And the common people of the state were as yet no concern of anyone's. The programme of reform, which had already been started by Salar Jung, did not attract much notice from Canning or elicit any praise from him, notwithstanding his repeated insistence on good government in Indian states. The new Hyderabad that was to emerge out of its medieval shell was the creation of her own people, and the lead was taken by her Minister, Salar Jung.

Canning was succeeded by the unremarkable Elgin, to whom he had given a somewhat 'modified approval' as his successor.[56] He had indeed wondered whether he should congratulate Elgin on his appointment as Governor-General of India: 'It is almost too solemn an event to carry much cause of felicitation with it.'[57] Although Elgin had made significant contributions as the Governor-General of Canada and led successful missions to China and Japan, this Scottish peer, scholarly, philosophical, hard-working and unglamorous, could leave little impact on India. One reason for this was that he ruled for too short a time, just a little over a year and a half. The other was that the domineering Wood reduced him to the level of a subordinate officer, trying to govern India largely by private correspondence.[58] Wood expected Elgin merely to carry on Canning's general policy and felt that anyone expecting a change would be altogether 'disappointed'.[59]

This was also what Elgin thought, at any rate, at the beginning. Before he came out to India he had almost humbly asked Canning for his suggestions regarding what had to be done in India. 'I shall be very grateful to you if you will direct my attention to any matter to which you think I ought to turn it before I leave England.'[60] On coming to India he felt that India was 'at peace'—thanks to Canning—and that the atmosphere was 'calm enough.' Canning had been 'very friendly and communicative' with him before his departure and Elgin assured Wood that he had no intention of departing from the great man's policy.[61] Regarding the policy to be followed towards the princely states, Wood had warned him that 'Canning's policy was right, and ought to be carried out and for Heaven's sake don't let yourself be unwillingly betrayed into anything which may undo the favourable impression on the minds of the chiefs which Canning's conduct has produced.'[62] Elgin, however, wondered whether Canning's policy regarding the relation between the Indian chiefs and the British Government was altogether 'correct' or 'complete'.[63] Unfortunately, untimely death claimed him before he could develop his own policy.

It was during Elgin's viceroyalty that Davidson died at the Hyderabad Residency in August 1862. He had served as Resident during a most critical period of Hyderabad's history from 1856 onwards. He had witnessed Hyderabad passing through the crisis of 1857-8, and had willy-nilly been instrumental in carrying out Canning's policy towards the state. He was a fair-minded man, with a sense of justice and fair play that could, and on many occasions did, rise above petty and selfish interests. He had tried his best to present Hyderabad's case before the Viceroy many a time, although he had met with little success. His death was a great blow to Hyderabad, and a personal loss to the Minister. The filling of the office of the Resident at Hyderabad required some thought, especially as Wood was distrustful of 'the fanatical Mahometans in that country.'[64] Finally, Sir George Yule, one of the famous Yule brothers, was chosen.

Yule came out as Resident at Hyderabad in 1863 and stayed on for four years. Fortunately for Hyderabad, he, like Davidson, proved to be a well-wisher of the state. He also became a personal friend of the

Minister, and this friendship continued long after he had left the place. He encouraged Salar Jung to go on with the scheme of reforms on which the Minister had already embarked, and appreciated the Minister's 'thorough honesty of purpose.' Yule was convinced that although the Minister had not been able to put an entire stop to all the evils in the state, he had checked and reformed many of them. He had stopped bribes and corruption, especially among government servants, the gross oppression of the ryots had been mitigated, and the financial credit of the Government restored. The Resident sent a detailed report of Salar Jung's reforms to Elgin. The Governor-General much appreciated the Minister's efforts and services 'to his country and to civilization'.[65]

Elgin died suddenly on 20 November, 1863 at Dharamshala. 'Three Governor-Generals [sic] in so short a time', commented Wood, 'is a sad reflexion.'[66] While two of them, Dalhousie and Canning, had proved themselves to be stalwarts of the British Empire, in comparison Elgin's viceroyalty was short, unexciting, uneventful, and an 'unfinished chapter' in Indian history. John Lawrence succeeded Elgin in January 1864. A trusted lieutenant of Wood and a prominent figure in his Council during Elgin's viceroyalty, Lawrence was the nominee solely of Wood. When the telegram of Elgin's death reached the Secretary of State, he told Algernon West, his private secretary, that the next Viceroy must be Stanley or Lawrence or himself. And Lawrence it was. Wood obtained the Queen's permission and gave Lawrence the news of his splendid appointment at Paddington railway station.[67]

Lawrence as Governor-General gave no evidence of the administrative ability or farsightedness that was expected of him. For the first half of his rule he was dominated by the energetic and despotic 'Maharaja Wood' (as he was called in India),[68] who turned him into a mere mouthpiece of the Government at home. During the second half, when cabinets fell and Secretaries of State were changed with surprising rapidity, he was unable to capitalize on the political instability at home. And yet, his viceroyalty witnessed significant developments in Hyderabad's relations with the paramount power.

Almost as soon as Lawrence arrived in India, an important aspect of Canning's policy came up for clarification. In 1864, when Nizam Afzal-ud-Daula was indisposed, an interesting question regarding succession was raised by the Resident, George Yule. The Nizam had no sons, but a half-brother, Roshun-ud-Daula, whom unfortunately he hated, and so he was likely to nominate some other member of his family as his successor. The question now was whether the Nizam had a right to nominate his successor, passing over the next heir or heirs. Yule refused to recognize this right. Canning's Sanad, according to him, implied that, so long as a natural heir survived, he could not be passed over in favour of a selected successor without inherited rights. Further, the recognition of the Nizam's right to order succession as he pleased could easily cause incessant intrigues in the state. Lawrence upheld Yule's interpretation of the Sanad, and authorized him to recognize Roshun-ud-Daula as the Nizam's successor in case the Nizam died.[69] Wood, too, wrote privately 'that the brother ought to succeed, and the Resident ought to contrive with Salar Jung that he should do so.' The Secretary of State, however, believed that succession in Muslim states was not quite so regular as it should be, and that the chief often selected from amongst his family the person whom he thought the best. If, therefore, any member of the family should be selected and supported by the family and the influential people, Wood would recognize him. He was in favour of recognizing anybody or any settlement amongst the members of the family which afforded the best prospect of avoiding confusion and promoting the well-being of the state. In his official dispatch, therefore, the Secretary of State, while approving Lawrence's policy in general, laid down that under certain circumstances the Viceroy was at liberty to exercise discretion to recognize any other suitable and popular member of the family.[70] Obviously, Wood wanted to keep the door open for the selection of a Nizam whom the British wanted in preference to others, should the occasion or need for this ever arise. It may be mentioned here that Roshun-ud-Daula never became the Nizam. A son was born to Afzal-ud-Daula late in life, in August 1866, and on his death he was succeeded by this infant son, Mir Mahbub Ali Khan.

Of far greater importance to the paramount power was the question of trade. By the 1860s *laissez faire* economics had established a strong grip over the British Government and the British Indian administration. Notwithstanding the treaty of 1802, transit duties frequently levied at different customs houses in Hyderabad irked traders and merchants, and numerous complaints poured in from the Governments of Bombay and Madras.[71] What was worse, under the threat of a famine the Nizam had prohibited the export of all grain from his dominion, a factor that caused a sharp rise in grain prices in the Bombay and Madras markets.[72] Besides, the Nizam had ordered his subjects to grow less cotton and more grain, presumably because he felt that Salar Jung, acting under the advice of the late Davidson, had deliberately encouraged the ryots to take up the cultivation of cotton at the expense of food crops. Yule personally believed—as he had earlier reported to Elgin—that there was no scarcity of grain in Hyderabad and that its high price was due to other causes. Yule had tried to prevent the Minister from interfering either with the prices or with the dealers and had told him that 'the prohibition did his master's subjects more harm than good.' Elgin had agreed with Yule: 'The tendency which seems to be growing in many native states to interfere with free trade in this article is certainly causing embarrassment.'[73]

It was after several interviews with Salar Jung that Yule succeeded— sadly, after Elgin's death—in persuading the Minister to propose to the Nizam the abolition of all transit duties in the state and the withdrawal of the prohibitory order against the export of grain.[74]

The Nizam could hardly be expected to appreciate why he should comply with the request since he had every right to do what he considered necessary for his state. He gave his reluctant consent to the proposal only when the Minister hinted at intervention by the Resident. Eventually, through a proclamation the Nizam announced the abolition of all transit duties in his state and of all duties on grain. He also withdrew the prohibition against the export of grain. Lawrence, the new Viceroy, and Wood, the veteran Secretary of State were very pleased.[75] These relaxations were understandably not popular with the Nizam's people. The prices of food-grains in the state rose inevitably due to a large export to Bombay, and the Minister had to compensate the lower Government officials by increasing their salaries[76]—an additional drain on the state treasury. The angry Nizam often taunted the Minister by saying—truthfully, if unkindly—that, as a result of the Minister's proposal, instead of coming into his country grain was mostly being exported.[77]

Nor was grain the only article on the Indian Government list. Free trade was pressing hard for the abolition or relaxation of duties on other goods as well. In order to compensate the treasury for the loss caused by the abolition of all transit duties, Salar Jung had imposed a 5 per cent tax *ad valorem* on every article, except grain, produced in the country, to be levied at the place of production. In December, 1864, Yule persuaded the Minister to remove this duty. At the same time, different rates of duty for different articles of export and import were fixed. The rates were subject to a ceiling of 5 per cent *ad valorem*— except on salt, on which higher duty was paid—and were to be levied once and for all at fixed customs points. Six places, situated on the main lines of communication with British Indian territory, were mentioned in the rules for the establishment of frontier customs houses.[78] The relaxation and regulation of duties doubtless increased the volume of trade in Hyderabad, but there was a corresponding increase of imports over exports.[79] With the slogan of free trade, British manufactured goods captured the Hyderabad market.

A less significant, although more irritating, measure taken by Lawrence's administration was the levy of fines on Indian states on account of mail robbery. With the extension of the Empire the security of British mail assumed increasing importance. The Government of India sought to protect its mail passing through the Indian states by enforcing upon them responsibility for the security of the mail. This was done by imposing a penalty for mail robberies committed within their territories and extracting compensation for valuable articles like jewels and bullion dispatched by mail or *banghy* post. The penalty realized was to be spent on improving police protection for mail lines.[80]

When this resolution was circulated to the political officers, Yule at Hyderabad made a spirited protest. 'Let us', wrote the upright Resident with striking candour, 'put ourselves in the place of the Nizam and his Minister and his subjects; would we not consider it as the deepest degradation if another and more powerful state fined us for robberies of the mails which ran through our territory for its own convenience, not for ours, and which, by the permission to carry valuables, it rendered an incentive to crime?'[81] Lawrence was unimpressed by Yule's argument. He ruled that every state was responsible for the secure passage of British Government mail and parcel post through its territory. If mail or parcels were plundered within its domain, it would have to extract compensation from the people of the area for the restitution of the value of the property plundered. It would also have to pay compensation to the men disabled, as well as to the families of· the men killed, either in defence or in the carriage of Government mail.[82]

Salar Jung resented the implication of subjection underlying the rules and was anxious to have an assurance that they would not apply to his state. He had taken every step, he reasoned, to protect the mails and his state did not merit the humiliation. Nevertheless, Lawrence was not prepared to make any exception in favour of Hyderabad. If exceptions were made, the whole arrangement would fall apart. He merely assured the Minister that the case of each state would be duly considered and decided on merit.[83]

Although not opposed to Lawrence's general policy, the Secretary of State, Cranborne (later Salisbury), was nevertheless critical of the Viceroy. By his own admission, Cranborne had 'no particular sympathy' for the princes. They would, he believed, 'certainly cut every English throat' if ever they could do so safely. And yet, Cranborne was anxious that the British Government should be 'temporarily just to them', and give them no reason for saying that the British treated their promises lightly. 'I do not think', admonished the Secretary of State, 'any good purpose can be served by using publicly languages of a humiliating kind towards them.' And the language of the mail-bags robbery proclamation was 'to say the least, peremptory and austere.' The velvet glove, regretted Cranborne, had somehow slipped off.[84] Lawrence must have received the Secretary of State's remonstrance with considerable annoyance. He tried to defend himself by claiming that sometimes 'a little severity in the way' saved 'the necessity of more severe action.'[85] Even so, Northcote, Cranborne's successor, could not uphold the Viceroy either. Unwilling to disturb the arrangements already made, he permitted the rules to continue, but requested Lawrence to enforce them with great discretion, and only in extreme cases.[86]

There was one issue, however, on which Lawrence's Government treated the Hyderabad durbar on a footing of equality, and that was the question of extradition of criminals. Not infrequently, the Nizam's subjects committed offences in the state and fled to British territories. Similarly, criminals fled from British territories to the Nizam's domain. The Anglo-Nizam treaties were virtually silent on the subject of extradition and only Article 7 of the treaty of 1798 provided for some kind of extradition in the case of 'Sepoy deserters'.[87]

Usually, the principle of reciprocity was observed in practice between the Nizam's Government and the Government of India in respect of the surrender of notorious criminals, who, being subjects of one state, took refuge in another. In accordance with the prevailing practice, Salar Jung in 1862 requested the Bombay Government through the Resident to hand over one Mahadeo Hutkul, accused of murder in the Nizam's territory and apprehended in British territory. The Bombay Government refused to oblige, but requested the Resident to furnish the magistrate of Sholapur with enough evidence to satisfy the Bombay Government of sufficient grounds for the charge against the accused so as to justify his surrender. The Government of India supported the Bombay Government's stand. Since the British had to deal with a number of states and their different laws, they had to make sure, in order to guard against injustice, that there was reasonable cause for the apprehension and surrender of an accused person.[88] Soon, the Nizam's Government and the Bombay Government came to an understanding on the subject. It was decided that British officers seeking extradition of a criminal from the Nizam's territory were to forward their applications along with evidence against the offender to the Resident, who would request his surrender from the Nizam's Government. Similarly, the Minister would send his application supported by evidence for the surrender of a criminal through the Resident to the Bombay Government.[89]

Lawrence's Government felt that the question of extradition of serious offenders should be solved on a formal basis. It instructed Yule to negotiate an extradition treaty with the Nizam based on terms of strict reciprocity and on the model of the extradition treaty with Nepal. Salar Jung was initially exceedingly averse to the conclusion of a treaty 'from dread of his master', who disliked the British and their innovations. He was ultimately persuaded by Yule to present the proposal to the Nizam. The Nizam was extremely annoyed. Under the proposed treaty, he maintained, the 'criminals required by the British Government would all be delivered up, but none claimed by us would be surrendered.' He was already annoyed because he had been persuaded by Salar Jung to agree to withdraw his order prohibiting export of grain from Hyderabad. He rebuked his Minister angrily: 'You have taken all the grain out of my country, and now you propose to take away all my people.'[90] But, gradually, he came to see that there was no point in opposing the treaty which, unless accepted gracefully, would be imposed on him. A draft treaty was prepared by Yule and Salar Jung, but Yule left Hyderabad before its final execution. Yule's successor, Sir Richard Temple, sent the final treaty to be signed and sealed by the Nizam *on the day on which it was sent to him.* Salar Jung fowarded it to the Nizam, with the request that 'as the Treaty bears this date, no delay should occur in returning it.' The Nizam signed, and Lawrence duly ratified it (May 1867).[91]

The treaty provided that either Government could make a requisition on the other for the surrender of any of its subjects accused of having committed a heinous crime[92] within its territory, and that the Government into whose territory the criminal sought refuge would, on receipt of such requisition, hand over the accused to the requisitioning Government. No Government would surrender the criminal unless a requisition was duly made by the Government seeking the surrender, and unless enough evidence of the crime alleged to have been committed was produced, so as to justify his apprehension and surrender.[93] This was one of the fairest treaties ever concluded between the two Governments on the basis of equality and reciprocity. The Secretary of State was satisfied with the treaty and hoped that its provisions would be carried out by both parties in a spirit of co-operation.[94]

Presently, an embarrassing situation in Hyderabad attracted the attention of Lawrence's Government. In 1867, one of the periodical crises between the Nizam and his Minister broke out. When negotiations for the extradition treaty were going on, the Nizam began to show his displeasure against his Minister and decided to get rid of him. At Hyderabad, all communication between the Nizam and his Minister, except on durbar days, were concluded through two *vakils*. Here a few words about the role of the *vakils* in Hyderabad may not be out of context. In accordance with the prevalent custom, members of the nobility seldom met the Nizam or each other directly. All business was usually conducted by their *vakils* on their behalf. A regular exchange of friendly messages, greetings and gifts through *vakils* helped maintain cordial relations between the Nizam and his nobles and between the nobles themselves. The *vakil*, therefore, was a crucial factor in the Hyderabad political system.[95] On the death of a particular *vakil*, the Nizam appointed to the vacancy Lashkar Jung, 'a man of bad character', and an avowed enemy of the Minister. The Minister, quite understandably, refused to acknowledge him as a *vakil*, at which the Nizam asked the Minister to resign formally, which he did. The letter of resignation was actually written, the Minister said, 'in obedience to His Highness's order', and on his insistence, and the Minister immediately informed Yule of this development. Once again, almost like a repeat performance of an oft-staged drama, the British came to his rescue. Yule, a staunch ally of Salar Jung, refused even to think of his resignation. He at once asked for an audience, clearly with a view to persuading the Nizam to take the Minister back. This constant and obvious aid from the Resident, which enabled Salar Jung to retain office, lowered his self-respect and his influence over the people of the country. It seemed as though Salar Jung was being forced upon his master through alien interference, which he was. But Salar Jung's retention in office, Yule felt, was of the very greatest importance in the interest of good administration, and if this could not be brought about by the Minister himself, then he, Yule, would strain every nerve to achieve this objective.[96] He tried to impress on the Nizam through the Amir-i-Kabir,[97] the head of the nobility in Hyderabad and related to the Nizam through marriage, that the Minister was supported by the British because of his efficient administration, that his removal would lead to anarchy in the country, that it would definitely disturb the friendship between the two Governments. The Government of India could not afford to sit back and watch with indifference the disturbances in the Nizam's territory, as these could very well spread to its own. George Yule thus virtually threatened the Amir-i-Kabir with British interference in case Salar Jung was removed. On the Amir-i-Kabir's suggestion Salar Jung sent a humble apology to the Nizam. No reply came. Yule then requested the Nizam again for an audience, and Salar Jung sent a message to the Amir-i-Kabir to bring the business to a speedy conclusion.[98]

The Nizam was, or at least appeared to be, pacified by Salar Jung's apology. Lashkar Jung was dismissed and Salar Jung restored to favour. On 15 March 1867, the Nizam, at the Resident's request, held a durbar at which he invested both the Minister and the Resident with the insignia of the Knight Commander of the Star of India, which the Queen had bestowed on them.[99] On 15 April in another durbar he honoured Salar Jung with jewels, a pair of diamonds, a *sirpesh* of diamonds and emeralds, a pair of *dustabands* set with diamonds, and a diamond ring, the whole cost being Rs.50,000. 'His Highness was in good humour', the Minister reported to the Resident, 'and very gracious when presenting the jewels, fixing the bracelet on with his own hands.' This was considered a mark of great regard and the Minister came back from the durbar in 'high spirit' at the open restoration of his master's favour.[100]

It will be quite clear by now that Salar Jung never really meant to resign. He had sent in his letter of resignation on the Nizam's insistence. But he knew of the Resident's support for him, he knew that the Nizam would have to take him back whether he liked it or not, and he probably knew also that the Governor-General would approve of Yule's policy. It is obvious from the interesting letter he wrote on 27 April 1867 to Sir Richard Temple, George Yule's successor, describing the whole incident, that he had had recourse to external pressure on his master to retain office. Although he denied 'having desired or invited British interference' on the 'unpleasant' occasion of the Nizam's 'displeasure' with him,[101] he had, in fact, kept in constant touch with Yule and relied fully on the Resident's timely intervention on his behalf. But it must be said in the Minister's favour that, although he tried to maintain his position through foreign intervention, he was perfectly loyal to the Nizam. He showed the reverence which his countrymen felt for their master and would have undergone any labour for the welfare of his liege. The Nizam had kept him in a state of thraldom; he was almost a prisoner in his own house, and could not move beyond the outer gates of his courtyard without his master's permission. Despite such humiliations, his 'genuine regard' and 'heartfelt' deference for his 'ungracious lord' surprised Richard Temple on many an occasion.[102]

Lawrence approved of Yule's proceedings in dealing with the Hyderabad crisis. He reported to the Secretary of State, Cranborne, that there had been a split between the Nizam and Salar Jung and the latter had resigned. 'Yule very properly deprecated this measure.'[103] Notwithstanding the support to Salar Jung, Lawrence was a little critical of the Minister's unco-operative attitude towards the Nizam, and did not want to encourage him against his master too often. Nothing could be further from his wishes than to maintain the Minister of any state in power after he had ceased to give satisfaction to the chief himself.[104] An admirable sentiment, but in this particular case Lawrence's decision was dictated not so much by any consideration for the Nizam's feelings as by his own annoyance with Salar Jung. The Hyderabadi Minister had already taken his first bold step—indicative of future policy—by asking for the restoration of Berar. Lawrence had considered this an 'audacious' request.[105] He must have felt that it would be wise to keep the Minister under some check in order to prevent him from becoming too daring or ambitious. While, therefore, he sent a *khureeta* to the Nizam urging him to keep someone who was as able and good a Minister as Salar Jung, no copy of the *khureeta* was sent to the Minister. Salar Jung, although none too pleased, agreed quietly that 'it was far better' and more appropriate that he should receive a copy of the *khureeta* from the Nizam rather than the Resident.[106]

The Nizam was not too unhappy with the Governor-General's *khureeta*. 'What appears to have chiefly contributed to this is, I think,' wrote the Minister to the Resident, 'the certainty expressed of my loyalty and obedience to him in the Viceroy's *khureeta*.'[107] The Nizam assured the Viceroy that he had always found his Minister submissive, subordinate and loyal and that he would always give his Minister his confidence and support.[108] Sir Stafford Northcote, the Secretary of State, doubted 'the sincerity of the reconciliation,'[109] and many others shared his feeling.

Meanwhile, Sir Richard Temple replaced Yule, who had gone to join the Governor-General's Council. Yule, Lawrence reported to the Secretary of State, had been 'unwilling' to leave Hyderabad until the Nizam-Salar Jung crisis was resolved. 'I do not think this need keep him there and have told him so.'[110] Lawrence was perhaps slightly annoyed with Yule for his complete support to Salar Jung on every issue, including Berar. Richard Temple, who took Yule's place, was, in the words of Elgin, under whom he had earlier served, very 'able and energetic'.[111] Lawrence had first met Temple in 1851 as a very young British officer and had at once recognized in him the most promising officer in the Punjab. 'He can understand what I say, and put it into first rate form', Lawrence used to say of Temple to his friends.[112] When Temple was sent by the Governor-General to Hyderabad he was Chief Commissioner of the Central Provinces. The news was received by his friends with surprise, since it was doubtful whether the new post was as desirable as the old one. It was widely rumoured that the real object of his being sent was to procure the annexation of Berar to the Central Provinces.[113] He did not achieve that, nor is there any proof that he tried to do so. But he faithfully carried out Lawrence's instructions in Hyderabad. It was he who had received, as the Resident, Lawrence's *khureeta* to the Nizam enjoining the retention of Salar Jung in office. Salar Jung had at that time wished that the Resident sought a private interview with the Nizam, and had practically suggested it. 'I have every hope that in your private audience with His Highness you will speak to him so that he may be favourably disposed towards me as my only anxiety is to secure His Highness's kindness and good will.'[114] Temple, however, did not seek a private audience, and the Minister did not press him any further.

On coming to Hyderabad, Temple assessed the situation shrewdly. His first official business was to transmit Lawrence's *khureeta* to the Nizam. It was reported to him that when the Nizam's secretary read out the opening sentences which were highly complimentary, the Nizam had been silent, but at the mention of Salar Jung's name he exclaimed with the utmost disgust, 'Oh! it's once more Salar Jung.'[115] When Temple visited the Nizam to present his credentials, the Nizam received him with a demeanour not haughty but calm and almost impassive. Salar Jung accompanied the Resident, and was made to feel thoroughly subdued in the presence of His Highness. After a chilling pause, the Nizam began the conversation with the usual inquiry about the Governor-General's health. In order to say something civil and polite, Temple congratulated the Nizam on the good government which existed in his country. The Nizam immediately replied in a tone of slight displeasure, 'It has been good from the first and it is still good.'[116] The Resident realized that the Nizam interpreted his compliment as an indirect recommendation of Salar Jung, and that he had aroused his sensitive jealousy. Under these circumstances, Temple's policy was, as his chief Lawrence wanted it to be, two-fold: to retain the Minister in power and yet not allow him to become too independent. He insisted that, while he would support the Minister, he should have full communication with the Nizam. And he told Salar Jung discreetly that it would be advisable if everything were done nominally in the Nizam's name so that His Highness might feel that he had a personal share in the credit of success.[117] This the Minister perfectly understood. Thus, while government was to be carried on nominally in the Nizam's name, it was Salar Jung, still the Anglophile Minister, who was to run the administration with the advice and support—and under the control—of the Resident.

Temple's tenure of only a few months at the Hyderabad Residency witnessed a significant rise in the power of the Resident, to which he contributed more than any other Resident since the time of Metcalfe. He described his position thus: 'As British Resident I was virtually the Atlas on whose shoulders the Hyderabad state rested.'[118] Though perhaps a somewhat exaggerated evaluation of his importance and power, Salar Jung's demi-official correspondence with him, as well as his own political diary, clearly reveal that Temple enjoyed tremendous power and influence in the state and successfully projected his image as representative of the paramount power. He was also able to build up a very good understanding with Salar Jung, whom he considered to be a really good Minister.[119] The Minister, too, consulted him on every important occasion. 'I shall take care not to take any step of importance without consulting you, which is a privilege I shall highly value', he promised. The Minister also sent the Resident confidential reports in English through his English secretary, and forwarded to the Resident detailed information about his own civil administration, which he was trying to reorganize and reorientate. Salar Jung reformed every part of the state's administration, the land revenue, the dispensation of justice, the police, education, sanitation, and, above, all finance. In all this, Temple gave him active guidance and encouragement, and Salar Jung was grateful for the 'excellent suggestions' he often made.[120] It may be said that Hyderabad made real progress towards modernization under the Salar Jung-Temple programme of reform.

But the programme was based on European principles, and the reforms ran on western lines. The people of Hyderabad did not appreciate such quick and Europeanized changes made under British influence. There existed in the state a deep-seated resentment and hostility against the British, and in 1867 an attempt at insurrection was made. A person known as Ram Rao and representing himself as a connection of the Satara family, tried to induce the local people to supply men and arms for the subversion of British and Muslim rule in the Deccan. Salar Jung took adequate measures as soon as the report of the conspiracy reached him and Ram Rao and a few others were arrested near Bhalki. The Minister forwarded the prisoners to the Residency and agreed to be guided by the Resident's views. The preliminary investigation was conducted under the supervision of the Assistant Resident and the result showed that the rising was not really important. Hence, the prisoners were returned to the Minister with a request to try them in the Hyderabad Criminal Court on the ground of treason against the Nizam's Government. The Court passed the sentence of imprisonment for life against Ram Rao. The Resident, however, felt that the British could not afford to ignore even abortive attempts like this one in Hyderabad, and so altered the sentence to one of deportation.[121] Thus, the Bhalki conspiracy failed miserably. Its only importance was to demonstrate the existence in Hyderabad of a section of people who were enemies of the British and who would clearly not hesitate to subvert the alien Government.

That this hostility was aimed not only against the British but also against their chief ally, Salar Jung, came to light with a desperate attack on the Minister in early 1868. The Minister was proceeding to the durbar at the Nizam's palace through a narrow street when a man in the crowd fired two shots, one of which grazed his turban, and the other killed a peon.[122] The assassin was arrested and eventually sentenced to death. He was a Muslim, long without any employment, and his motive was a hatred of change and anti-English feeling. The Nizam, greatly annoyed at this, took the unusual step of advising the kotwal to proclaim that no unemployed man should hereafter be allowed to carry arms in the streets. He did not enforce this measure, much to the regret of the Resident and the Government of India.[123]

Temple was prepared to overlook such minor lapses, but he could not quite ignore the reorganization of the Nizam's army or, rather, the Reformed Troops. In Hyderabad the army comprised (1) the Reformed Troops and the Reorganized City Regiments, and (2) the Irregular Troops, apart from the *Surf-i-khas* and *Paigah* troops, used only for police purposes. The Irregular Troops, consisting of Arabs, Rohillas, Sikhs, Rajputs, Baluchis and other tribes, were employed on escort and guard duties, like escorting mail and in helping the police prevent dacoity and highway robberies.[124] They carried old-fashioned arms and were innocent of drill or discipline. Besides the Nizam, each chief nobleman maintained armed retainers, who were equally indisciplined and badly armed. Their number was constantly being swelled by fresh infiltrations of Arabs and Rohillas into Hyderabad. The British Government was greatly concerned about this lawless element, and pressed the Hyderabad Government for the reduction of their number.[125] While Salar Jung complied with this request, he at the same time continued to organize the Reformed Troops.[126] He had started his military reforms in the days of Davidson, and proceeded with great vigour under the positive encouragement of Yule. The Reformed Troops were placed under the command of a European officer and disciplined after the model of the Hyderabad Contingent, obviously with a view to dispensing with the services of the Contingent in the not-too-distant future.

To Temple this trend seemed to be alarming. Determined to assess the situation for himself, he decided to review the Reformed Troops.[127] Salar Jung was apparently delighted with the idea, but sought to be excused from accompanying the Resident. 'For various reasons, I would prefer not applying to His Highness for permission to do so, at least for the present. I think on the present occasion if you honoured the troops yourself, it would be sufficient.'[128]

Temple reviewed the troops in the parade ground on 30 May. The Brigade was commanded by Capt. Rocke, formerly of the Royal Artillery. The Brigade's movements were well and smartly conducted, noted Temple. The artillery firing was rapid and precise and the cavalry well-mounted. The general result of the review as regards the troops was satisfactory. 'Whether such a body of troops', commented the Resident in his private political diary, 'are wanted at all in the place where they now are, is quite another question.'[129] Here Temple, was, of course, following the pattern of thought of his masters. Since the days of Wood and Canning the British Government had distrusted the armies of the Indian princes, notwithstanding their loyalty during the Rising of 1857. The British felt no need for the states to keep any military force beyond what was required by internal circumstances. Although a rising of the princes was not feared, a cautious attitude towards their military power still lingered. Hyderabad, in particular, was not to be trusted. 'Hyderabad is the only place likely to give us trouble', Lawrence had confided to Denison, the Governor of Madras, who promptly agreed. 'We have the Nizam with a strong force of his own, and our own Contingent would probably join him in case of an outbreak.'[130]

Unaware of Temple's private observation or the Governor-General's confidential correspondence, Salar Jung thanked Temple for his kind 'commendation' of the Reformed Troops. 'It is a matter of the highest satisfaction that they have obtained your approval. of which they will doubtless be proud and encouraged to go on improving themselves.'[131] Temple, however, was no Yule, and did not give any encouragement to further improvement or organization of the army. Nevertheless, he did not openly discourage the Minister. He left Hyderabad with a genuine feeling of sadness, having parted with Salar Jung after a hearty and tender embrace in oriental fashion, on 3 January 1868. Lawrence left India exactly a year later.

III

By the time Lawrence left in January 1869, some significant changes had rapidly taken place in the Home Government. Wood was no longer ruling the India Office. This latter-day Mughal had to leave his post on 16 February 1866 thanks to a fall while hunting at Hickleton. He professed himself 'very sorry' to quit office, which he described as 'the most interesting in the Government from the large sphere of its action'. 'I have been connected with Indian administration so long', he wrote to Frere, 'that I feel the interest in everything connected with India.'[132] Wood had ruled India despotically for well-nigh seven years, and was more responsible than any other person for shaping Britain's India policy of the time. Even after his retirement from India Office, he continued to exercise tremendous influence on the making of that policy.[133] *The Times* commented on his retirement that it would be difficult to find another man 'possessed of that extent and variety of knowledge, that quickness, industry and versatility, that acquaintance with matters financial, military, naval, judicial and political' to deal with the destinies of 150,000,000 of the human race.[134] It is, however, difficult from Hyderabad's point of view to compose such a panegyric on Wood. Whatever his other qualities might have been, he ruled Hyderabad solely in the interest of the British, and particularly of Manchester. He obstinately refused to look at any problem from the point of view of Hyderabad, and clung to his own ideas regarding British paramountcy. The ruler and the ruled in Hyderabad had nothing to thank him for, apart from the tightening of British control.

Wood was followed in quick succession by three Secretaries of State. The first was Ripon, whose tenure ended in June 1866 with the fall of the Russell Cabinet. The third Derby Government saw Cranborne as Secretary of State, and Cranborne resigned his post, on the death of Derby, owing to differences with Disraeli over the household suffrage reform bill. Sir Stafford Northcote, a close friend of Disraeli, took Cranborne's place in the Conservative cabinet, headed for the first time by Disraeli. It was Disraeli who had the opportunity of choosing Lawrence's successor in India, and he chose Lord Mayo, his Chief Secretary for Ireland, to fill the post.[135] Before Mayo arrived in India, Disraeli had yielded place to the Liberal leader, Gladstone. It was rumoured that Mayo would be recalled, but no such step was taken. India was not really a party issue; neither the Liberals nor the Conservatives had any great knowledge or understanding of Indian problems and the Indian people. Both parties followed the same sort of policy towards India, without any fundamental difference, and the Viceroy, be he a Mayo or a Northbrook, was expected to carry that out.

In the India Office, of course, a change had to be made. The Secretary of State held a cabinet position. The Conserative Northcote was replaced by the Liberal Argyll, who warmly thanked Gladstone for the position. 'India Office has long been *the* office that I liked the thoughts of best. I need not tell you that its value is enhanced by its being held under you.'[136] Argyll also promised to accord to Mayo his unqualified support. 'Indian politics', the Secretary of State frankly wrote to the Viceroy, 'are fortunately for the most part unconnected with party struggle at home, and I hope that there will be nothing to prevent me from having open and confidential communication with you on every question affecting the Government of India.'[137] Argyll was no Wood. Although he held office for six years (almost as long as Wood), he could not and did not exercise as much influence on

Mayo or his successor, Northbrook, as Wood had done on Elgin, Lawrence or even Canning. Lacking in initiative and energy, he was content to leave the affairs of India in the hands of the Viceroy and his men.

Lawrence stayed on in India until 12 January 1869, having informed Northcote that Mayo should not arrive in Calcutta earlier than that day: 'I wish to make my full term'.[138] On 12 January Mayo arrived at Government House in Calcutta, a man of self-confidence and enthusiasm after the ineffective Elgin and the cautious Lawrence. His physical and mental toughness was often concealed behind a winning smile and a personal charm which was all his own. This Irish nobleman, born of an originally Norman baronial family, was relatively unknown in England when he was offered the Indian Governor-Generalship. He was delighted with it. India promised splendid opportunities to those connected with its administration. Mayo knew his mind and formulated the details of his policy himself, often with, and more often without, the advice of the Duke of Argyll. That policy in general was, of course, to entrench British rule firmly on Indian soil and to assert British paramountcy over the states; but Mayo also combined with it a desire to see the country well governed, and to give it an able, firm and efficient administration.

Towards the Indian princes Mayo's attitude was imperialistic, but paternal. He would not dream of giving up British paramountcy over them but intended to use that authority to promote good administration. 'If we support you in power, we expect in return good government' he told the princes in a famous speech at the Ajmer durbar.[139] Much like Canning, the original founder of the policy, Mayo looked upon the princely states as an integral part of the British Empire and constantly exhorted their rulers to govern well. But Mayo out-matched Canning in his conception of the future role of the Indian chiefs. He established Mayo College at Ajmer for the princes and chiefs of Rajputana with a view to bringing them in close contact with European ideas and teachers. The new generation of Indian princes would be westernized which, Mayo believed, would infuse them with a high sense of public duty. It would also serve another and more important purpose, that of securing for the British powerful and staunch allies, imbued with British ideas and familiar with British manners and customs.

Mayo had been in India barely a month when on 26 February 1869 the Nizam, Afzal-ud-Daula, died. A rule marked on the one hand by the dominance of the paramount power, and on the other by the inauguration of an era of reform and progress in the state, came to an end. Afzal-ud-Daula died suddenly after a brief illness leaving his only son, Mir Mahbub Ali Khan, an infant of only two years and eight months. The British, who seldom failed to seize an opportunity favourable to themselves, recognized the new situation as a chance to assert their rights of paramountcy and further their interests by assuming the guardianship of the infant Nizam. C.B. Saunders, who had been appointed the Resident at Hyderabad in 1868, understood what his role required of him. Regarding Mir Mahbub Ali's title to rule there was no doubt under the terms of the sanad granted to Afzal-ud-Daula. At the Minister's request, Saunders sanctioned the proclamation of the boy as Nizam, subject to the order of the Government of India regarding guardianship and administration of the country during his minority.[140] With most commendable promptitude he next availed himself of the first opportunity to abolish an old etiquette in the Nizam's court which required officers of all ranks to take off their boots before coming into the Nizam's presence. Out of respect for the Nizam, successive Residents at his court had followed this custom, albeit unwillingly, for more than half a century. If the custom was regarded as an admission of inferiority to the Nizam on the part of the British representative, like the kowtow before the Chinese Emperor, it could be objectionable. But if regarded simply as a part of court etiquette, which all who visited the court were to observe, the practice was not so offensive. On his visits to the Nizam Richard Temple had not demanded any departure from the old custom. About his first visit to the Nizam he writes in his diary, 'On arriving at the threshold of the Nizam's room of audience I took off my boots (which was easily done in a moment) and walked forward'.[141] Nevertheless, Saunders was not prepared to follow any alien custom which might throw some doubt on his *de facto* superior position. He informed the Minister that on the occasion of his visit of condolence to the infant Nizam, and at the subsequent installation of the Nizam, he would not, excepting under his own Government's order, observe the old humiliating custom of taking off his shoes and sitting on the ground. The durbar must be held henceforth according to the rule followed at all other courts, and chairs must be provided for him and other British officers.[142] The Minister and the Amir-i-Kabir did not quite relish the idea and gave way somewhat reluctantly. At the time of the Resident's visit of condolence to the Nizam the Indians divested themselves of their shoes, while the

British party sat on chairs of European manufacture with their boots on.[143] After a few days, at the more formal durbar installing the new Nizam, the same procedure was followed. Thus, a practice which was not considered consistent with the British position in India and with the dignity due to the paramount power, was quietly dropped. The Nizam himself was much too young to disapprove, but the nobles at his court must have been extremely vexed.

The Nizam was installed by the Resident at a crowded durbar. The Resident assisted in placing the Nizam on the *musnud*—a symbol of his assistance and protection to the ruler. Everything passed off satisfactorily, with the Resident and British officers accomodated with chairs.[144] Saunders's actions were fully approved and appreciated by Mayo. 'The Nizam's death is a fortunate event', felt the Viceroy, 'Saunders had done right well as far as I can judge.'[145] Mayo was pleased that the Resident had 'acted with much judgment and courage' and that he had succeeded in relieving British officers from the 'humiliating ceremony' of taking off their shoes and sitting on the ground in the Nizam's presence. He happily reported to Argyll, 'Saunders had behaved with great firmness....and I have told him so.'[146]

Since the Nizam was only an infant, a Council of Regency had to be proclaimed. Roshun-ud-Daula, now a disappointed man without any hope of becoming the Nizam, claimed that the office of the Regent should be conferred upon him. The Resident was, of course, not prepared to lend an ear.to his pleading. Previous history might have led one to believe that Salar Jung, a friend of the British, would be installed practically as the sole ruler. But the British also decided against him. It was felt that one man could not possibly be invested with so much power for a continuous stretch of fifteen years. Time had taught the British that in India it was wiser to place two men in key positions in order to watch and check each other, and this fact, coupled with the slight unpopularity of Salar Jung with the Government of India for having posed the Berar question, convinced the British of the necessity of associating some other nobleman with the Hyderabad administration. The Amir-i-Kabir, the head of the *Paigah* forces and the principal nobleman, who also represented dynastic interests, was the obvious choice. This arrangement also suited Salar Jung. He must have realized that the association of the Amir-i-Kabir with his administration would help win the support of the common people as well as the nobles.[147]

At the Resident's invitation the Amir-i-Kabir, Khurshed Jah, the

Amir's nephew,[148] and Salar Jung came to the Residency to discuss the administrative measures to be adopted during the Nizam's minority. After the discussion the Minister submitted a scheme which proposed i) that the state be administered by Salar Jung and Amir-i-Kabir conjointly; ii) that the domestic charge of the Nizam be given to the Begum Sahiba, while his education was to be conducted under the direction of the two nobles; iii) that the Crown estates be managed by the two nobles; iv) that the functions of the Dewan be discharged by Salar Jung, who would consult his colleague on all important matters; and v) that the Resident would be consulted in every emergency and all important matters. While recommending the proposals to his Government, Saunders suggested that whatever system might be finally instituted to govern the state during the Nizam's minority, it must be held to have been derived from or impressed with sanction by the paramount power.[149]

The Government of India, while approving the proposed scheme of administration, enunciated in a dispatch to the Resident, the basic principles of its policy towards the Nizam's Government during the period of his minority. While unnecessary interference was ruled out, the Resident's right to offer advice on all important occasions was asserted. It was not the wish of the Governor-General that the Resident possessed more direct control over the internal affairs than he had hitherto done. But on all important occasions, he must offer to the Minister and the Amir such advice and support as he might think desirable in order to assist them in carrying on their important duties. The position of the Resident, as representative of the paramount power in India, must always be one of commanding influence and power, but this power and influence would not be used except for the maintenance of order and the welfare of the subjects. To ensure a succession of intelligent and able Ministers, the Resident was advised to encourge young men to take an interest in public affairs. The young Nizam was to be given a sound and liberal education, and an English gentleman was soon to be entrusted with the duty of supervising this. The Governor-General also expressed his keen interest in the good administration of Hyderabad, the reduction of its army, the organization of a new police and works of public utility, and the all-round development of the state.[150]

This 'very important' dispatch which Mayo had 'drawn up with great care' would, he hoped, be approved by the Queen's Government.[151] This dispatch, indeed, outlined for the first time the ideas which Mayo

later developed with greater sophistication and finesse towards the
Indian states. The first was to secure good local administration. This
would be ensured by Salar Jung's retention of dewanship. Salar Jung,
Mayo believed, was 'one òf the ablest and wisest men in India'. With
him and a series of able Residents the Nizam's territory ought to have
'a chance of real good Government for the next 15 years.'[152] This
dispatch also enshrined the concept of westernizing the Indian
princes. The infant Nizam was accordingly brought under English
guidance and supervision. But undeniably the most important aspect of
this policy was to ensure and preserve unfettered British paramountcy
over the state. Mayo himself was greatly pleased that Salar Jung, after
initial hesitation, had consented to the proposals made by the Government of India with regard to the education of the young Nizam and the
administration of the state during his minority. 'I think, therefore,' he
wrote to Argyll, 'that your Grace might with advantage recommend
him at a fitting opportunity to H.M. for the first class of the Order of the
Star of India.'[153]

In Hyderabad the British now became all-important. They wielded
tremendous authority, as though entitled to do so by treaty. Even the
infant Nizam, although undeniably the legal heir, was not proclaimed
until after a reference on the subject had been made to the Resident,
and the latter's sanction coupled with a special proviso reserving for
the Government of India the right to decide the future mode of
administration. The scheme of administration was drawn up by the
Minister with the Resident's consent and placed for the Viceroy's
approval. The scheme, while investing the two nobles with the power
to conduct day-to-day administration, made no attempt to conceal
where the real power lay. Both the Amir and the Minister assured the
Resident that in difficult undertakings and matters which could not be
carried out except with the support of the Resident, his advice would
be taken. Salar Jung further elucidated upon the subject and said that,
although it was said on paper that the Resident's advice would be
sought in all necessary and important matters, in practice no new
measure would ever be initiated without the Resident's approval.[154]
Thus, the image of the two noblemen governing the state was outwardly upheld, but the real power lay in the hands of the Resident.
While the executive was in Salar Jung's hands, and the Amir-i-Kabir
was the 'prestige' man associated with him, the Resident controlled
affairs and the whole of Hyderabad found itself in the firm grip of
British paramountcy.

CHAPTER III

Paramountcy Challenged

I

The friendly understanding with which Salar Jung and the British co-operated and the cordiality which existed between them had a short life span. Salar Jung, now firmly established as the most powerful man in Hyderabad and having wielded that power well, cherished great ambitions for his master as well as for his state. As long as Afzal-ud-Daula was alive, Salar Jung had not asserted too great an authority. He had considerable regard for Afzal-ud-Daula, a Nizam of the old school, and was genuinely awed by him. He was seldom admitted to the Nizam's presence, and when he was, he would almost pale with trepidation. Even so, he had embarked on a programme of reform for which he received only grudging and reluctant approval from Afzal-ud-Daula. His chief strength lay in the support provided by the British Residents. He had a constant foreboding that there would come a day of reckoning between him and his master, and his hope was that 'as the British flag waved over him', he would be safe.[1] With the infant Nizam on the throne, and Salar Jung being the chief member of the Council of Regency—the Amir-i-Kabir played merely a secondary role—Salar Jung's position became absolutely secure in the state and his ambitions grew correspondingly. An ordinary politician would tend to advance his own personal career and prosperity, but Salar Jung was no statesman of the common run. He began to cherish ambitions for his state, as well as for his master, to the detriment, as will be seen later, to his own interests. He started devoting far greater attention to the affairs of the state than he had hitherto done; he improved its administration and rejuvenated its army.[2] He dreamt of a strong Hyderabad which, enlightened and improved under his guidance, could be restored to its former autonomous position.

Here it is necessary to say a few words about Hyderabadi society and politics. Salar Jung was no doubt functioning in a state that did not have representative institutions, and was thus not subject to pressures from organized public opinion. But he had to take into account the interplay of domestic politics, internal economic compulsions and social prejudices. Within the state itself there were systems of relation-

ships between the Nizam, the Minister, the Resident and the local
nobility. There were rival groups and people with differing aims; their
rivalries needed adjustments and they inevitably reacted to the Government's policy in all its dimensions, including its relations with the
British.

To make the situation more complicated, in his zeal for modernization and the construction of a new centralized administration, Salar
Jung tried to staff his bureaucracy with men from British India. This
was unavoidable, at least temporarily, since the local nobility or
mercantile classes, not to mention the common people, lacked at this
stage the necessary skills. The process, however, gave rise to the Mulki
and non-Mulki conflict—the legacy of which surfaced in the recent
Telengana agitation[3]—the Mulkis being the countrymen of
Hyderabad and the non-Mulkis the men brought into the state. These
new men were mostly English-educated, familiar with the administrative practices in British India. There were Europeans amongst them,
but most were Muslims from north India, quite a few being associated
with Syed Ahmed Khan and Aligarh Muslim University. 'They established an Anglo-Indian bureaucracy and became a new social categ-
ory.' They naturally tried to secure their interests and prevent the
infiltration of the local nobility into the administration. Equally naturally, the local nobility grew jealous of them and resented them.
Significantly, Salar Jung, himself a member of the old nobility, was
careful to deny these new men any political power, which they seized
after his death, during his son's dewanship. He kept them completely
isolated from the local nobility, the Nizam as well as the Residency
officials, and under his own absolute control. He did not totally
dismantle the Mughlai bureaucracy, nor did he displace hereditary
personnel, but he viewed the old nobles as threats to the centraliza-
tion of power by the Dewan, and believed that they had hitherto
exercised power disastrously for the state. He worked for 'an increasing erosion of the nobles' political power in the state'. Not unnaturally,
Salar Jung alienated the nobles, so far the pillars of the state and equal
to him in power and rank. These men headed the conservative group,
became his enemies and opposed his reforms.[4]

Throughout his rule Salar Jung managed to follow a double-edged
policy. In his internal administration he took every precaution to keep
the non-Mulkis away from politics and to maintain a balance between
the old nobility and the new officials (though inclining more towards
the latter); but in his relations with the British, the non-Mulkis, espe-

cially the Europeans who came from outside the state, became his chief collaborators. He utilized them to carry out his plans for the greater glory of Hyderabad and to improve its status before the outside world.

This concern for the status of Hyderabad made Salar Jung undertake a careful and thorough study of the treaties between the Nizam and the British. He was convinced that the Nizam's subordinate position vis-à-vis the British was not warranted by them. He thus began to question the validity of the rights of suzerainty exercised by the British since the beginning of the century. It became his aim to raise the Nizam's status to the level it had enjoyed at the time of the earliest treaties, and to obtain recognition of his independence. Moreover, he was consumed with a passionate desire for the restoration of Berar, and appeared to stop at nothing to realize this goal.

The entente was now becoming rapidly uncordial. Salar Jung's ambitions were too clearly pronounced to be ignored by the British, as these were inconsistent with their own claim to paramountcy. Mayo, a staunch upholder of British paramountcy, had almost a missionary faith in the justification of British imperialism in India. 'I feel you will agree with me', he once wrote to Argyll, 'that the line of duty is very plain—and that we ought never to depart from it ... that we have no right to be here at all unless we use all our power for the good of the Blacks.'[5] He had an equally deep-rooted faith in the permanence of British rule in India, an illusion that dominated British thoughts about India throughout the nineteenth century.[6] Such a man was unlikely to look indulgently on any challenge to British paramountcy offered by Hyderabad. Mayo's successor, Northbrook, no less an imperialist and always suspicious of the loyalty of Muslims, felt that Hyderabad, the premier Muslim state in India, was rapidly developing into a source of danger and that its Minister was a trouble-maker.[7]

Salisbury, who suceeded Argyll as Secretary of State, shared with Northbrook the fear and distrust of Muslim power and, like him, felt the need to curtail the ambition of Salar Jung.[8] Lytton, the Conservative successor of Northbrook, was inclined to agree with the Secretary of State. In his view, Salar Jung's undisguised object was to build in the heart of British India a strong, independent Muhammedan power. But 'we cannot afford', Lytton asserted, 'to encourage the development of a strong Muslim state in the centre of our power.' The situation was further complicated by reports of a Muhammedan rising in Turkey and of Sher Ali of Kabul[9] exhorting all Muhammedans to act in unison. It was not known whether Indian Muslims would unite with those outside if the latter decided to 'unfurl the green flag', but the possibility of their doing so certainly existed. The British would, therefore, have to be on guard against any future disturbance.[10] Under these circumstances, Salar Jung, with his hopes and plans, ideas and ambitions, was looked upon as a potential threat to British paramountcy.

II

Friction first started when the Government of India and the Co-Regents in Hyderabad disagreed over the education of the young Nizam. At the time of his accession there had been some discord between Salar Jung and Saunders over the issue of British officers taking off their shoes and sitting on the ground in the Nizam's presence. Salar Jung had yielded gracefully, although it had been clear to Saunders that he might be a little more 'difficult' in future. And he was.

While sanctioning the scheme of administration during the Nizam's minority, the Government of India had stipulated that the young Nizam would be given a sound and liberal education under an English teacher to prepare him for the important duties of his future life. His education was to be European as well as liberal, so that the Nizam might grow up under British influence, learn to obey an Englishman—his tutor—and remain a friend of the British. His state, the most important of the allied Indian states, would thus prove in times of trouble a source of assistance and strength to the British. The Resident was accordingly instructed by the Government of India to appoint an English gentleman of learning and ability who should be entrusted with the duty of superintending the Nizam's education and of selecting other subordinate teachers in the different branches of education. He was to be selected by the Co-Regents with the Resident's advice.[11]

But the Co-Regents' ideas were very different on the subject. They disliked the thought of an Englishman taking charge of the Nizam. They regarded with suspicion any arrangement which would tend to bring the Nizam under British influence, and feared that a European tutor appointed with so much power might interfere with the Nizam's religious observances. They wanted the teacher of the infant Nizam to be a Muslim, who would select all the teachers except the one for the study of English. The role of the latter would then be solely that of a tutor, not a superintendent. The Government of India rejected this suggestion.[12] It did not fit Mayo's scheme of bringing up young Indian princes under British influence and supervision.

Further consideration of this matter was postponed for the next two or three years as Mayo's mind was taken up with another, and more important project, viz., the introduction of the railways in Hyderabad and the settlement of the terms and conditions regarding it.[13] It took the Viceroy some time to persuade Salar Jung to accept his terms, and in his anxiety to settle this issue he left the Nizam alone. Before he could turn his attention back to the child's education, he was suddenly assassinated on 8 February 1872 by a Muslim convict from Peshawar, while visiting the Andaman Islands.[14] It was a calamity for the British. 'It is impossible to describe the horror and grief', reported Strachey, a member of Governor-General's Council and Mayo's right-hand man in India, to the Secretary of State, 'with which the intelligence of Lord Mayo's death has been universally received by all classes of Europeans, and I think I may add, of natives. I never knew a man who had made himself so evenly popular with all that in any way came into contact with him.'[15] In Britain the Queen was deeply affected by the death, and Argyll, who had never met Mayo, paid him fulsome tribute. Disraeli, now in opposition, expressed genuine sorrow in a few, simple, poignant words.[16] Although Mayo had not been too generous to Hyderabad in his co-regency arrangements, and had been extremely unfair in his railway settlement, it cannot be denied that, viewed from the general Indian standpoint, he was amongst the ablest Viceroys of India. He combined the energy of a Dalhousie and the political sagacity of a Canning, and impressed people by his brilliance, his zeal and courteous behaviour.

On Mayo's death, Northbrook was chosen by the Liberal Party in power to head the Indian administration. His nomination was urged upon Prime Minister Gladstone by Sir Charles Wood, now Viscount Halifax, Lord Privy Seal in Gladstone's cabinet.[17] Argyll had some reservations about him, but Gladstone upheld Halifax's choice. And Argyll, usually reluctant to assert himself in Indian affairs, gave in to his chief.[18] Northbrook himself had at first been doubtful about his qualifications to fill this magnificent post. When, however, Argyll formally offered it to him on 20 February, he accepted the next day.[19]

Northbrook came from the well-known Baring family, which had acquired a name for itself in the fields of financial enterprise and politics. He had served his political apprenticeship under Wood, a close friend of his father. Brought up on the Wood model, he had all the cynicism and reserve of his teacher, but none of that statesman's

brilliance or his quick mind. Although formally belonging to Gladstone's Liberal Party, as an Indian ruler he was not liberal in any sense
of the term. He was as conservative in outlook as Mayo had been—
probably more so—but much shrewder and more impassive. The
main object of his policy in India was, as expressed to a later Viceroy,
Dufferin, to let things go quietly on and to seek no change.[20] In the
context of these facts, if Salar Jung hoped that arrangements for the
Nizam's education decided upon during Mayo's time would not be
enforced, he was to be soon disillusioned. Northbrook was unlikely to
introduce a change in that policy or to deviate even slightly from the
concept of British paramountcy. Saunders was thus merely asked to
maintain the status quo in Hyderabad.[21]

For once, Argyll took the initiative. He called upon the Government
of India to invite the Nizam's Ministers to propose a definite scheme
for the education of the young prince under European superintend-
ence. Following this suggestion, but without giving Saunders any time
to interfere, Salar Jung wrote to a few of his friends in England to form
a committee to propose the name of a suitable person for the post of
the tutor to the Nizam.[22] The prompt action of the Minister made it
obvious that he aimed to secure a nomination of his own choice and
not that of the Government of India. 'I shall take care', decided the
Minister, 'to insist on our right to nominate the tutor and not accept
any officer appointed by the British Government to undertake this
important duty.'[23] The choice of the selection committee, thus formed
quickly, fell upon Captain John Clerk,[24] son of George Clerk, a
member of the India Council and a friend of Salar Jung, and the
selection was approved by Northbrook.[25] No tangible results emerged
from this appointment. The Captain assumed his role in January 1875,
but thanks to various religious ceremonies in the state, and the
Nizam's weak health, he was unable to make any headway with the
boy's education. When he soon lost his wife he returned to England. In
his place, his brother, Captain Claude Clerk,[26] was appointed at the
Minister's wish and with the approval of the Government of India.[27]

In the meantime, the sudden and crushing defeat of Gladstone at
the polls in 1874 brought the Conservatives back to power under
Disraeli, who persuaded Salisbury to accept the post of the Secretary
of State. Northbrook was retained in India; further proof that the
affairs of India were quite distinct from English party-politics. Northbrook warmly thanked Argyll, the outgoing Secretary of State, for
giving him 'general confidence and support', and felt confident that he

would be 'safe in Salisbury's hands'.[28] However, relations between the Viceroy and the new Secretary of State did not remain cordial. The masterful Salisbury tried, like Wood before him, to rule India by private correspondence with the Viceroy and to reduce him to the status of a mere ambassador or departmental officer. This was resented by the strong-willed Northbrook. When differences in policy matters, both internal and external, were added to a basic difference in outlook, Northbrook asked to be relieved of his office.[29] He would, however, stay on until the conclusion of the proposed visit of the Prince of Wales (later King Edward VII) to India. He planned to do all he could to make the visit 'successful and agreeable'.[30]

The only opposition to the smooth implementation of the Viceroy's plans came from the Minister of Hyderabad. By now Salar Jung had been thoroughly alienated from Northbrook. He had tried repeatedly and untiringly to convince Northbrook of the validity of the Nizam's claims to the restoration of Berar, but each time his proposal had been rudely brushed aside by the Viceroy.[31] He found himself thwarted, and hampered by the Government of India whenever he wanted to assert Hyderabad's claims, however just they might be. At each major move to strengthen its hold over Hyderabad, the Government of India, in its turn, encountered Salar Jung's opposition. And the Minister, piqued by his frustrations, decided to create difficulties for them once again over the visit of the Prince of Wales.

As soon as news of the Prince's proposed visit got round, most Indian princes expressed a desire to pay their respects to him, but the Nizam's voice in the matter was conspicuously silent. Yet it was quite well known that Salar Jung was 'in communication' with the Prince of Wales' people about his visit to Hyderabad, without the slightest reference of the subject to the Resident or the Viceroy. Northbrook was thus forced, rather unwillingly, to make the first advance.[32] Saunders was instructed to let the Viceroy know whether the Nizam would like to visit the Prince at Bombay or at Calcutta. The Minister, who at heart was opposed to either, replied that the boy was not well enough to make the journey, and suggested that a deputation be sent on his behalf.[33] This plea was rejected outright by Northbrook as being 'insufficient'[34]—perhaps because he realized that Salar Jung did not want the Nizam to pay homage publicly to the Prince of Wales as his suzerain. That was possibly true. Nevertheless, it was equally true that the Nizam was in fact weak and delicate, and that the strain and excitement of the journey to Bombay could prove too much for the boy, who had 'never been five miles away from his capital.'[35] The Viceroy, however, asserted that in the interests of the Nizam, and 'for various other reasons', the Nizam should make the visit to Bombay. Salar Jung was accordingly given the 'opportunity' of withdrawing his reply, and 'retreating' from the position he had taken in the matter. Several demi-official and private letters were exchanged between the Resident and the Minister, who finally agreed to allow the Nizam to visit the Prince at Bombay.[36] The pressure exerted on him on this occasion by the Resident is clear from Captain Clerk's private letters to Northbrook. He informed the Viceroy that 'by a succession of threats' about the consequences that Salar Jung personally would have to face and the injury that must result to the Nizam, and finally, by making it 'entirely a political question', Saunders had succeeded in making Salar Jung accept the proposal.[37]

Northbrook was elated, as he reported to the Queen, that the invitation had at last been accepted.[38] Privately, he confided to Salisbury, 'I am glad I gave him [Salar Jung] the opportunity of reconsidering the matter.'[39] To Northbrook's great annoyance, however, the news of the Minister's initial unwillingness had become common public knowledge. It was 'most unfortunate', the Viceroy grumbled, that the difficulty about the Nizam's visit should have leaked out through the Prince's people. 'It has given rise to just the sort of newspaper gossip here which does harm.' Northbrook was himself doubtful if, after all, the boy would be able to go. The Residency surgeon would finally decide, but the official acceptance instead of refusal of the invitation made all the difference in the position of the Nizam towards the Prince of Wales.[40]

Salar Jung had yielded, although not gracefully. There was something, Salisbury warned Northbrook, 'not entirely pleasant' about his mode of procedure. 'He may not mean mischief, but he will make it if the chance occurs'.[41] On this point the Viceroy was at one with the Secretary of State, notwithstanding their differences in other matters of Indian administration. He requested Salisbury to give a hint to the Prince of Wales not to be 'over-civil' to Salar Jung, and to avoid any discussion of politics, specially of the Berar question, and to give the Prince's staff distinct orders to that effect.[42] Following this advice, Salisbury went to see the Prince before his departure for India, only to discover that the Prince had already received communications on the subject from others and 'been subject to pressure in an opposite sense'.[43] Both Salisbury and Northbrook were bewildered at the 'wonderful' influence Salar Jung had upon Englishmen.[44] However, this influence was confined only to unofficial circles, for officialdom appeared to be impervious to his charm.

By this time all preparations were being made for the Nizam's trip to Bombay. Unfortunately, the boy suddenly became indisposed, and Dr Wyndowe advised against the proposed journey.[45] There were some in the viceregal circle, like Sir Henry Norman,[46] who felt that it was easy to make a sickly boy indisposed.[47] In Northbrook's view Dr Wyndowe was 'a good man', and the Viceroy accepted the doctor's advice.[48] A deputation consisting of Salar Jung, three principal noblemen—the Vikar-ul-Umra,[49] Bashir-ud-Daula[50] and Mohtashim-ud-Daula[51]—and the *Peshkar*, Narayan Bahadur[52] represented the Nizam at Bombay.

The Minister wished to welcome the Prince of Wales in Hyderabad where the Nizam could meet and receive him, but Northbrook was adamant in his opposition to this. The people of the city, he argued, were a 'rough lot' and all armed, so that there might be some risk to the Prince.[53] When Saunders, rather thoughtlessly, if truthfully, assured him that there was no such risk, and that the Prince's visit would prove 'a most popular one',[54] Northbrook lost patience. 'It seems to me that you have not thoroughly understood', he rebuked the Resident, 'that the visit to Hyderabad is out of the question.'[55] Northbrook actually felt that the Prince could not, 'without seriously diminishing the position of the British Government', visit Hyderabad territory until the Nizam had already visited and paid his respects to the Prince.[56] Northbrook knew also that Salar Jung had been in touch with the Prince for some time past, and he saw no need to further the acquaintance. So he also rejected Salar Jung's suggestion of a meeting between the Nizam and the Prince at Gulburga in the Nizam's territory. The Prince would be happy, the Minister was told, to accept an entertainment on the Nizam's behalf at some place on the line of the route between Jabalpur and Bombay. Since this would not be in Hyderabad territory, Northbrook reported to Salisbury with his characteristic dry humour, the suggestion was 'evidently unpalatable' to the Minister.[57] Salar Jung's plan of receiving the Prince in the Nizam's state was quietly dropped, to the great disappointment of the Minister. One can conclude that there was some truth in Northbrook's cynical remark. Salar Jung probably wanted to receive the Prince in the Nizam's territory because it would give him an opportunity to influence the Prince in favour of the restoration of Berar. The Prince's official visit to meet the Nizam would, moreover, look like the visit to an ally, not a feudatory, and thereby increase the Nizam's prestige.

If Northbrook was being stand-offish, and Saunders high-handed, Salar Jung was not too obliging either. He had promptly published all the correspondence between himself and Saunders which had earlier forced him to accept the invitation for the Nizam to visit the Prince of Wales at Bombay despite the boy's delicate health. The offensive tone and impolite language of the Resident's letters raised a storm of criticism both in India and in Britain. *The Friend of India* commented that the Prince's visit had been made an occasion for giving 'serious annoyance' to one of the principal princely states, and that 'downright terrorism and threats' had been employed by the Foreign Office to secure the Nizam's consent to go to Bombay.[58] In England, too, the correspondence was received with 'general disapprobation'. Salisbury was furious at the 'clumsy' handling of the affair by the Resident. Saunders had contrived, by his 'imperiousness and un-couthness of expression' to give Salar Jung a distinct diplomatic advantage. Few party-critics could unravel the rights and wrongs of an Indian question, but anyone could see that the Resident had been 'uncivil'. Salisbury even suggested changing the Resident at Hyderabad. Northbrook was unwilling to throw Saunders out, for, after all, the Resident had really carried out his orders. At Salisbury's insistence, however, the Viceroy removed the Resident. Salisbury was 'convinced that it is necessary that Residents should learn the use of the velvet glove more than they have hitherto done'.[59]

Richard Meade, who replaced Saunders in Hyderabad, was re-garded by Salisbury as the man 'with the glove of velvet, and the hand of iron.'[60] Northbrook, it is said, chose men of caution and reserve.[61] But Meade was neither reserved, nor cautious, and he did not put on the velvet glove either. From the moment he landed in Hyderabad, Salar Jung found himself face to face with a truly formidable adversary. Meade's avowed object was to cultivate good and friendly relations with Salar Jung, but his real intention was to put an end to the Minister's show of independence and to become the master of the situation himself. 'This Salar Jung is only a Minister, and our obliga-tions are to the Prince himself'[62]—this one sentence in one of his office notes sums up his attitude to the man who, more sincerely than anyone else, had been looking after the interests of the state and his master for over twenty years.

Before the arrival of Meade in Hyderabad, Salar Jung had planned and arranged a European tour for himself. The Prince of Wales' visit had given him the opportunity to fulfil his ambition of paying a visit to England. Once there, he could contact his English friends who would help him resurrect the Berar question and bring it to the forefront. He informed the Government of India that he would be going to England at the invitation of the Prince of Wales. On meeting him, Meade found him determined to make this trip,[63] which Northbrook feared (not without cause) would be utilized to push forward the claims to Berar. Northbrook also resented the fact that Salar Jung had informed the Government of India of his intention, instead of asking for its permission, to go the England, and was himself making arrangements for the administration of Hyderabad during his absence. It meant that he was trying to take a position which was 'inconsistent' with the authority of the Government of India. The Resident was asked to remind the Minister that the approval of the Government was necessary both with regard to his leaving Hyderabd and to the administrative arrangements during his absence. Salar Jung readily admitted the Government's point, and Meade in his turn found that the arrangement proposed by Salar Jung for the administration of Hyderabad during his absence was the only one apparently practicable. Even so, Northbrook ordered the Resident to make it clear to the Minister that all the arrangements were to be made and sanctioned by the Government of India. It was responsible for seeing that the arrangements worked well, and might alter them if the necessity arose.[64]

Meade required no prompting and conveyed Northbrook's message to the Minister. It was finally arranged that during the Minister's absence the administration would be carried on by Mookaram-ud-Daula[65] and Bashir-ud-Daula conjointly, with the assistance of the Amir-i-Kabir. Northbrook sanctioned the arrangement and gave his permission to the Minister to leave Hyderabad for England.[66]

Shortly after the Hyderabad matter had been settled, Northbrook resigned as Viceroy. His brief rule of four years had done more damage to Salar Jung's plans and ambitions than any other previous rule. Northbrook effectively checked Salar Jung's schemes for the restoration of Berar and crushed every attempt of the Minister to restore the Nizam's prestige or increase his independence. This, instead of making Salar Jung dispirited, only made him more resentful, more independent and much bolder in his attitude towards the Government of India. Salar Jung, too, had caused Northbrook enough worry and embarrassment. Before his final departure from Calcutta,

Northbrook gave a piece of advice to his successor, Lytton. 'He thinks', Lytton faithfully reported to Salisbury, 'I may have to set Salar Jung aside and says he has prepared the way for this, in case it should become necessary.'[67] Northbrook, thus, created a precedent for Lytton and chalked out a policy towards Hyderabad which Lytton followed and developed.

Lytton, diplomat by profession and poet by nature, was only forty-four years old when he received the magnificent offer of the Indian viceroyalty. In him the Conservative Party leaders had found a man who would implement their imperialist policies in India with competence, enthusiasm and a touch of imagination. A loyal Disraelian, with all his master's sentimental attachment to the Queen, this witty and domineering Viceroy came to India to translate Disraeli's visions into a reality and to carry out the principles of the new Conservative imperialism. If he defeated his own purpose by arousing great public discontent in India, the failure lay in the policy itself. Pomp and glitter attract people but cannot win them, and blatant imperialism inevitably evokes popular opposition.

Towards the princely states Lytton developed further Canning's policy of collaboration with and domination over them. His attitude towards the princes was admirably simple. He placed all of them in one class, that of feudatories, and regarded the social structure of the Empire as 'essentially feudal', and eminently fitted for the application of the salutary military principle of the feudal system. 'Here is a great feudal aristocracy', he reported to his party chief, 'which we cannot get rid of, which we are avowedly anxious to conciliate and command, but which we have as yet done next to nothing to rally round the British Crown as its feudal lord.'[68] He was convinced that British relations with the feudatory states and princes could be so modified and ameliorated as to contribute largely to the consolidation and security of the Empire as well as to its resources.

It would be a good policy, he decided, to use the revenue of some of the states, use the armies of the same states or others, and at the same time give certain selected princes military commands under the British Crown. Of course, this principle could not be applied indiscriminately. Kashmir could be made Warden of the Marches, but the Nizam could not be treated with the same confidence. In his anxiety to build up an entente with the principal feudatories he departed radically from the policy of another Conservative Viceroy, Mayo, and from the policy of Canning, emphasizing good administration in the Indian states. He wrote in a particularly interesting and illuminating letter to Salisbury:

I am convinced that the fundamental political mistake of able and experienced Indian officials is a belief that we can hold India securely by what they call good government ... Politically speaking, the Indian peasantry is an inert mass. If it moves at all it will move in obedience not to its British benefactors but to its native chiefs and Princes, however tyrannical they may be. The only political representatives of native opinion are the Baboos, whom we have educated to write semi-seditious articles in the Native Press and who really represent nothing but the social anomaly of their own position.... But the Indian Chiefs and Princes are not a mere noblesse. They are a powerful aristocracy.... To secure completely and efficiently utilize the Indian aristocracy is, I am convinced, the most important problem now before us.

Lytton seemed, however, to be more convinced on another point. 'While on the one hand we require their cordial and willing allegiance, which is dependent on their sympathies and interests being in some way associated with the interests of the British Power, on the other hand, we certainly cannot afford to give them any increased political power independent of our own.'[69] In other words, Lytton would use and utilize the princes, but would not allow any enlargement of their political rights or powers.

To a man with such pronounced views on imperialism and the role of the princes in the Empire, Salar Jung of Hyderabad was bound to appear a dangerous man. Salar Jung's hopes and aspirations were the perfect antithesis of the policies and interests represented by Lytton. The Viceroy summed up the situation with striking clarity. 'The chief objects which he has, I believe, at heart, are of a kind which we are bound to oppose and prevent. There is no chance of his relinquishing his insistence on them, or of our relinquishing our resistance to them, and therefore it is not likely that our relations with him can ever be satisfactory. ...Salar Jung's object is to build up a strong Mahomedan State in the heart of British India—ours to prevent that State from ever becoming inconveniently strong.'[70]

Sparks of hostility flew the moment they met. When Lytton landed in Bombay on his way to Calcutta, Salar Jung, ready for his departure to England, sought a private interview with the new Viceroy. Lytton received him on condition that no business would be discussed. The meeting was anything but cordial. Lytton disapproved of the Minister's desire to visit St Petersburg and Constantinople (on his way to England) at a time when there were reports of Muslim rising in Turkey. Sher Ali of Kabul, too, was calling upon all the Muslims to come together. To make matters worse, Salar Jung was known to have been involved in 'sinister intercourse' with Arabia. Obviously his object was to enlist external Muslim support for the establishment of Muslim power in Hyderabad.[71] Lytton was determined to deter and defeat any such move.

The Viceroy's distrust and resentment of Salar Jung grew on reading the reports of what he considered to be the Minister's 'impudent utterances' in England, once the Minister arrived there. Salar Jung seemed to have lost no opportunity to impress upon the English public the image of Hyderabad as an independent power in alliance with England. This was where the real conflict lay. The Nizam was not independent, Lytton argued, and his political relations with the British Crown were the same as those of the other Indian feudatories. Lytton was also extremely suspicious of the Minister's moves with influential men in Britain to secure their support for his pet scheme about Berar. The exasperated Viceroy urged the Prince of Wales not to encourage the Minister to press his demand for the restoration of Berar and begged the Queen not to receive privately any communication regarding it. Salar Jung had taken with him to England a large quantity of money and extremely valuable state jewels. Reportedly, the Minister had spent over Rs 70 lakhs in England, and this not counting the jewels. Lytton suspected that the money and gifts had been used in endeavouring to corrupt the press and Parliament.[72] Salisbury, while regarding the news as 'gloomy', was less worried. A shrewder politician than Lytton, he rightly calculated that the more money Salar Jung spent on these useless expenses, the less he would have to spend on other dangerous and military preparations.[73] Lytton insisted that the best way out of this complex situation was the removal of the Minister from office, if it could be effected by his colleagues during his absence. In a very confidential letter, he asked Meade whether this would be desirable or practicable, and whether Meade could prepare and promote such an event without compromising his own position or openly appearing as the author of it.[74]

Much to Lytton's regret, Meade advised against the scheme. In his view it was not at all desirable, because Salar Jung was the only person in Hyderabad who was capable of running the state efficiently and successfully. He enjoyed great influence and authority in the state, having introduced order and beneficial reforms. There was no one who could replace him, and it was impossible to say what would happen if he were removed. The Minister's removal with the consent of his colleagues, all loyal to him, was also out of the question. The Resident could probably create some hostile elements against the Minister, but he could not do so without compromising his position. Meade's unhesitating conclusion under the circumstances was that any attempt to drive the Minister out of office would be 'impolitic' and in its effect 'disastrous'.[75]

Salisbury was inclined to agree with Meade. While apprehending considerable trouble from Salar Jung, he pointed out that it would not be expedient to dismiss the Minister at that time. It would shock a good deal of opinion in England, and if the result was a deterioration in the condition of the state, the complaints would be very loud, and might make it 'difficult' for the Viceroy to interfere with another Prince in some other case. The Secretary of State, however, promised to do all he could to checkmate Salar Jung's moves to get back Berar.[76]

Thus, despite the animated speculations it created and the hospitality with which he was universally treated, Salar Jung's European trip was a failure. He did not go back with 'the restored Berars in his pocket', as the *Friend of India* crisply commented. He was, on the other hand, 'courteously but decisively snubbed' by the Secretary of State,[77] and sent home with many fulsome compliments and with half a promise to reconsider the issue on his return to India. Meanwhile, the storm clouds were gathering which would later lead to the inevitable clash between the Minister and Lytton. A frustrating series of incidents began. The first seriously disturbing event took place on the occasion of the Imperial Assemblage in Delhi in January 1877.

III

Despite strong Liberal opposition, the Royal Titles Bill had been passed by Parliament, now dominated by Disraeli, and it had received royal assent on 27 April 1876. By this new Act the Queen assumed the title of the Empress of India, *Kaiser-i-Hind*. The title originated in Disraeli's wish—graciously supported by the Queen—to embellish his concept of imperialism with a symbol.[78] The Conservative leader felt that it had been a serious omission on the part of the party not to add a new title to the Crown in 1858. He therefore persuaded Parliament to endow Her Majesty's title and authority in India as the paramount power with a new adornment.

In India, Lytton was no less enthusiastic about the royal title. He did not agree with the opposition critics that the title had been created out of caprice or as a covert design against the rights of the Indian princes. 'It is essential', he wrote to the Queen, 'for the dignity of your Majesty's position.[79] As ardent an imperialist as Disraeli, and with a predilection for pomp and grandeur, Lytton proposed to announce the new title with great solemnity and dazzling public ceremony in a special durbar. This would not only imprint the Queen's authority upon the throne of the Mughals, which had been associated for centuries with the splendour of a supreme power. To the Viceroy this also presented an opportunity of inaugurating a policy of identifying the Crown of England with the hopes and aspirations, sympathies and interests of the Indian aristocracy, and of defining more distinctly the subordinate position of the Indian states. The necessity of the Assembly was also greatly enhanced by recent events in Europe. If the British were, as appeared to be, on the eve of a war with Russia in Central Asia, it was of vital importance to rouse the enthusiasm and loyalty of all the feudatories in India. For political purposes, asserted Lytton, the people of India were 'dumb', and as a body-politic, the seat of its motive power was in its head, the aristocracy. 'As the head wills, so the body will move.' 'If we have with us the Princes, we shall have with us the people.'[80]

Salisbury supported Lytton in this effort to secure the loyalty of the Indian aristocracy. The Indian people were liable to rise against the British if the opportunity presented itself. It was, therefore, worth winning over the aristocracy and the princes. 'If they are with us, we can hardly be upset. ... Their self-interest must strongly be on our side. The point is to get their sentiment with us too.' The Secretary of State was, nevertheless, a little doubtful about the immense expenditure to be made on the Assembly while a famine was raging in South India and Bombay. The Indian press was protesting loudly against this heartless expenditure on mere display at a time when hundreds of people were starving. It was also being rumoured that the idea of the Assembly was unpopular with the Indian chiefs on account of the expenses they had incurred so recently in connection with the Prince of Wales's visit.[81] Lytton assured his chief and the Queen as well—although not with strict regard for truth—that public opinion strongly favoured the Assembly and the Indian chiefs, without exception, were so exuberant that the problem was to check their ardour and keep expenditure within limits![82]

It was decided that the Assembly would be held in Delhi on 1

January 1877. The occasion would be utilized to abolish the system of exchanging presents between the Viceroy and the Indian princes, but the presentation of the *nuzzur* or tribute by the princes would be retained as a salutary symbol of feudal allegiance. Instead of personal gifts from the Viceroy, medals commemorating the occasion would be presented by him in the Queen's name to all the chief dignitaries present at the durbar. The medals would be stamped on the obverse with the effigy of the Queen in high relief, and on the reverse with the inscription 'Victoria, Empress of India'.[83] The Queen was enthusiastic about the idea and took great interest in the medals, to the extent of sending Salisbury a drawing in order to ensure the proper rendering of her profile.[84] Lytton, pleased with the way his schemes were going, asked the Home Government to authorize the Viceroy to present guns and banners as well to the princes. These would not cost much, but would be even more effective than political concessions, since the Indian nobility was easily affected by sentiment and was susceptible to the influence of symbols.[85] All Lytton's suggestions were approved by the Home Government. Only his plan for the creation of a Privy Council for India consisting of the major Indian princes and members of the Viceroy's Council was first rejected, and later modified beyond recognition, by the India Council and the British cabinet.[86]

Invitations to attend the durbar were dispatched to all the princes and chief officials in India. It was anticipated that Salar Jung would be unwilling to let the young Nizam go to Delhi and thus publicly acknowledge the Queen's sovereignty over him. Lytton was anxious to ensure the Nizam's presence in Delhi. The refusal by any prince of an invitation addressed personally by the Viceroy would be 'a very inappropriate slight' to the British Government. What was more important was that the Minister's recent assertions to the English public that Hyderabad was an independent state in alliance with England made it absolutely necessary that the Nizam should appear in Delhi in his 'proper character as feudatory'. Lytton was determined not to allow Salar Jung to come to the Imperial Assembly unless he brought the young Nizam with him. 'On one thing I am resolved', he informed Meade, 'under no circumstances will I allow the Minister to represent his master at Delhi on the 1st. *Aut Caesar aut nullus.*'[87]

As anticipated, Salar Jung thoroughly disliked the idea of the Nizam's attending the durbar in Delhi. He started raising objections on grounds of the risk that would attend if he did so. Meade explained to the Minister that the Nizam was duty bound to attend, and after a prolonged discussion with him, Salar Jung accepted the Viceroy's invitation to the Nizam.[88] Lytton was pleased. All the chiefs, including the Nizam, who had been considered the most doubtful, would now come to the durbar. The success of the show was assured. To prevent the Nizam from becoming ill again (as he had been on the occasion of the Prince of Wales's visit), the Residency surgeon was asked by the Resident to see the boy twice a week. The Nizam kept well, and along with Salar Jung prepared to leave for Delhi.

Just before his departure, Salar Jung submitted a fresh application for the restoration of Berar. The timing seems to have been rather unfortunate. Not that Berar would have been returned to Hyderabad had the Minister chosen a more appropriate moment. But he might have been spared the personally humiliating and frustrating series of incidents that followed the submission of the memorial. Lytton was understandably furious with the Minister. At a time when every other Indian chief was trying to make the Assembly—Lytton's dream child—memorable and successful, 'that rascal' (Lytton actually used the expression!) Salar Jung had dared to sing a different tune.[89] He had revived the much debated Berar issue, which was bound to raise a note of discord between him and the Government of India, and to vitiate the peaceful and ceremonial atmosphere in Delhi. Salar Jung was peremptorily ordered to withdraw the application and asked to submit a fresh one after the Assembly was over. The whole affair thus had a rather unpleasant start.

But there was more to this episode than mere unpleasantness. The story of the clash of ambitions between the Viceroy and the Minister, of one's refusal to co-operate with the other, and of the pressure and humiliation that the Minister had to undergo emerges from notes of the conversation between Salar Jung and Meade and Meade's private letters to Northbrook and Lytton. Since Salar Jung had chosen to re-open the Berar question at a time when all the princes had been invited to pay homage to the Empress, Lytton telegraphed Meade on 22 December 1876 that he would be unable to receive the Minister with cordiality in Delhi unless the Minister assured him personally of the loyalty of the Nizam's Government to the Crown. Salar Jung felt humiliated at this demand and claimed that he had Salisbury's permission to re-open the issue on his return to India. On Meade's suggestion, Salar Jung wrote a letter embodying all the details of the Berar case for the Viceroy's information. The Viceroy, however, repeated his earlier demand, and required in the letter the insertion of a paragraph

that distinctly acknowledged the Queen's supremacy over the Nizam.
It is clear from Meade's private letter to Northbrook (who still continued to take a great interest in Indian affairs), that this insistence on
written recognition of the Nizam's subservience to the Queen was all
Lytton's own. Meade personally had nothing to do with the Viceroy's
message of 22 December or with raising the question of supremacy.
The Resident felt that the Nizam's presence in Delhi was so practical an
acknowledgement of the point that there was no real need for written
admission from Salar Jung of the Queen's supremacy. Lytton,
nevertheless, was adamant in his demand. At his order, Meade had to
take back the Minister's letter for necessary alteration. In course of the
discussion that followed Meade suggested that the word 'suzerain' be
put in the letter. Salar Jung, on asking the meaning of the word, was
told that suzerain was the equivalent term of sovereign. Although he
admitted the British power as the supreme power in India, he could
not give Her Majesty this title in reference to the Nizam, because it
would relegate the Nizam to the status of a subject of the Queen.
Making this subtle difference between the Queen's 'supremacy' and
her 'sovereignty' Salar Jung sent the letter to the Resident without
making the suggested alteration.[90]

The interviews between Meade and Salar Jung had been most
unsatisfactory from the former's point of view. Throughout the discussions, Salar Jung had revealed a persistent refusal to acknowledge in
writing the Queen's supremacy over the Nizam. He admitted it ver-
bally to Meade, but would not put it in writing. He based his stand on
the existing treaties and refused to recognize a position for the Queen
which would in any way affect the Nizam's independence regarding
internal administration. He strove for the restoration of the relations
which had existed between the Nizam and the East India Company up
to the end of the eighteenth century, and for the preservation of
autonomy in the internal administration of his country as guaranteed
by the treaty of 1800. There can be no question that technically the
Minister was right. It could not be truthfully argued that the Nizam had
at any time or by any treaty surrendered his internal autonomy to the
British or had declared himself a feudatory of the Queen. The Crown's
representatives in India had set about to do just that—to deprive the
Nizam of any real power and to relegate him to the position of a feudal
vassal. In their view great changes in the relative position of the two
Governments had taken place between 1800 and 1877, and the position which the Minister claimed for the Nizam was not consistent with

the unquestioned and indisputable paramount position which the British enjoyed in India.

The most effective platform for establishing this fact was furnished by the durbar and its accompanying ceremonials and formalities in Delhi. Before the actual day of the durbar the Nizam, on arriving safely in Delhi, paid a visit to the Viceroy on 26 December. Such visits to the Queen's representative were undoubtedly public acts of obeisance to the supremacy of British power. The Viceroy on that occasion presented the Nizam with a silk banner and a gold medal bearing the Queen's portrait, and said that these two symbols, he hoped, would always remind the Nizam of the loyalty of his House to the Queen.[91] The Nizam accepted the tokens of feudal allegiance, and Lytton had every reason to be satisfied now that his purpose of accomplishing the Nizam's subordination to the Queen had been served.

The year 1877 began with the gorgeous durbar of Delhi. At a time when hundreds of people were dying of famine in the south and west of India, no less than Rs 19,54,000 were spent on this magnificent show.[92] Here the Indian princes and chiefs assembled to recognize the Empress of India, and heads of provincial governments and other important officials in British India came to pay homage to the Empress. Ranged in a vast semi-circle in front of the viceregal throne were all the provincial ruling chiefs, and in the centre of the semi-circle sat the young Nizam with Richard Meade beside him. Close by, but slightly in the rear, sat the faithful Minister.[93] About the contrast between the Viceroy, the Queen's representative, and the Nizam, her subordinate, there was no room for doubt.

The Proclamation, formally declaring the Queen to be Empress of India, was read first in English and then in Urdu. At its conclusion a salute of 101 guns was fired. After a brief pause the Viceroy rose and addressed the Assembly. In his speech he emphasized the Queen's concern for the welfare of the Indian people, and her regard for the rights of her feudatory princes. At the end of this speech, Sindhia rose and congratulated the Queen as the *Shah-in-shah Padshah* and formally recognized her power to give the absolute order or *hukumat*. Other chiefs, like the Maharajahs of Udaipur and Kashmir, expressed similar sentiments, after which there was an expectant pause, while the durbar awaited a few words from the principal Muslim chief or his Minister.[94] For a moment the silence was both eloquent and ominous. At length Salar Jung spoke. He obviously had no desire to speak. But the Vikar-ul-Umra 'nudged' the Nizam and whispered in his ear. The

Nizam turned to the Resident, who talked to the Minister, who then rose and spoke a few brief words,[95] and the Viceroy thereafter left the dais.

Despite that uncomfortable moment, the Assembly had gone splendidly from Lytton's point of view and he deserved Salisbury's warm congratulations for its success. Lytton himself had no doubt that the political effects of the Assembly would be far-reaching, and he was particularly happy that its general result had left British relations with Hyderabad more satisfactorily defined than before.[96] Despite his various preoccupations during those busy days, Lytton had not for a moment forgotten the letter which Salar Jung had earlier sent back to him without having made the required alteration recognizing the Queen's suzerainty over the Nizam. Immediately after the Assembly, the Viceroy returned the letter to the Minister through Meade with instructions to alter it in accordance with his wishes. After much discussion and argument, Salar Jung eventually wrote that he supported the dignity of the Empress of India 'whose supremacy of position over His Highness the Nizam according to existing treaties' he had never questioned. Notwithstanding the qualified admission of the Queen's suzerainty, Lytton found the letter acceptable, perhaps because he felt that his triumph over Salar Jung had been complete. The question of the Queen's supremacy over the Nizam had indisputably been settled at the durbar.

Salar Jung was most unhappy. The whole episode was thoroughly disappointing and frustrating for him, and he retaliated in the only way open to him. He printed his version of his conversations with Meade, just as he had done earlier in the case of his correspondence with Saunders, and sent it to his friends in England. The Duke of Sutherland, a special friend, was particularly requested to place the notes before the Prince of Wales.[97] This was an error and a fruitless exercise. Salar Jung failed to realize that no real help would or could ever come from England. The Minister's move only served to alienate Lytton and Meade even further. Meade started quiet inquiries and found out that during the Delhi durbar Salar Jung had held several private interviews with Sindhia and Holkar, and that after returning from Delhi he had, by a special messenger, sent to them copies of his memorial on Berar as well as of the notes of conversations with Meade. It was well known that Sindhia had grievances against the British regarding Gwalior Fort, and that he took much interest in the Berar question, in the hope that, should Salar Jung succeed in securing the restoration of Berar to the

Nizam, his plea for a reconsideration of his claims might be admitted. And, if Salar Jung had sent these papers to Sindhia and Holkar, who knew that he had not sent them to other chiefs as well? Clearly, his object was to create mischief, or so Meade concluded. On the basis of these reports, the Government of India started suspecting a combined intrigue of the Indian princes against the British rulers.[98] The exasperated Viceroy reported to the Queen that Salar Jung was behaving 'abominably' and that he was trying to incite Sindhia and Holkar to support his Berar claims and agitate for their own as well. 'If such claims were entertained', the Viceroy added shrewdly, 'Your Majesty would not have a rood of ground left in India, for your Majesty's Indian empire is composed entirely of territory from Native States.'[99] To Salisbury, Lytton's expression of anger was more frank and uninhibited. 'Salar Jung will, I suspect, be a thorn in our flesh till he reaches the world where the wicked cease from troubling.[100] Salisbury agreed, as he almost always did with the Viceroy of his choice. Some sort of mischief was 'brewing' in Salar Jung's 'dreamy brain' and he would certainly give them incessant trouble as long as he lived.[101] Assured of the support of the Home Government, Lytton awaited a favourable opportunity to curb the Minister of Hyderabad.

The opportunity came soon enough. In April 1877 the Amir-i-Kabir died, giving rise to two important problems.[102] Who would inherit his titles and estates? And who, if anyone, would succeed him as Co-Regent? The Amir-i-Kabir's brother, Rashid-ud-Din, the Vikar-ul-Umra, claimed a right to the Amir's titles and estates against those put forward by the Amir's two nephews, Mohtashim-ud-Daula and Bashir-ud-Daula, to whom the Amir had in a will bequeathed his property. Salar Jung had to act quickly to prevent the Vikar-ul-Umra, his life-long enemy, from becoming the most powerful nobleman in the state. In the politics of Hyderabad the Vikar-ul-Umra was the head of the retrograde party; opposition to Salar Jung and a dislike of his policy had been the key-note of the Vikar-ul-Umra's plans for many years. Salar Jung and the Vikar-ul-Umra represented two opposite policies and two opposite factions. Taking advantage of a somewhat vague letter from the Resident, the Minister, therefore, cleverly managed to have the estates conferred on the Amir's nephews by the Nizam in a durbar. The Vikar-ul-Umra and the Resident were both furious, and ultimately, at the Resident's intervention, the dispute was settled by the bestowal of the family titles on the Vikar-ul-Umra and the confirmation of the estates on the nephews. Rashid-ud-Din, the former

Vikar-ul-Umra, thus became the Shums-ul-Umra Amir-i-Kabir.[103]

A far more complicated issue than the inheritance to the late Amir's estates was succession to the co-regency. On the death of the Amir, Salar Jung informed Meade that there was no need to appoint a Co-Regent to succeed the late Amir, as he had decided to run the administration as the sole Regent and with the advice and assistance of the Resident. He also submitted a scheme for administering the state during the remaining years of the Nizam's minority.[104] *Prima facie*, this proposal could appear as an attempt by Salar Jung to assume supreme power in the state for himself. Yet it was a perfectly justifiable decision. The late Amir-i-Kabir had taken merely a nominal part in the administration and Salar Jung was, as friends and foes alike admitted, quite capable of running the show himself. A new colleague would certainly mean a restriction of his power, and worse still, he might not co-operate with his schemes of reform in the state and the restoration of Berar to the Nizam.

Not unnaturally, the British had 'very grave objections' to making Salar Jung the sole Regent. He had given them enough trouble and there was no need to encourage him in the belief that he could dictate his 'decisions' to the Government of India.[105] The prospect of appointing this 'slippery customer' as the sole man in charge of Hyderabad was unthinkable to Lytton.[106] His plan was to support Salar Jung's arch-enemy, the Vikar-ul-Umra, for the co-regency. This would ensure that the man working along with Salar Jung would not co-operate with the Minister and would obey the British out of gratitude for their support.

Meade, aware of Salar Jung's determination not to work with the Vikar-ul-Umra,[107] had, in his official letter of 28 May 1877, proposed the recognition of Salar Jung as the sole Regent.[108] Although no friend of Salar Jung, Meade recognized his administrative ability, and realized that the Vikar-ul-Umra's nomination, if followed by the Minister's resignation from office, would be 'unfortunate' for Hyderabad. He also surmised that this would cause 'a general howl' in the Indian press and most European journals, and that the Government would have to face trouble at home.[109] But Meade was forced by Lytton to alter his official letter and recommend the Vikar-ul-Umra's nomination to the Hyderabad Government.

The Viceroy declared that Salar Jung was 'the most dangerous man in all India, and like a horse or a woman that has once turned vicious, thoroughly irreclaimable'. He must be suppressed even at the risk of loud protests in Britain. If the Vikar-ul-Umra was appointed, the advantage would lie with the British, whether Salar Jung resigned or not. If he resigned, the British would be rid of an implacable enemy. Should he not, his power would be restricted by his colleague.[110] Lytton could not take the step of removing the Minister from office with only indirect proof of his misconduct. He needed direct evidence of disloyalty for that. In a letter to Meade, Lytton directed the Resident to procure, in the name of the Viceroy, certified copies of Salar Jung's letters to the Vikar-ul-Umra or to Sindhia on the subjects of Berar and the Queen's suzerainty over the Nizam. No member of Parliament, Lytton was sure, would dare to espouse the cause of any Indian state that could be proved to be conspiring against the suzerainty of the Queen.[111] Unfortunately for Lytton, Sindhia denied having received any communications from Salar Jung,[112] and the Vikar-ul-Umra obviously failed to produce convincing enough evidence. Lytton felt that it would be a 'God-send' if Salar Jung voluntarily resigned on the issue of the Vikar-ul-Umra's appointment. The Minister would find it difficult to justify his resignation on the mere ground of personal dislike for his colleague.[113]

There were other considerations as well for the Minister's removal. 'In the present excited condition of Muhammedan sentiment throughout India', explained Lytton, 'coupled with the danger of any combined opposition from the Native States to our proposed salt measures, which will probably bring Hyderabad, as well as the Rajputana States indirectly under British taxation, we cannot afford to play with our eyes open into the hands of an intriguant.'[114] The present moment seemed particularly favourable for the British. Parliament was not sitting, and Salar Jung's friends in England would be disarmed for some months. The attention of the English public was 'absorbed in the Eastern war'. Salar Jung's removal or resignation would cause less trouble now than at any other time.[115] On these calculations, Lytton decided on the nomination of the Vikar-ul-Umra as the Co-Regent, secretly and fervently hoping that it would lead to the Minister's resignation.

Lytton was not alone in his desire to get rid of Salar Jung. Salisbury shared his views. But the polished and diplomatic Secretary of State made it clear that if the Vikar-ul-Umra was to be appointed, it was to be done with the 'utmost civility' and such 'expressions of good will' towards Salar Jung as would prevent him or his friends from saying that he had been insulted into resigning. If he did resign on the issue, it would then seem to everyone that he was demanding a change from the old arrangement. The Government of India, on the other hand, was simply adhering to the *status quo* and appointing to the vacancy a man whose relationship to the deceased and whose position among the Hyderabad nobility naturally marked him out for the post. 'If he took offence at some innocent cut on our part and resigned, we should be relieved from a good deal of anxiety.'[116]

Thus, the Governor-General in Council, supported by the Secretary of State, decided that the delegation of full administrative power to any single Minister, and to Salar Jung at that, was inadmissible. Since Salar Jung's personal dislike alone was hardly any sufficient ground for rejecting the Vikar-ul-Umra's claim, the Governor-General appointed him as the Co-Administrator (this term was used in place of Co-Regent, on Meade's suggestion) of Hyderabad.[117]

Salar Jung still declared that it would be impossible for him to carry on the administration along with the Nawab. 'We are now like the two goats on the bridge', Lytton with a touch of humour aptly described the situation to Salisbury.[118] When Meade urged Salar Jung to accept the Viceroy's decision, the Minister refused either to do so or to resign. He declared, with considerable courage and determination, that he was the Nizam's Minister and not the Minister of the Government of India from whom he needed to receive no orders and to whom he owed no account of his conduct. He had been appointed Minister by the grandfather of the present Nizam and to resign his position of trust was impossible. He told the Resident that he would resist the Indian Government's decision, which was so insulting to himself, and would not be responsible for the consequences. Meade, taken aback by the Minister's stand, reminded him that he had received his present appointment as Co-Regent not from the Nizam but the Government of India, whose order he was bound to carry out. The Resident further warned the Minister that any attempt on his part to create disturbances in Hyderabad might imperil the independence of the state, and advised him to avoid a scandal 'which would destroy his credit and probably ruin himself and his family'. Yet the warnings had little effect on Salar Jung, who refused to yield or make any concession. The Minister was most obstinate, Meade privately wrote to Northbrook, 'and I was of course compelled to speak in a firm and resolute tone. It was an altogether painful scene'.[119]

Salar Jung was fighting on new ground on this occasion. In the course of his unequal duel with the British, he had gradually developed a new approach and policy. Gone were the days when he wrote to Yule and Temple soliciting their support. He now stood proudly on his own strength and his own ability, and asserted spiritedly his position as the guardian of the state during the minority of his master. In this, he was also indirectly asserting the authority and independence of the Nizam whose servant he declared he was. The Nizam's Minister was bound to serve his own master, and not the foreign rulers of India.

This challenge from Salar Jung incurred the wrath of Lytton. 'If the Government now flinches an inch, or shows the slightest hesitation to enforce its decision', Lytton decided, 'after the bullying tone adopted by Salar Jung, its position throughout India will be shaken to its foundation.' He asked Meade to summon the Hyderabadi nobles as well as Major Neville, the Nizam's commandant, and Captain Gough, the Nizam's Military Secretary (these two were to be reminded of their loyalty to the Queen and their duty to her Government). In their presence, Salar Jung was to be asked either to accept the order of the Government of India or to resign. If he refused to do either, Meade was to request the Vikar-ul-Umra to form a ministry and choose a colleague in his place. Meade was to take every precaution against any surprise move of Salar Jung's, to seek a guarantee of support from influential people, and to consult the Vikar-ul-Umra on measures to be taken in the event of forcible resistance from Salar Jung. He was also advised to keep in touch with the officers in command of the force at Secunderabad and quietly strengthen the Residency before acting.[120]

Still unaware of the conspiracy between Lytton and Meade, Salar Jung sent two long letters to the Resident reiterating his determination not to receive the Nawab as his colleague and remonstrating with the Resident for his high-handedness.[121] Following the letters, Meade sent Smith, his First Assistant, to the Minister with a final letter asking him to put an end to fruitless resistance and obey the Viceroy's order, and that same evening the First Assistant returned with a message from Salar Jung, who had finally agreed to accept the Viceroy's decision.[122]

This sudden *volte face*, appearing almost like an anti-climax, can, however, be explained. Salar Jung himself justified his altered stance by admitting that, though his views were unchanged, he had no power to offer resistance and that it was his duty to remain by the side of the Nizam during his minority.[123] An article published in the London *Statesman* a few years later, however, offered another explanation. It indicated that after Meade's return from a visit to Lytton a message was conveyed to Salar Jung to the effect that, if he refused to acquiesce in the final order, his arrest and deportation to Madras would follow.[124] Salar Jung, when asked about the truth of the report, denied having received any threat of deportation but admitted that, previous to Smith's visit, rumours were afloat that either Sir Dinkar Rao[125] or Sir Madhav Rao[126] would succeed him. He also confirmed that even after he had agreed to the Vikar-ul-Umra's appointment as Co-Regent, there were vague rumours that, in the event of his refusal to do so, the Assistant Resident had orders to take him to the Residency in his own carriage.[127] One has only to read between the lines to realize the magnitude of the pressure that compelled Salar Jung to yield. In a private letter to a friend Salar Jung offered an explanation for his action:

> I am afraid my friends do not give me my due when they think I was not firm enough in the matter of the appointment of a colleague. No Native State, I believe, has ever dared to show such a front as I did, on any question. I resisted to the last, until the Resident took the extraordinary step of announcing the appointment of the Ameer Kabir and others independent of myself. Where was the use under the circumstances of further resistance? They would probably have set me aside altogether, if I had not given in then or, worse still, made that a pretext for assuming the Government. What could Parliament have done in the matter? Parliament would have felt itself compelled to support the policy to which the Indian Government had committed itself, however much as a body it might regret its spirit and tendency. For the present I believe it would be wise to keep quiet and let the ill blood and bitterness be laid before taking any fresh step in the matter.[128]

It is clear from this letter that Salar Jung meant to surrender only temporarily. His spirit was still rebellious and willing to fight again if and when the opportunity presented itself.

In the meanwhile a notification issued by the Resident on 24 September 1877 proclaimed that the Governor-General in Council was pleased to nominate the Amir-i-Kabir (formerly the Vikar-ul-Umra) as Co-Administrator during the Nizam's minority, and that, while the general conduct of affairs would rest with Salar Jung, the concurrence of his colleague would be necessary in all important matters.[129] Despite the Minister's desire to avoid a durbar,[130] the new appointments were announced in a special durbar on 29 September—appropriately held by the youthful Nizam in the British military cantonment of Secunderabad.[131] Two generals and nearly fifty British officers accompanied Meade on the occasion, perhaps as a precaution against any unforeseen disturbance or opposition, and everything went off smoothly. The presentation of the Vikar-ul-Umra before the Nizam by the Resident was symbolic of the whole relationship between the Resident and the Nawab, who had literally been led by the hand of the Resident to that high post in the state of Hyderabad. Thus the 'pitched battle' with Salar Jung ended in his complete defeat and unconditional surrender. Meade believed that the Minister had steadily been increasing his authority and influence in a manner that would have made him the real master of the state. Now, with the Nawab firmly seated in his office, Meade hoped that 'the whole game will be in our hands'.[132]

Although Lytton would undoubtedly have preferred the total dismissal of the Minister from office, he, too, agreed that much had been gained by the victory. It left the Minister weakened and shorn of personal prestige, the Resident correspondingly strengthened, and the Government of India placed in its proper position in Hyderabad.[133] Salisbury was impressed by the efficient handling of the Hyderabad affair by Lytton. Salar Jung's conduct had been inconsistent with loyalty to the suzerain power. 'In such a context', Salisbury warmly wrote to Lytton, 'there is no question you did right not to yield one inch. It would be as dangerous as yielding to a restive horse.'[134]

It cannot be denied that Lytton's proceedings were highhanded and imperialistic. His successor, Ripon, could not bring himself to agree with this policy concerning selection of the Vikar-ul-Umra as the Co-Administrator. 'All that I have read and heard of the transactions of 1877', Ripon wrote, 'leads me to the conclusion that the course which was then pursued towards him [Salar Jung] was ill-advised, and my only surprise is that it did not produce worse consequences.'[135] Nor was the press reaction favourable. *The Friend of India and Statesman* criticized the 'arbitrary proceedings' of the Government of India. The London *Statesman* actually hinted at Meade's corruption and the Nawab's bribing his way to the Regency.[136] There is no evidence in the papers, official or private, to suggest that this was the case, although the Vikar-ul-Umra's earlier history reveals that bribing the Resident was a tried technique with him.[137] Whatever the truth, it is certain that the Nawab's appointment was not as popular in Hyderabad as the Government of India wanted to make it out to be. Even the Nawab himself was not confident of his own strength. Asked by Meade, as late as 23 September, he could not say what reaction would follow the Minister's resignation or removal or who should succeed to the ministerial office.[138]

In fact, the new arrangement was totally unworkable from Hyderabad's point of view. The two Co-Administrators had the greatest personal dislike for each other and any co-operation between them was out of the question. The Resident's policy was to strengthen the Vikar-ul-Umra's hands and to encourage him to claim for himself more responsibilities and share in the administration than his elder brother had ever done. It was reported in the press of Calcutta, Bombay and London that the Vikar-ul-Umra literally seized every opportunity to oppose Salar Jung's policies.[139] The Minister felt himself hampered at every turn by the activities of his unco-operative colleague and by the belief that it was the Amir-i-Kabir whom the Resident would always support. This dampened the Minister's energy and restricted his plans for improving the administration. Steuart Bayley, Meade's successor, who had an opportunity of observing these effects closely, neatly summed up the situation. 'The double arrangement', he asserted, had 'more evil consequences than Sir Richard would perhaps allow. ... it has I think hampered seriously his [Salar Jung's] internal policy, it has checked his anxiety to introduce new reforms and to complete old ones; it has made each step difficult.'[140]

The entire episode represented intervention in the internal administration of Hyderabad. Lytton claimed on this occasion that the Nizam–British treaties had made the Government of India the supreme protector of the state, that in the exercise of such a power it had assumed in 1869 the guardianship of the young Nizam and was now acting in that capacity.[141] This view could quite well have been disputed on legal grounds. No treaty with Hyderabad ever gave the British guardianship over the state. On the contrary, the treaties had explicitly debarred them from exercising control over internal administration. Lytton had imposed his will on the state by virtue of superior might, unmasked by civility and tact.

V

The enemy had been defeated, if not totally crushed, and Lytton wanted to follow it up by 'a series of light cavalry charges' on the Minister's position.[142] For a beginning, he brought up a charge against Salar Jung's Secretary, Arthur Oliphant. Oliphant was the son of J. Oliphant, an old friend of Salar Jung's and a former Director of the East

India Company. Meade had discovered that Oliphant had been selected by Salar Jung in order to help him organize a press party, and to build an 'underground communication' with influential men in Britain. He had assumed the role of a political adviser to the Minister in the latter's differences with the Government of India, and encouraged him on the co-regency and suzerainty questions. What was worse, he had forwarded the Minister's views privately to an officer in the India Office. Meade had warned Oliphant about the consequences of such anti-Government proceedings, but Oliphant had dismissed the warning by stating that, as a servant of the Minister, he was bound to do as the Minister desired.[143] The Government of India, not unnaturally, took the strongest exception to this view. Lytton's Council was unanimous that the permission previously given to Oliphant (in 1876) to accept the appointment of Private Secretary to Salar Jung should be withdrawn. Not content with this, Lytton sought the dismissal of Oliphant from Hyderabad territory as well.[144]

In Lytton's view the question of European employment in Hyderabad posed a major problem for the Government of India. The Minister employed quite a number of Englishmen to serve in various capacities under the Nizam. His army was organized by an Englishman, and his Public Works Department was full of them. The statutory rule which prohibited the employment of the Queen's European subjects in Indian states had been relaxed in favour of Hyderabad at a time when the Minister enjoyed the confidence of the British. He had, therefore, established 'a kind of right of way through the British reign' and surrounded himself with a group of English agents whose chief service was to assist him in creating and managing influences in England that were hostile to the authority of the Government of India. All the 'native durbars', Lytton observed, were watching the activities of these men with considerable interest and it would be weak and foolish on the part of the British to allow them to continue. Sindhia and Holkar, who also had grievances of their own, were amongst those watching the tactics adopted by Salar Jung. If these were even partially successful, the repercussions would be serious and spread beyond the boundaries of Hyderabad. Lytton was convinced that the employment of Europeans by the states was 'purely mischievous in its effects', and decided to reduce the unusual number of Englishmen in the pay of the Hyderabadi Minister.[145] His first attack was launched against the Minister's principal assistant, Oliphant.

The Government of India instructed the Resident to call upon the

Minister to dispense with Oliphant's service in conformity with the treaty of 1798 (Art. 6). The reluctant Minister was persuaded to abide by the order. The Government of India declared that in future no employment of a European in Hyderabad would be sanctioned until the applicant signed a declaration that he would not encourage any measure opposed to the policy of the Government of India.[146] Meade further suggested that the Nizam's Government, if it ever wanted the service of a European, should be restricted to selection from the officers under the Government of India. Unofficial Englishmen tended to be mischievous and disloyal.[147] Once more Lytton had won a battle with Salar Jung. Deprived of his able assistant, and checked by his colleague, the Minister would be quite powerless to do any harm to the British. The elated Viceroy jubilantly wrote to his Prime Minister, 'In India, at least, the power and prestige of that restless schemer are now completely extinguished.'[148]

Very different was the tone of the India Office. It was nervous about facing embarrassing questions in the House of Commons. The India Council considered that Lytton had gone 'too far'. Even Salisbury, who had always supported Lytton's Hyderabad policy, felt that the Viceroy in this particular case had been rather Draconian. Though Oliphant's conduct and his role in Hyderabad could hardly be described as ideal from the point of view of the British, there was no distinct proof against him that would justify more than a serious warning. Salisbury sent a telegram to Lytton suggesting a revocation of the order of Oliphant's dismissal,[149] but before the telegram reached Oliphant had left Hyderabad.

The unceremonious removal of Oliphant gave rise to a great outcry in England. A good deal of private agitation went on, and the Secretary of State had to answer several awkward questions from the Queen herself.[150] The subject came up for discussion in Parliament.[151] Salisbury, however, took 'high ground'. In an attempt to protect Lytton officially—despite his personal disapproval—he refused to submit the relevant papers upon the table of Parliament or to enter into any discussion of the question on grounds of public interest.[152]

If Parliament concerned itself with Oliphant's removal, a far more important matter demanded the attention of Lytton. This was the Nizam's army. Ever since Yule's days, Salar Jung had consistently carried on his military reforms almost openly, without any challenge from the Residents or the Foreign Department. Although Northbrook had felt—and Salisbury had agreed—that Hyderabad should not be permitted to become a strong military power,[153] no effective step had been taken in this regard during Northbrook's viceroyalty. It was left to Lytton to curb the military as he had curbed the political ambition of the Hyderabadi Minister.

As early as mid-1876 Salisbury had posed the problem to the Viceroy. 'I am fully sensible', he wrote, '... of the importance of disarming Hyderabad, if it could be done. Or, is it impossible? And if possible, is not the time too high?'[154] Alarming reports were also pouring in from Hyderabad about the increasing strength of the Nizam's army and, worse still, about the manufacture of breech-loading ordnance and rifles in the state. Lytton became almost panicky. In his dramatic way he informed the Queen, 'Salar Jung keeps a large arsenal for the manufacture of all kinds of arms, quite out of all proportion to the legitimate wants of a state protected by British troops'.[155] To the Secretary of State, too, the Viceroy expressed great concern. The matter of the arsenal was 'extremely awkward'. Besides, apart from the Reformed Troops, the number of private troops maintained by various amirs in the state was reportedly about 60,000. If the maintenance of the Reformed Force was used as a pretext for secretly drilling and disciplining these unrecognized troops, and the arsenal for equipping them with modern weapons, 'the Nizam must now be in possession of a tolerably powerful army' declared Lytton.[156]

Subsequent inquiry by Meade, however, proved the fears about the arsenal to be unfounded. The Resident had sent Col. Fraser, his Military Secretary, to inspect the two military workshops believed to be actively functioning in the city. Fraser had found in one a steam-engine (procured in 1873) adapted for the manufacture of rifles, but it had not been set up. At the other military workshop under Maulavi Mahmoud, Fraser had found a small engine at work and a mere model breech-loading ordnance. Perhaps the manufacture of breech-loading ordnance had been contemplated, but 'nothing *was* done beyond making a model'. Even if some breech-loading rifles had actually been made, Meade was obliged to conclude, they must have been only rough weapons made by hand and not by machinery.[157] Salisbury was only half-relieved. If the manufactory was 'inefficient', he agreed, it was 'not worth a fuss'. Nevertheless, it should be carefully watched, for the danger involved was no trifle. 'At the risk of any offence to native feeling, native princes must not be allowed to manufacture arms of precision'—this was his clear order to the Government of India. As

regards the Reformed Troops, Salisbury affirmed that the limits within
which the Nizam might maintain his troops ought to be defined with
precision, and when defined, rigidly observed.[158]

Following London's instructions, the Government of India asserted
its right to watch and limit the growth of the Nizam's troops, and
demanded periodical and accurate returns of the strength of the
forces. The force was not to be further organized, nor were Europeans
to be employed in the military service of the Nizam without the
permission of the Government of India. Salar Jung seems to have
quietly agreed to abide by this order, although reluctantly,[159] presumably because he was still hoping for the restitution of Berar.

Notwithstanding this apparent submission, the Minister had never
given up his project of army reorganization. In mid-1877, Meade
found him bent on putting the Nizam's army on an efficient basis.[160]
The Resident lost no time in faithfully reporting to his master that he
had received secret information that the Minister had had a scheme
elaborated and completed to organize a force out of the Irregular
levies along the same lines as the Reformed Force. Under Moulavi
Mahmoud, the man reputed to be the 'active promoter of the military
reforms', young and efficient men from the levies were being trained
and new hands enrolled. Infirm men were being replaced by young
men; drill instructions were being given to them by men formerly
belonging to the British service. The Vikar-ul-Umra had apparently
disclosed to the Resident that this military reorganization was undertaken as 'the surest means of compelling the British Government to
restore Berar'. Meade was not prepared to accept that Salar Jung was
merely trying to bring a disorderly and worthless body of troops into
some sort of moderate efficiency, without infringing the Indian Government order. He was convinced that these proceedings formed part
of a deliberate project, which could eventually menace British supremacy in India. Meade had considered giving a stern warning to the
Minister, but decided to wait until the co-regency question was
settled.[161] When that problem was solved it was time to deal finally and
firmly with the whole question of the Nizam's army. 'I think', Lytton
happily wrote to Salisbury, 'the opportunity for dealing with
Hyderabad is favourable. Salar Jung has been obliged to cave in and
submit to the appointment of a colleague.'[162]

It was not, however, the Nizam's army alone that concerned the
Viceroy. He intended to shape the Indian Government's policy to the

armies of the Indian states in general. He was dissatisfied, as we have
seen earlier, with the existing relations between the Government of
India and the princes. In his view, it would be good policy to make the
princes contribute to the consolidation and security of the Empire.[163]
He set up a committee, the Native States' Armament Committee, to lay
down the broad foundations on which the relations of the princes'
armies to the Government of India might be practically remodelled.
The Committee, however, was not at one with Lytton. It questioned the
expediency of permitting the states to maintain military establishments in excess of their internal needs. That excess, the Committee
held, could not be conveniently utilized in the interests of the Empire
and could, on the other hand, be a source of anxiety for it. In particular, the Committee was strongly against giving arms of precision to the
states. Nor did it approve of the employment of Europeans in a
military capacity by the princes. Hyderabad came in for special comment by the Committee. The number of Reformed Troops in the state
was far in excess of its requirements. The state was, after all, protected
by the subsidiary force and the Hyderabad Contingent. The Committee suggested that the Reformed Troops and the Reorganized City
Regiments should be disbanded and the Irregular levies reduced.
The arsenal in the city could, however, be maintained if no arms of
precision were manufactured there, and if it was inspected from time
to time by a British officer.[164] Lytton's Government accepted the
recommendations of the Committee and instructed all Political Officers to submit annual reports regarding the military establishments of
the Indian states.[165]

Meade needed no persuasion. He conveyed his Government's
views to Salar Jung and demanded limitation of the strength of the
Reformed Troops and reduction of the Irregular levies. The strength
of the Reformed Troops must not exceed two hundred and forty men
in the artillery, one thousand in the cavalry and two thousand in the
infantry. The number of troops in the Reorganized City Regiments was
to be limited to two thousand only. Salar Jung calmly accepted the
order.[166] Aware of his impotence against the ruthless Resident and his
subservient ally, the new Co-Administrator, he did not obviously
consider it worthwhile even to put up a show of resistance. This was
the end to Salar Jung's ambition of building up an efficient and
organized force in the Nizam's state.[167]

It was to the Nizam himself, or rather his education, that Lytton now turned his attention. Meade was not satisfied with the young prince's progress, as shown in Clerk's report for 1877 and 1878. He was convinced that the Nizam's late tutor, Captain John Clerk, the present tutor's brother, had been appointed by Salar Jung with a view to influencing the British court on behalf of the Minister.[168] Captain Claude Clerk, too, was not above suspicion. Meade believed that he was working in league with Keay, one of Salar Jung's paid agents, for private objects of their own.[169] Salar Jung had earlier tried to secure Lytton's permission for the employment of Major Percy Gough as tutor to the Nizam under the direction of Clerk. Lytton disallowed the appointment as he felt that, in asking for a man like Gough who had never been educated at a university, but who had military experience and some influence in England, Salar Jung's motive lay elsewhere. 'The real objects of his asking for Mr Gough are, first, to get two European officers instead of one into the pay of the Nizam's Government and second, to strengthen Salar Jung's interest in England.'[170] Meade had dittoed this view. And now, thoroughly sceptical of Claude Clerk's role in Hyderabad and Salar Jung's intentions about the Nizam's education, Meade advocated the appointment of a more qualified tutor than the Captain. Here, again, Lytton agreed. He was convinced that Salar Jung's object was to reduce the Nizam to 'a cipher' so that all the power in the state might remain concentrated in his own hands. For this purpose the Minister kept the boy secluded, almost a prisoner in the palace. Salar Jung visited him daily, but everyone else was excluded from his presence and he was rarely allowed to leave the palace. This deprivation from exposure to healthy, external influence, Lytton felt, was not conducive to the development of a sound mind and body.[171] It was decided, therefore, that a properly qualified Assistant Tutor, whom the Co-Administrators would select subject to the approval of the Government of India, should be appointed to help Clerk. Salar Jung first regarded the proposal with considerable disfavour, but Meade managed to obtain his assent to the appointment of Dowding, at that time the Principal of Rajshahi College in Bengal, as the Assistant Tutor.[172]

At about this time the young Nizam was removed from the zenana and made to live and work in a separate wing of the palace where he would have only selected male companions and attendants.[173] The Nizam acquired a colloquial knowledge of English, and his pronunciation was unusually good. His progress in the field of oriental studies was not so rapid, and Meade, ignoring the advice of Clerk and Salar Jung, did not allow him to learn Arabic.[174] The Nizam was to be educated with a certain object in mind, which was only too obvious from the nature of his curriculum, his daily routine and the supervision so well exercised on him. What Salar Jung, the nobles and the people of Hyderabad might have wanted their Nizam's education to aim at was never a very important consideration for Lytton and Meade.

Meanwhile, Salisbury had left the India Office to become Foreign Secretary in April 1878. He had been a pillar of strength to Lytton, and had always given him vigorous and unqualified support. 'I shall retain long', he wrote to Lytton, 'a very pleasant recollection of my association with the certain years of your viceroyalty.'[175] Salisbury's departure was a personal loss for Lytton, although Salisbury's successor, Viscount Cranbrook, a person who left no mark in Indian history, gave him free rein. Lytton's own days in India, too, were numbered. In April 1880 Gladstone came back to power. Lytton resigned. Between him and the new Prime Minister or his Secretary for India, Lord Hartington, any co-operation was out of the question. Lytton complained to the Queen that Hartington had twice declared in Parliament, that 'I was personally as well as politically unfit to exercise that high function, being everything which a Viceroy ought not to be.'[176]

In Lytton's view the most serious danger during his time was the 'Hyderabad conspiracy'.[177] 'There is in all India only one native', he warned his successor immediately after his own departure, 'whom I believe to be positively dangerous. This is Salar Jung. ... And if you do not desire the steady growth undetectable till too late, of an unmanageable, strong and practically independent Mahommedan state in the heart of India, I would say, "Beware of Salar Jung".'[178] This was certainly an exaggerated and theatrical assessment of the situation. And yet, the four years of Lytton's viceroyalty witnessed a fascinating duel between the masterful and obstinate Viceroy and the equally determined and ambitious Hyderabadi Minister. The fight—Lytton regarded it as a personal war—was an unequal one, not because the vanquished was any less capable than the victor, but because he was at a great disadvantage. Lytton's victory was in the long run pointless. No doubt the Minister's powers were temporarily crippled and his so-called conspiracy checked. Nevertheless, Lytton's policy served to alienate the state and the people of Hyderabad along with its Minister. As *The Friend of India and Statesman* commented, it proved 'detrimental' to the friendship between the two Governments.[179] It aroused mutual distrust and enmity where it should have cemented an alliance.

Ripon relieved Lytton in India on 8 June 1880. Trained from childhood in diplomacy, son of a Prime Minister (born in 10 Downing Street during his father's short premiership), and with previous Indian experience both as Under-Secretary and Secretary of State, he was a good choice for India. Sober, honest, shrewd, and a man of integrity, Ripon was the perfect antithesis of Lytton. As much an agent of Gladstone as Lytton had been of Disraeli, he thoroughly disapproved of Lytton's Indian policy. 'If you only knew what I know now of the spirit which animated the late administration of this country and the means which it employed, you would feel even more strongly than you do now from which mischiefs the late election delivered us', he wrote to Gladstone soon after his arrival in India. His mission was, he declared, to convince the people of India that 'we desire to govern them in their own interests and to promote their welfare and not any selfish or narrow national objects of our own'.[180]

Notwithstanding this lofty idealism, Ripon was as much a supporter of the paramountcy of the British Government as his predecessor. He was, however, far more tactful and diplomatic. He disliked Lytton's treatment of Salar Jung—'foolish and violent to a high degree'—and was anxious to be on better terms again with the Hyderabadi Minister. His views were neatly summarized in a private letter to Hartington: 'The true way to deal with the subject is ... to take a new departure in regard to British relations with Salar Jung, without of course abandoning the watchfulness which it is necessary to maintain in the case of a person who is evidently so prone to intrigue as Sir Salar Jung, or allowing him to assume the uncontrolled power at which it seems evident that he formerly aimed.'[181]

When Meade left Hyderabad early in 1881, Ripon appointed Bayley, in whom he had great confidence, as the Resident there with clear instructions to place British relations with Salar Jung on a better footing than they had lately been. Bayley was as good a diplomat as his Viceroy, and was sympathetically inclined towards Hyderabad. He was able to 'manage' local politics very well and to build a friendly understanding with the Minister. This pleased the Viceroy. Bayley was doing 'excellently' in Hyderabad,[182] and he became Ripon's chief adviser on Hyderabad affairs, a position he retained even after ceasing to be the Resident.

Bayley's most immediate anxiety was the Nizam's education. The

Nizam had only three more years to go before attaining his majority, and these three years were naturally of crucial importance from the British point of view. In conformity with the wishes of the Government of India, Bayley persuaded the Minister and his colleague to sign a formal resolution of the Nizam's Government regulating the education and training of the Nizam. By this document, the superintendent of the Nizam's education was invested with great authority. He was empowered to regulate the place and hours for the Nizam's study and recreation, the number and composition of his attendants, and the expenditure on his private allowance. The resolution satisfied the Viceroy, and the Secretary of State agreed that its principles were likely to serve their purpose.[183] At long last, the tricky question of the Nizam's education was settled.

Yet another problem of crucial importance demanded the attention of the Government of India. To explain this, it is necessary to digress a little. The revenue on opium, derived from a duty both on its local consumption and export, contributed, next to land revenue, the largest amount to the British Indian exchequer. The bulk of India's opium was exported to China to pay for China tea for the English market.[184] There were two sources of supply of opium in India— Bengal opium, or that grown in British India, and Malwa opium, or opium grown in the princely states of Central India and Rajputana. The Government of India had a monopoly over Bengal opium, which was sold at a profit by auction to merchants who exported it to China. The Malwa opium was permitted to be shipped to China through Bombay on payment of a duty. To prevent smuggling, it was necessary to ensure that the duty on, and the selling price of, Malwa opium imported into the British provinces and princely states for local consumption should not be less than its export duty.[185] The Government of India wanted to maintain parity between internal and export prices of opium, and also to keep the price within the princely states at the same level as in British India.

In this respect, Hyderabad posed a serious problem. In the first place, opium was cultivated in Hyderabad, though the amount was not enough for the local demand. The state imported opium from British India, but levied no duty on the import. The difference in the price of the drug in British India and the Nizam's state naturally tempted smugglers. Lytton's Government had suggested that the Nizam prohibit the cultivation of poppy in Hyderabad.[186] Salar Jung had hesitated then, but now he agreed to the proposal. New rules were framed for the state after consultation with the Resident. The cultivation of poppy and the manufacture of opium in the state were prohibited. So was its export. The import of opium into Hyderabad was allowed only under a licence, obtained by the Nizam's Government through the Resident from the opium agent at Malwa, on payment of the duty thereon. The duty was at that time Rs 700 per chest of 140 lbs *avoir dupois*, as in the case of Malwa opium intended for export by sea. This duty, after deducting the cost price of opium, was to be credited to the Nizam's state treasury.[187] These rules obviously served the purpose of the Government of India well. The price of opium was kept high enough in Hyderabad to prevent its smuggling into British territory, and British opium interests were preserved.

Presently another important issue came up before Ripon's Government. The Amir-i-Kabir died on 12 December 1881. The Government of India was immediately faced with the choice of either electing a successor or leaving Salar Jung as the sole administrator. On this issue the Viceroy was guided by the advice of Steuart Bayley. Bayley judged that the appointment of a Co-Regent in 1877 had a decidedly injurious effect on the administration of Hyderabad and that the reasons which had led to the appointment no longer existed. For instance, the Minister had been reconciled to the Government's directive regarding the Nizam's education, and the Berar issue was apparently shelved. He no longer insisted upon expansion of the Nizam's army, nor did he try to create trouble for the Government of India by intriguing with people in England. On the other hand, he was working in harmony with the British. The Nizam's minority had only three years to go—too short a time to consolidate the Minister's power and position. And no one knew better than Salar Jung himself that his relations might be difficult with the new Nizam (as they had been with his father) and that his position in future would again depend on the extent of British support. He would, therefore, be an ally rather than a foe of the British. On these considerations Bayley advised against the appointment of any successor to the Amir-i-Kabir as Co-Regent.[188]

This was a shrewd assessment of the situation. Ripon wholeheartedly agreed with his Resident; he was himself anxious to make an arrangement that would be 'less disagreeable' to Salar Jung. He was convinced that Salar Jung was not likely to forget the lesson of 1877, or to rely upon those influential friends in Britain who had failed him so signally then. The shadow of the Nizam's majority was also falling upon him. Ripon's instructions to Bayley were clear enough. Bayley was to tell Salar Jung,

We see that there are objections to the introduction of a fresh element into the administration for the short period which will elapse before the Nizam's majority, we fully recognize your experience and ability in the management of the state, and we are prepared to abstain from insisting upon the appointment of a Co-Regent, if you on your part will give us satisfactory assurances of your determination to act in loyal co-operation with the Government of India, and to place your reliance upon them, and also of your intention to conduct the young Prince's education in a manner which will remedy the defects and obviate the evils, of which we have had so much cause to complain, and which will tend to fit His Highness for the responsible duties upon which he will enter before long.

This was the guideline set before Bayley, and as to its details and mode of execution, Ripon left his Resident considerable latitude.[189] At the same time he strongly put forward his plea to the Secretary of State to take advantage of the situation created by the death of the Amir-i-Kabir to place British relations with Salar Jung on a more cordial footing. 'I feel pretty sure, that, if we can do this, it would have a good effect not only at Hyderabad, but throughout India.' Besides, the Viceroy judged, it would do more than anything else to stop the intrigues of which Salar Jung had for some time been the centre. Ripon's Council, too, unanimously accepted Bayley's recommendation and decided to discontinue the dual Government in Hyderabad. No successor was appointed to the Amir's place as Co-Administrator. Salar Jung was to be regarded as responsible for the judicious control of the states affairs and for the education of the young Nizam. He was left the sole Regent until the Nizam came of age. Ripon was confident about the wisdom of his decision and was sure that this step would put British relations with Salar Jung upon a 'better footing' than they had been on for the last few years.[190]

Ripon had calculated rightly, for Salar Jung much appreciated his gesture.[191] Salar Jung's expectations, which had led him to act against the British, had remained expectations only; his plans had failed, and his cherished schemes had been frustrated. He was an embittered and unhappy man now—apparently 'ageing rapidly'[192]—but resigned to the fact that at best he could accept reality and carry on the administration with the advice of the Resident. The co-operation between the two was restored once more and Salar Jung again devoted his whole-hearted attention towards the improvement of the state. He drew up with renewed energy an elaborate scheme of administrative reorganization and consulted Bayley on every point. In November 1882 the notification for the changes was issued.

At about this time there was talk of the visit of the Nizam, accompanied by Salar Jung, to England.[193] Unfortunately, before anything could materialize, Salar Jung died tragically of cholera on 8 February 1883. He was attacked by the disease about midnight. Bayley's successor, Jones, heard of his illness the next morning, but did not treat it seriously. The Residency Surgeon, Dr Beaumont, examined the Minister at about 2 p.m. and by 6 p.m. Hyderabad had lost the statesman who had guided her fortunes for nearly a third of a century.[194] The people of Hyderabad mourned the death of the great statesman who had struggled all his life to promote the interests of Hyderabad. He had not always maintained his popularity with the people, but for the most part had been a loved and greatly respected man. Public offices were closed for three days in respect for the memory of the nobleman 'whose generosity, courage, justice, charity, kindness and modesty were known to all, whose faithfulness and attachment to his sovereign were unequalled, who was ever willing to sacrifice self for the well being of his country and his fellow-subjects.'[195]

Salar Jung was undoubtedly one of the foremost administrators and diplomats of India. He came to rule the most misgoverned state in India at the young age of twenty-four years. Industrious, honest, with a single-minded devotion to duty, and a noble purpose before him, he served his country magnificently through thirty long years. Not that his service was totally devoid of self-interest—during the early part of his career he enjoyed and clung to his position of power at the cost of alienating both his chief and the Hyderabadi population. But this love for power never became a primary consideration, nor was it ever allowed to stand in the way of Hyderabad's progress and improvement. He was quite free of any desire to better his financial position, so much so that, while he made a tremendous improvement in the finances of his state, he himself died heavily in debt (Rs 26 lakhs).[196] 'I always knew', remarked Bayley 'that Salar Jung would die a poor man, and that he had not made anything for himself or his family out of the state, but I had no idea he was so surrounded in debt as this.'[197]

Salar Jung sacrificed his own powers and standing with the paramount power in the interest of his state. In his relations with the

British, he fought to the last to realize his twin aims—the recovery of Berar for Hyderabad and the restoration of the internal independence of the state. He failed in both, but the failure lay in the logic of history, since he set out before him unattainable goals. In this respect, Salar Jung was probably more a dreamer than a realist or a statesman. He dreamed of the Hyderabad of the past century and failed to take in the real significance of the fundamental changes in India's body-politic by the middle of the nineteenth century.

The British could not afford to give up Berar, nor could they allow Hyderabad to enjoy internal autonomy. Their policy towards Hyderabad was part of the larger aims of imperialism, which dictated all their schemes in all the Indian states. It was futile to expect any deviation in favour of Hyderabad. The process of empire-building embraced significant political, economic and cultural dimensions, and had its own inexorable logic. Whether a Liberal or a Conservative, a Canning or a Mayo, a Lytton or a Ripon, one was expected to play a game of which the pattern had already been set.

Salar Jung or his state had neither the man-power nor the material resources to fight against this force, to turn back the tide. His defeat, therefore, was a foregone conclusion. Yet that he dared to fight, that he did fight, without self-interest, elevates him far above the rank of ordinary politicians. And his contribution to the internal development of Hyderabad (in its effect more significant than his futile fights against the British) stamp him as unquestionably the greatest Minister Hyderabad ever produced.

VI

Salar Jung's sudden death created a serious situation for the Government of India. A major concern was making fresh administrative arrangements for the state, at least during the Nizam's minority. As for Hyderabad, everything was in a turmoil. Apart from various other problems, serious conflicts broke out immediately among differing groups and sub-groups, especially between Mulkis and non-Mulkis. In the process of centralizing the administration, Salar Jung had made the Dewan's position crucial in the power-structure of the state.[198] A scramble for dewanship was, therefore, only natural. The Resident advised the formation of a provisional Government (until the Nizam came of age) consisting of Bashir-ud-Daula and the *Peshkar*. Laik Ali,[199] Salar Jung's son, was to be associated with the *Peshkar* as an assistant.[200] Bayley, now a member of the Viceroy's Council, but possessing an intimate knowledge of Hyderabad affairs, was, on the other hand, convinced that the main need was to keep things going as they had hitherto been. He, therefore, suggested privately to the Foreign Secretary, Grant, that Laik Ali should be made the Dewan and that the *Peshkar*, an old and experienced man, should be associated with him. The two cousins, Bashir-ud-Daula and Khurshed Jah should form a Council of Regency. He felt that this was what the Nizam and his people would like. The Indian Foreign Office, however, was not inclined to accept the suggestion. It upheld the claims of Khurshed Jah, the eldest son of the late Amir-i-Kabir, to be the chief administrator in Hyderabad during the Nizam's remaining minority.[201]

Bayley, therefore, proceeded to Hyderabad to confer with the Resident for a working arrangement which would be acceptable to all. Finally, it was decided that the administration would be carried out by the two joint administrators, the *Peshkar* as the senior and Laik Ali as the Junior. A Council of Regency presided over by the Nizam was to be set up. Its members were to be Bashir-ud-Daula, Khurshed Jah and the *Peshkar*, with Laik Ali as the Secretary. The Council was to advise on all important matters which the administrators might lay before them.[202] Ripon was pleased—Bayley had 'done his work capitally', he said.[203] And Kimberley, Hartington's successor and a close friend of Ripon, considered the arrangements to be extremely satisfactory.[204]

But it was not a happy arrangement. Despite Bayley's strong private recommendations that Laik Ali should succeed his father—all the people loved him, reported a contemporary visitor[205]—Laik Ali was not granted the dewanship. Perhaps the memory of his father's fighting spirit made him undesirable to the Foreign Office. A half-hearted compromise was merely sought between the differing interests in the state. The compromise proved to be unworkable. The *Peshkar*, fond of power and 'jealous' of Laik Ali, denied him his proper share in the administration.[206] Cordery, Jones's successor as Resident, supported the *Peshkar*, reminding Laik Ali that he was 'subordinate' to his older colleague.[207] Khurshed Jah also tried to capture the real power. Hyderabad, in short, became a nest of intrigue.

In this setting Ripon decided to invest the Nizam with full power as soon as he came of age. Although Cordery strongly advocated making the *Peshkar* the sole Dewan,[208] Ripon, more fair minded than his Resident or Foreign Office, decided to be guided by the Nizam's wishes. 'The appointment rests with him, and under the Treaty of 1800 the British Government has no right of interference in the matter.'[209]

He sent Bayley to ascertain the Nizam's views and the Nizam chose Laik Ali.[210] Ripon next invited the Nizam to visit him in Calcutta. There, at a private interview (at which the Viceroy was much 'impressed' by the young Nizam) he gathered from the Nizam that he would like to have Laik Ali as the Dewan. Ripon approved of the choice. 'I must say', he wrote to Kimberley, 'that in spite of his youth, which is, I admit, a serious drawback, he seems to me to be the best selection that can be made out of the lot from which we have to choose.' Ripon only suggested that a small Consultative Council should be appointed composed of the principal men in Hyderabad whom the Nizam should consult on all important questions. The Nizam readily accepted the suggestion.[211]

On 5 February 1884, the Nizam was vested with full powers of administration at a gorgeous ceremony which was graced by Ripon's presence, and Laik Ali, now Salar Jung after his father's death, was given the dewanship. The people were happy, the Nizam jubilant and Kimberley approving. Ripon had won a diplomatic victory and a new ally. A difference of opinion with the Nizam on the subject of the appointment of his Dewan would not have been worthwhile. It was hoped that the Nizam would prove to be 'a tolerably good ruler' and the new Salar Jung a capable administrator.[212]

The death of Sir Salar Jung had removed the last obstacle in the path of absolute British domination over Hyderabad. Laik Ali was but an inexperienced youth of twenty-one and the Nizam was hardly more than a boy. It was possible now to conduct the administration virtually from the Residency and to shape the contours of the policy from Simla and Calcutta.[213] The Resident had wide powers, with a young Dewan and a younger Nizam, both totally dependent on him. It was only natural that Hyderabad would now be easy to manage. And it was.

Colonel C. Davidson

Sir George Yule

(Photo: Elliott & Fry, Baker Street, W.)

Yours very truly
Richard Temple

Sir Richard Temple

J. G. Cordery

C. B. Saunders

Sir Richard Meade

Sir Stuart Bayley

W. B. Jones

Nawab Mohammad
Rafi-ud-Din Khan

Nawab Rashid-ud-Din Khan

Nawab Sir Khurshed
Jah Bahadur

Nawab Mir Laik Ali Khan,
Salar Jung II

646.

My dear Sir Rd Temple

I have received your note about the Railway business — I shall wait till the Durbar is over to make the necessary representation to H.H. on the subject —

Yrs very truly

Salar Jung

12 Dec /67.

Letter from Sir Salar Jang I to Sir Richard Temple

Nizam VI as a child

Court scene of the child Nizam

Hyderabad Residency

عبارت سابق

فرزند مرتبه بلند جنگ گوشه نِجان سیونه میر تینیت علیخان بهادر فتح جنگ نظام الدوله نظام الملک
آصفجاه سپه سالار یار و فادار مظفر الممالک رستم دوران ارسطو زمان فدوی سلیمان اقتدار
کشور ستان محمد بهادر شاه بهادر پادشاه غازی

عبارت حال

آصفجاه نظام الملک نظام الدوله میر تینیت علیخان بهادر فتح جنگ سپه سالار
مظفر الممالک رستم دوران ارسطو زمان

١٢٦١

The Nizam's Seals
(*Above*: before 1858; *Below*: after 1858)

CHAPTER IV

The Question of Berar

Berar may be regarded as the principal axis round which the history of Hyderabad-British relationship revolved during the second half of the nineteenth century. The issue had both legal and emotive overtones. For Hyderabad, it was a question of justice and the return to its fold of the most prosperous area of the Nizam's erstwhile domain. For the British, regardless of any legal connotation, the annexation and retention of Berar came to be symbolized with imperial power and glory. The duel was bitterly fought for many years.

Although by the treaty of 1853 the Government of India had obtained a temporary assignment of the province,[1] its restoration to the Nizam had clearly no place in the settled policy of the British. Their desire to cling to Berar was understandable. It provided employment for British people in high positions; it also kept the Lancashire textile industry supplied with raw materials when its existence was threatened by the American Civil War. But above all, the motivation was territorial expansion, albeit by the back door.

There is no denying the fact that the province of Berar was exceptionally well-administered by the British and prospered beyond recognition. Cotton cultivation, naturally, was the centre piece of this prosperity with enhanced acreage under plantation.[2] Grain production also witnessed remarkable growth. Taxation was light and the existing cumbersome land-revenue system was replaced by the new, efficient ryotwari system followed in Bombay.[3] When railways were introduced in British India, Berar was covered from east to west by the Nagpur branch of the Great Indian Peninsular Railway. From this main line branched off two state railways from Khamgaon and Amraoti, both managed by the Great Indian Peninsular Railway Company.[4] Roads were constructed connecting the railways with important trade centres in the interior of Berar, and commerce developed rapidly. Paper currency replaced the multiplicity of coins in use and helped create a uniform standard of exchange and in avoiding troublesome fluctuations in value.[5] Mines were explored and exploited thoroughly; the structure of the judiciary underwent a sweeping change; the police forces were made effective. Schools, which had been neglected by the Nizam, were granted aid by the Government of India. The gains from all these reforms were reflected in the Census Reports of 1867 and 1881. The total population rose from 2,227,654 to 2,672,673 in 1881. Cultivated area increased by 50 per cent and land revenue by 42 per cent. Nominally under the Nizam, Berar was virtually administered as a part of British India and looked upon with pride as a model province.[6]

And this is where the trouble lay—a prosperous Berar was the root of dissension between Salar Jung and the British. Despite their earlier amity, they could not agree over the Berar policy. Salar Jung's mission in life was to retrieve Berar, and he struggled for its restoration throughout his tenure as Minister of Hyderabad. 'My first desire', he declared to a friend, 'is to see Berar restored.'[7] The painful scene of the Nizam's humiliation in 1853 was 'indelibly imprinted' on his memory.[8] A sense of deep injustice to his state rankled in his mind and he resolved to see justice done. Besides his conviction that the Nizam was the rightful owner of Berar and should get it back, he also had a personal involvement in the issue. 'The assignment of Berar', Yule wrote to Lawrence, 'sat and sits very heavily on him and his master, and I know that he considers the assignment was the cause of the death of his uncle Sooraj-ul-Moolk by whom the treaty was made and has left a stain on the family name which the restoration of Berar effected through his means would efface.'[9]

An additional, and more important, factor fuelled Salar Jung's resentment, and that was his immediate anxiety to find resources for his impoverished state. If he secured Berar its revenues could meet the increasing expenditure on administration and railway construction. His arguments were neatly summarized by Richard Temple in a private letter to Northbrook:

> The Deccan wants money. Berar, its most remunerative province, is in British hands. It might be administered much more cheaply than it is. Although the results of the expensive British administration in developing the revenues may be admitted, still when the Raichore Doab was restored to the Nizam and native substituted for British administration at a saving of full half of cost, and yet the Raichore Doab yields as much now as it did then. If he could recover Berar he would halve its expenses and still maintain its revenue.[10]

Both Nasir-ud-Daula and Afzal-ud-Daula exhorted Salar Jung again and again to do his utmost to recover Berar, and he tried every means to achieve this end. 'I shall go on bothering, bothering', he once wrote to Northbrook, 'until I get a favourable reply. It appears to me that there are three courses before me—either I must recover Berar, or I must be convinced of the justice of reasons for withholding Berar—or I must die.'[11]

Salar Jung's feelings over the loss of Berar really surfaced at the end of the Rising of 1857. He had hoped, as we have seen, that the British would restore the province in recognition of the Nizam's loyalty during the Revolt. His faith in the British sense of justice received a rude shock when his maiden effort to retrieve Berar for the Nizam was frustrated.[12] In 1866, Salar Jung, hitherto the staunchest ally the British could hope to have, showed the first signs of rebellion and discontent. Coincidentally, intensive discussions were going on in England about the annexation of Mysore. Despite his earlier half-promise that on his death the kingdom would be bequeathed to the British, the childless Maharaja now wanted to adopt a son and heir. Wood was keen to annex the kingdom on the death of the Maharaja. 'Somehow or other', the Secretary of State confided in Denison, one of his principal advisers in India, 'we must retain possession of Mysore.'[13] While pleading his case, the Maharaja had also pointed out that the cession of Mysore to him in 1799 was a joint action by the British and the Nizam, and that the Nizam, therefore, had a claim to half his territory.[14] None too pleased with this plain speaking, Lawrence denied outright the Nizam's claim to any part of Mysore. He argued that the Nizam's help in the Mysore expedition had been merely nominal and that he had been granted concessions for this assistance far exceeding his due.[15]

Salar Jung was greatly offended by this rejection of the Nizam's claim to a share of Mysore. He felt, as did the Maharaja of Mysore, that if in 1799 a Hindu Raja had not been chosen by Wellesley for Mysore, the Nizam would have had a share of the state as the ally of the East India Company in the joint conquest. The fifth article of the Partition Treaty declared that the cession of Mysore was an act of the Nizam and the British Government 'mutually and severally'.[16] On its lapse, therefore, the Nizam should receive his due half share.

In a private interview with the Resident, Yule, Salar Jung pressed this claim for the first time. With considerable excitement he told Yule, 'I mean to go to England. I do not care whether His Highness agrees or not. I mean to go.' It would be futile raising in India the claims of the Nizam to a share of Mysore, if the British Government annexed it on the Maharaja's death. The matter was going to be discussed and settled in England.[17] If he made no claims now, his silence would be construed as acquiescence.

In reality, the claim to Mysore was only peripheral to Salar Jung's main objective, the recovery of Berar. He would willingly withdraw any claims to Mysore, he said, if the British Government, in satisfaction of this claim, would consent to return Berar, and pay the Contingent themselves. That would be a charge of Rs 25 lakhs only (the expenses on the Contingent having been reduced in 1853), while Mysore yielded upwards of a crore. Yule pointed out that, since the Nizam's claim to a share of Mysore had already been disallowed by the Government of India, Salar Jung's proposal would be totally futile. This the Minister refused to accept. 'There were the treaties which proved His Highness's right.'[18]

The Nizam had claims on the Government of India on other accounts as well. The Nizam had a justifiable right to the whole of the Kurnool Nawab's estates minus the *peshkush*, though the British had taken them all. By the treaty of 1800 only the *peshkush* of Kurnool was ceded, and not the revenues of the entire district, which remained in possession of the Nawab of Kurnool, a feudatory of the Nizam. On the conquest of the area in 1839, it should have become the property of the Nizam whose seigniorial rights were never ceded. The Minister also urged the Nizam's claim to half of Goomsoor, as the Nizam's troops had assisted in its conquest in 1835-6. According to the terms of the secret articles of the treaty of 1800, the contracting parties were to participate equally in the division of territories conquered by their united arms.[19] Having taken into consideration all these factors, Salar Jung sent in a formal application to the Resident pressing the Nizam's claims and asserting that the Government of India had incurred, or was about to incur, liabilities to the Nizam to the extent of Rs 60 lakhs per annum.[20] He would be prepared to barter these against Hyderabad's liabilities on account of the Contingent and other payments, and would also want Berar back. He was, he added, 'pleading' for 'only an act of justice', and hoped that, as the British Government had declared its intention to do 'strict justice' to the Indian princes and carry out the Queen's Proclamation, his 'just claims' would be met.[21]

Yule recognized the basic logic of Salar Jung's point. In his official letter to the Foreign Office, he rejected Salar Jung's claims to Kurnool and Goomsoor, but refrained from making any observation on the Nizam's claim to Mysore.[22] Privately, however, he justified Salar Jung's stand on this issue. 'As regards the Nizam's claim', he wrote to Lawrence, 'its righteousness is clearly proved by the reason for which the Mysore Raj was set up, viz., to prevent the Nizam becoming too powerful, that is, getting a share of Mysore as of other conquests, and if that right existed then, it must exist now.'[23] But the Viceroy's ideas were very different. Lawrence, who sought no change, and certainly did not support the restoration of Berar, considered Salar Jung's letter 'very audacious', and expressed surprise that Yule should 'take up the cudgels' for such a cause. Mysore, he was convinced, fell to the British 'by the right of conquest', a right which they had waived under certain specific conditions and limitations. And, now that it was going to revert to them through a failure of the purpose for which it had been set up and the absence of a natural heir, it was 'a fair lapse' to the British. The Nizam had 'no valid claim to a share of the country'.[24]

Lawrence was equally adamant about Kurnool and Goomsoor. He argued that Kurnool had become a fief of the Government of India under the treaty of 1800 when the Nizam had ceded all his possessions south of the Tungabhadra. There was no reservation of any reversionary interest in the treaty, and so the Nizam's claim was totally baseless.[25] Goomsoor was also to be denied to the Nizam on the specious ground that the Nizam had surrendered his rights to it by treaties with the British in 1766, 1768 and 1823. The argument ran that the Nizam had helped in the campaign of 1835-6, as a friend and not under any treaty obligations, because the zemindar had fallen behind with his rents and hence committed a misconduct. Ergo, he could not legally demand half of its revenue.[26]

As to Berar, Lawrence was quite clear that the Nizam had 'no case',[27] and here the Secretary of State, Cranborne, agreed. Cranborne had read Salar Jung's proposals 'with very great surprise'. The Minister should be told in no uncertain terms that the British Government had no intention of substituting Indian for British rule in Berar and that, whatever claims the Nizam might have had at any time upon the British, were now more than satisfied.[28] Salar Jung was accordingly informed in a lengthy document that his claims, 'altogether baseless', were rejected with censure. The alleged debt of the Government of India to the Nizam was non-existent, and as the essence of the arrangements of 1853 and 1860 was the retention in British hands of a permanent source of income to meet certain expenses, the Government could see no opening for any modification of the existing assignment of Berar.[29] Northcote, Cranborne's successor, apart from wondering what the effect of the Viceroy's 'plain-speaking' on the Nizam would be, was quite happy to go along with Lawrence's proceedings.[30]

Though upset, Salar Jung, remained undeterred by the rebuff. Confronted with the suggestion from Yule that the Minister would not improve his position with the British Government by making such claims, he apparently admitted the truth of this, 'but what could he do, he must do what seems right and his master wished'.[31] For the moment, however, he suppressed his annoyance and impatience, and quietly awaited a favourable opportunity to press forward his claim again. Salar Jung's claim to half of the revenue of Mysore turned out to be a lost cause anyway. Mysore was not annexed to the British Indian Empire. Northcote, less land-hungry than Wood, decided to accept the Maharaja's adopted son as the legitimate heir.[32] Salar Jung, therefore, had no option but to abandon this aspiration.

There was yet another cause for grievance against the Government of India. Besides retaining Berar unfairly, the Government did not stand by its promise to make over the surplus revenue from Berar to the Nizam. It was not paid for the first six years after conclusion of the treaty of 1860. Lawrence privately admitted this failure and attributed the lapse partly to inattention and partly to the Berar finances having been inadvertently mixed-up with those of British India. He directed that henceforward separate accounts be maintained and that the Nizam be paid every third year a portion of the surplus, keeping the rest for current expenses.[33] In 1867 only Rs 5,00,000 were paid, though the surplus amounted to Rs 17,07,814-12a-4p.[34] Regardless of repeated remonstrances from Salar Jung and notwithstanding the Hyderabad Commission Report recommending restriction of expenditure and payment of a reasonable surplus to the Hyderabad durbar,[35] the cost of administration soared rapidly and steadily.[36] The fair-minded Northcote felt that it was not unreasonable for Salar Jung to expect the Berar administration to be made more economical. 'I don't want to sacrifice the interests of Berar to Hyderabad', he wrote to Lawrence, 'but neither do I think we ought to spend all on Berar while the other provinces are in need.'[37] Argyll, who replaced Northcote as Secretary of State, was less generous. When informed of the payment of Rs 10 lakhs as surplus to the Nizam in 1868, he wondered why a larger sum than the Government had spent had not been utilized for the building of roads and works of irrigation so that the Nizam's surplus could have been reduced.[38] Little wonder that it became the standing policy of the

Government of India not to leave too large a surplus for the Nizam Berar, after all, was not administered for the Nizam's benefit.

In order to further their own interests in Berar the British decided to tighten their hold by consolidating their territory. As explained earlier, by the treaty of 1860 and subsequent boundary readjustments in 1861, they had been able to secure a natural boundary for the province except in the west. More readjustments of the frontier of Berar were necessary to make the boundary a scientific one on all sides. As early as 1867 Richard Temple had drawn the attention of the Government of India to the irregular nature of the line which separated the southern and south-western frontier of the Assigned Districts from the territories directly under the Nizam's Government. The British officers in the border districts frequently complained of difficulties faced by their police and of occasional complications in jurisdiction. To straighten out the frontier of the Assigned Districts, Resident Saunders in 1871 persuaded Salar Jung to agree to an interchange of territory on the border, on the distinct understanding that this interchange would not in any way affect the Nizam's title to sovereignty over these areas. Eighty-eight villages valued at Rs 19,628 were transferred from the unassigned to the assigned territory and sixty-two villages whose value was assessed at Rs 21,253 were transferred to the unassigned territory. Along with the transfer, a stipulation was made with the Minister whereby the existing land revenue settlement, which had been introduced by the British and had prevailed for thirty years, should be scrupulously maintained by the officials of Hyderabad following the transfer of these districts to their administration.[39]

Prima facie it seems that from Hyderabad's point of view it was a profitable transaction in as much as the revenue of the villages it got exceeded that of the villages it gave. This impression is not quite correct. The total area of the villages Hyderabad gave was 87,844 acres and of those it got 70,703 acres. While the total cultivated land in the former was 25,393 acres, in the latter it was 35,902 acres. The population in the former was only 6,630 and in the latter 11,129.[40] The resources in the villages that the Nizam got were clearly well-tapped, and consequently, showed a larger revenue. The British on the whole made a good bargain and at the same time straightened the boundary of Berar.

Meanwhile, Salar Jung continued to plan his strategy, which would make the rendition of Berar possible in the future. He devoted himself whole-heartedly to the administration and reorganization of his state. It could not any longer be justifiably argued that Berar was better administered than Hyderabad and that Indian rule was inferior to British. Apart from this administrative reorganization, Salar Jung trained the Reformed Troops as a future substitute for the Hyderabad Contingent, by which he sought to demolish the *raison d'etre* of British possession of Berar.[41]

Salar Jung's original idea seems to have been to ask the Government of India for either the disbandment of the Contingent or transferring the Contingent to the Nizam. Having lost his earlier faith in the sense of justice of the Government of India, he tried to manipulate this scheme through pressure from the Home Government and influential British people. He sent Palmer as his paid agent to England in order to secure the services of those Englishmen who might help him politically and legally to attain his objective. In three interesting letters (the drafts of which are available) he gave unequivocal and precise instructions to his agent. It is clear from this correspondence that at that stage he did not wish to visit England personally and was anxious to keep on good terms with the Government of India. He preferred to settle the matter quietly through private negotiation and influence without taking the unpleasant step of going to a court of law or appealing publicly to Parliament. 'If my claim for the return of Berar to the Nizam and the disbandment of the Contingent or its transfer to the Nizam is granted, I agree to pay you 16 lakhs of H.S. Rs', so Salar Jung promised Palmer.[42]

Palmer accepted the offer, but soon realized that neither of Salar Jung's two proposals would be accepted by the British Government. There was no question of the Contingent being handed over to the Nizam, since the British Government was determined not to increase the military power of any Indian state. The other proposal, the disbandment of the Contingent, might have been entertained but for the Commander-in-Chief's remonstrance against military reduction in India. 'The military reports from India', Palmer informed the Minister, 'are all averse to the reduction of the army, and from what I have learned the present Government will never consent to the Contingent being maintained by your Government.' Under these circumstances, Palmer advised Salar Jung 'to treat with the Government upon a pecuniary basis'. He suggested offering a money security in lieu of the territorial security which the British then had, for the regular payment of the Contingent.[43] Salar Jung accepted the suggestion but did not have enough money in his treasury to meet his obligations. To mitigate the situation he authorized Palmer to negotiate a loan from the Oriental Bank of England. By early 1872, a sum of £60 million was successfully arranged[44]—the sum considered by Salar Jung sufficient to cover his cost for maintaining the Contingent.

It was now time for Salar Jung to act, or so he felt. To add to the concatenation of favourable circumstances, Northbrook had come to India as Viceroy. Palmer, now Salar Jung's chief adviser on the Berar issue, encouraged him to go to the new Viceroy with his proposal. The Indian Foreign Secretary, Aitchison, who belonged to Dalhousie's school of annexation, was not expected to be on the Minister's side, but Northbrook, Palmer assured Salar Jung, 'cannot but see the justice of supporting your application'.[45]

Full of hope now, Salar Jung submitted a fresh application for the recognition of the Nizam's claim to Berar. In a lengthy and carefully composed letter to the Resident, which he sought to be forwarded to the Viceroy, the Minister quoted extensively from past documents to establish his case. The claim was based on three main arguments : (i) the arrangement of 1853 was only a temporary one. To prove the point he referred to paras 39 and 52 of Dalhousie's minute of 30 March 1853, and Col. Low's letter of 4 May 1853 to the Indian Foreign Secretary;[46] (ii) the duration of the treaty and that of the Contingent depended upon the pleasure of the Nizam; and (iii) as he was now offering a tangible security, there was no longer any need for the continuance of the assignment. This security consisted in a sum of capital offered by the Nizam's Government to the Government of India—a sum sufficient to secure the payment of the Contingent and to defray the minor charges referred to in the treaty. The Government of Hyderabad, Salar Jung added, wanted to finance this scheme by raising a loan, and, for this purpose, sought the British Government's permission to secure this loan from British subjects.[47]

Salar Jung had clearly miscalculated his chances. In claiming Berar, he had relied too much on the liberal creed of Northbrook. It is well to remember that when the treaty of 1860 was made, Northbrook was at the India Office as Under-Secretary for India, working with Wood, his old master. He must have played an active part in helping Wood to work out and formulate his policy towards Hyderabad. He was now 'sorry', he told Secretary of State Argyll, that Salar Jung had insisted upon raising the old question again. It was a 'difficult one' and 'would have to be very carefully dealt with'.[48] The Viceroy's decision was, of course, a foregone conclusion.

In answering Salar Jung's letter, Northbrook pointed out that the provision of territorial guarantee was one of the fundamental principles enshrined in the treaty of 1853 and, therefore, could not be waived, and that the security which the Minister offered would require the borrowing of a large sum of money from foreign sources, which would lead to serious complications.[49]

Salar Jung was not to be dissuaded easily from the path he had chosen for himself. Along with his colleague, the Amir-i-Kabir, he sent another letter to the Resident for submission to the Viceroy, a letter far more straightforward and bold than the preceding one. In it they argued that the treaty of 1853, unlike all other treaties between allies concluded with the free consent of the contracting parties, was accepted by the Nizam only under duress. He would never have accepted it had he not been threatened with military intervention.[50] Nor would he have maintained the Contingent (for whose upkeep the assignment of Berar had been made) at all, if he was allowed a free choice. In fact, the Contingent had been maintained by the Nizams of Hyderabad for the whole period from 1817 onwards under 'positive pressure'. In a private interview with Col. Low, Nizam Afzal-ud-Daula had distinctly told the British Resident, 'not my father, but Maharajah (Chandu Lal) maintained it'.[51] Official papers on the affairs of Hyderabad, written by no less a person than Lord Metcalfe himself, clearly indicated the real position of the Nizam and his Minister in regard to the Contingent. Chandu Lal had been established by the British in Hyderabad 'as a despotic ruler without the consent of his master' and the master had become 'a Prince held in subjection by a servant, supported by an irresistible foreign power'. It was in the interests of the British alone that the Contingent had been created and placed under British control. An enormous amount of Rs 40 lakhs per annum, or one-third of the gross revenue of the state, was appropriated for its support. As soon as Berar was assigned to the British the annual cost of the Contingent was brought down by several lakhs of rupees.[52] Had this reduction been made at an earlier period, the Nizam would not have been under any debt to the Company in 1853.

The Co-Regents then proceeded to question the validity of the debt itself. An analysis of the papers of the time, they maintained, clearly showed that in 1853, instead of the Nizam owing money to the

Company, it was the Company which owed money to him. In the first place, the subsidiary force was kept for a long time at a much reduced strength in relation to the number for which the Company had already received payment in advance in 1800. The saving in all fairness should have gone to the Nizam. Secondly, the Company appropriated the whole profits of the Secunderabad *abkaree* revenue (which formed part of the excise revenue of Hyderabad state), amounting to Rs 1 lakh annually for about forty-one years. That would have given the Nizam a credit of Rs 41 lakhs—without counting the interest payable on the sum—and would almost have offset the debt claimed to be due from him.[53]

Even so, the Co-Regents were not seeking to scrap the treay of 1853 or to disband the Contingent. Their point was that the assignment of Berar had been made only temporarily to provide a guarantee for certain cash payments. They now wished merely the substitution of a cash security for a territorial one. They offered, this time without any external aid, to place in deposit with the Government of India a sum equivalent to one, two or three years' payment in advance on account of the Hyderabad Contingent and the minor charges specified by the treaty of 1853, and to keep this deposit in British hands at all times.[54]

Not surprisingly, this proposal was not received kindly by Northbrook. It was all too clear to him that Salar Jung was determined to push the matter to the utmost limit. 'He will, I think', Northbrook warned Salisbury, 'if the present proposal be negatived, say that he can get on with the Reformed Troops and no longer wants the Contingent.' The Viceroy was very annoyed that Resident Yule had permitted Salar Jung to organize these troops. Unfortunately, there was little that could be done now about them.[55]

The problem did not lend itself to any easy solution. In his effort to resolve the issue, Northbrook hit upon a shrewd strategy. He declared, he was not prepared to discuss Berar and other similar questions during the Nizam's minority. In his private letters to Salisbury he elucidated further on his policy and the calculations that shaped it, and these reveal him in a rather Machiavellian light. In a powerfully argued letter to the Secretary of State, Northbrook observed:

If Salar Jung should play his last card, and ask us to reconsider the treaty on the ground that the Nizam no longer required the Contingent for whose payment the Berars have been assigned to us ... our reply, as it seems to me, should be that circumstances may arise which would lead us to agree to reconsider the treaties ... but that a minority, when nothing can be known of the character of the Prince upon whose will the welfare of the state must in a few years depend, is not a time when we could consent to deal with such a question. Moreover, we might add that the maintenance of the Contingent is a matter which depends not upon the will of the Nizam alone, but upon the joint determination of the two Governments and that we could not look upon it only with regard to the Berar treaties. It must be regarded with reference to the general position of the two Governments and to our other relations with the Hyderabad state. This general question might be considered and along with it the advantage of a rectification of frontiers and the necessity of the Hyderabad State maintaining any military force, excepting sufficient for ceremonial purposes, now that we can undertake its defence against enemies from without.

Northbrook doubted—and quite rightly—whether at any time the Nizam's Government would agree to enter upon the question upon such terms, and felt that this stand would strengthen the hands of those who would have to deal with this most embarrassing matter in future. He then requested the Secretary of State to send to the Government of India a dispatch about Berar so that Salar Jung might have his final answer, and advised that it would be well to make the answer 'as stiff as is consistent with politeness'.[56]

Salisbury, a Conservative and as much a lover of empire as his chief Disraeli, saw no cause to entertain Salar Jung's proposals now any more than when he had previously been at the India Office. He had read the Berar case then, and was already convinced that the Nizam had 'not the shadow of a case'. Lord Canning's dictum appeared to him to be unassailable, that so long as the British had a Contingent at Hyderabad, they must have Berar. Moreover, Salisbury was by nature suspicious of Muslim power and considered the Nizam a grave potential danger whom, if he could help it, he would never willingly strengthen. Salisbury looked at the problem from an international point of view. About that time the Porte had assumed a very 'unpleasant acerbity of tone'. At this awkward moment Muslim disturbances were occurring in several parts of India. Were these risings a mere coincidènce, or was there an outbreak of Islamic fanaticism in the offing of which the Porte was feeling the first pressure? Salar Jung's persistence pointed to the growth of an ultra-Muhammedan faction at Hyderabad and if this implied a recrudescence, whether spontaneous or organized, of Muslim fanaticism, then Salisbury was even less willing to embellish the Nizam's power with the restoration of Berar. 'As a matter of policy—I might almost say of self-defence ... I would not at this juncture aggrandise the Nizam.'[57]

In the dispatch of 17 July 1874 to the Government of India—made stiff in accordance with Northbrook's wishes—the Secretary of State totally rejected the Co-Regents' proposal on the ground that the abandonment of the territorial guarrantee could not be conceded. Nor would it be fair to the people of Berar to transfer and retransfer them according to the condition of the Nizam's exchequer from one system of administration to another. Her Majesty's Government, it was declared, was convinced that it would be neither right nor expedient to make any alteration in the treaties of 1853 and 1860. This was the final answer to all Salar Jung's applications for the restoration of Berar.[58]

The decision of the Secretary of State was conveyed to the Minister by Resident Saunders, not in a formal letter, as was usually done, but in a most unusual and offensive manner. Saunders invited Salar Jung, the Amir-i-Kabir and other leading members of Hyderabad durbar to breakfast. When the breakfast was over, he announced in an arrogant speech that Salar Jung's proposal had been rejected by the British Government. The assembled nobles heard the news silently. The lone voice of the Vikar-ul-Umra spoke in support of the decision.[59] Saunders's rude and undiplomatic behaviour found support only with Northbrook.[60] The judgement of others varied. Even Salisbury disapproved of the celebrated breakfast. Saunders had dealt with Salar Jung as a 'mere native', and had foolishly thought that he could suppress the Minister 'with a frown'.[61] The press, too, voiced strident criticism. The step was 'irregular', and the order was read out in the durbar 'in terms almost incredibly peremptory'.[62]

There can be no question that Salar Jung must have felt deeply humiliated. His resentment was boiling over. What the British Government termed 'expediency' was, he felt, 'only another word for self-interest'. Unable to reply to any of his arguments, it was just brushing them aside. He was not prepared to accept 'the sham decision of this kind'. To Richard Temple, an ex-Resident, he wrote, 'I am so confident of the equity of the claims that nothing will be satisfactory but that either justice should be granted or that I shall be proved to be in the wrong.'[63]

In fact, Salar Jung had already acted, even before the Secretary of State's decision was conveyed to him. Realizing that the Government was not prepared to accept financial, instead of territorial, security for the payment of the Contingent, he decided to strike at the very root of the problem, and questioned the origin and the maintenance of the

Contingent itself. In their next letter to the Resident the Co-Regents boldly asserted that, if their application for the restoration of Berar and the substitution of some other security for the payment of the Contingent was not complied with, no alternative would be left to them but to demand the disbandment of the Contingent. They wrote (i) that the Contingent 'for which the alleged debt was incurred' was an imposition on the Nizam and was kept on not by him but by the British and their stooge Chandu Lal; (ii) that its formation was un- justified, because the duties assigned to it were the same as those the subsidiary force was bound to discharge; and (iii) that the Nizam's consent to the treaty of 1853 was obtained by threat of war, and so the treaty was not morally binding on him. Moreover, the Nizam had given his assent on the specific understanding that the Contingent would be maintained as long as he might require it. The Government of India was, therefore, bound to disband it on demand and to restore the Assigned Districts.[64]

The arguments were indeed irrefutable, but Northbrook was not prepared to entertain them. He expressed annoyance at the dogged persistency of Salar Jung and 'the ill-advised manner' in which he raised yet again the question of the Contingent and the treaty of 1853.[65] It was not necessary, he decided in characteristic fashion, to send a reply to this letter, since the final answer had already been given by the Secretary of State's dispatch of 17 July 1874. The Resident was now ordered not to receive any further letter on the subject from the Minister. However, in two official dispatches to the Secretary of State, Northbrook clearly stated the arguments from the Government side, presumably with a view to preparing the case in the event of a Parliamentary discussion. He argued that (i) the reform of the Nizam's troops was not started by Chandu Lal, but by the Nizam's Minister Mir Alam and that the Contingent was maintained with the Nizam's con- sent; (ii) there was no provision in the treaty of 1800 which imposed upon the subsidiary force the services for which the Contingent was formed; (iii) regarding the *abkaree* revenue a just settlement had been made; it had been arranged that the surplus of *abkaree* revenue that arose after defraying the cost of collection and the maintenance of police and Bazar establishments, was to be used to meet the charges of the Thuggee Department and the Medical School; (iv) although the subsidiary force was maintained at less than the stipulated strength, this was compensated by the substitution of European for Indian regiments; and (v) the Nizam's minority was not the time to discuss these issues.[66]

Privately, an intensive debate ensued between the Viceroy and the Secretary of State. Salisbury would be more technical and rely upon the formal wording of the treaties. So far as the treaties were concerned, his views were well-formed; he regarded them as final. He was not prepared to look behind existing treaties or to inquire whether they ought to have been made. 'We cannot in India go behind existing treaties and reargue the controversies out of which they had arisen. Still less can we discuss whether they were or were not the result of compulsion. If a treaty is to be impeached by that circumstance', he asked, 'how many of our treaties in India can stand? How many in the world generally?' A treaty in his view was in most cases the result of force, openly applied or covertly threatened. On that ground, therefore, there was no question of revising Dalhousie's and Canning's settlements.[67]

Here Northbrook differed from him. He was convinced that the contracting parties to the treaty of 1853 had distinctly contemplated its revision, the reduction or abolition of the Contingent and the restoration of Berar at some future date as a possible event. 'I hold that we are already pledged by the negotiations which took place to consider a revision of the treaties as a possible event and that it is of no use to shut our eyes to the fact.' The Government was bound to revise the treaties, if the Nizam, having come of age, asked for it on the ground of equity.[68]

Salisbury did not share this view. 'I am not prepared to accept the application of the principles of the Court of Chancery to the Law of Nations. I do not think that the intentions of individual statesmen who negotiated a treaty ... can be held to bind his successors to forgo the plain wording of formal stipulation.' Lord Dalhousie's minutes were no covenant between the British and the Nizam, and what Low said was of still less moment. 'We uphold', he declared, 'Lord Canning's and Lord Dalhousie's treaties. We see in them no word to stamp them with a temporary character. Our right under them to administer Berar is as clear as our right to hold Bengal.'[69]

Salisbury put forward another argument as well. Determined that Berar should never be restored, he wanted to emphasize the fact that the province could not be returned to a personal Government. 'I am desirous to push forward the argument from the interests of the people more than has hitherto been done. I consider it to be our true

rule and measure of action and our observance of it, the one justification for our presence in India.'[70] A laudable sentiment, but not as
genuine or altruistic as it appeared to be. Nor was it diplomatic, and
on this ground the astute Northbrook could not quite endorse the
argument. How could they refuse to reconsider a treaty which was
made with a Government on the plea that it was a personal one? The
'interests of the people' argument was also dangerous as it would
frighten the princes. They would ask what the difference was between
keeping Berar and annexing any state under personal Government on
the plea of the 'interests of the people'.[71] There were other reasons as
well for Northbrook's reaction. The last administration reports on
Berar and Hyderabad did not indicate any superiority in the British
administration. Besides, it was not at all certain that the people of
Berar preferred British to Indian rule and if Salar Jung asked for a
plebiscite, the British Government would be in an awkward position.
Northbrook, therefore, strongly pleaded in favour of his earlier argument, that the Government should maintain that, as long as the Nizam
remained a minor, such discussions could not be entertained.[72]

Salisbury was hesitant to accept this argument, as it would practically amount to a pledge to revise the treaties when the minority was
over. 'I am not prepared to lay such a pledge on my successors.' The
very fact that the question was postponed would be an implied
admission that there was some justification for the demand and that it
could not properly be disposed of by a blank refusal. As to a plebiscite,
Salisbury's view was quite clear. He spoke of the interests of the
people of Berar, not their wishes, and the two were very different. 'It is
quite possible', he remarked cynically, 'that Salar Jung might get a
plebiscite in Berar in favour of the restoration to the Nizam. But he
would also probably get a plebiscite from the whole of India in favour
of the English being driven to the sea.'[73] Obviously, it was not the
people's wish, but what the Secretary of State considered to be their
interests, that must determine Berar's fate. Interestingly, as soon as the
adroit Northbrook pointed out that the 'interests of the people' argument would be inconvenient if in future the British wanted to exchange territories with Indian princes, Salisbury immediately yielded
on this point.[74] Nevertheless, it is clear that Northbrook and the
Conservative Government's Secretary for India were at one on the
fundamental issue—that Berar should not and could not be given up.
The point of the debate was what arguments, or in other words, what
excuses, were to be offered for its retention.

Strictly from the point of view of international law it was not necessary to go into the reason or motives that induced the signatories to sign a treaty. But it was scarcely an act of justice to impose an unfair treaty by threat of force on a protected ally and then to enforce its provisions on the ground that they were sanctioned by a treaty. Nor was Salisbury's pet theory of the interests of the people logical, as the Viceroy and the Foreign Secretary in India—the men on the spot—unhesitatingly pointed out. The administration of Hyderabad was fair and good, and it was known that the interests of the people in the Restored Districts had not suffered as a result of the transfer in 1860. There was absolutely no reason to apprehend that the people of Berar would suffer if placed under the Nizam's rule. It did not perhaps occur to Salisbury that it was not sufficient to give people what he thought was best for them. It was more important to consider what they felt to be in their interests. Even Aitchison, one of the principal Anglo-Indian administrators upholding the policy of annexation, felt that it would be difficult to set up 'our notion of what might or might not be for the interests of the people against the people's natural desire to return to their own Government'.[75]

Equally poor was Northbrook's 'the Nizam's minority' argument. When on an earlier occasion Salar Jung had objected to finalizing the railway settlement on the same ground, Mayo had told him that the Co-Regents had full powers to act. But now Mayo's successor was postponing the Berar question using the identical plea. Why was it, the Minister resentfully asked, that he would be forced to take steps in the interests of the British but would not be allowed to do what was in his own state's interests during the Nizam's minority?[76]

But the shrewdest excuse that Northbrook forwarded was that any revision of the treaty would involve not only Berar but several other aspects of the relationship between the two states, particularly the military one. The Hyderabad durbar knew from experience that any discussion and revision of the whole relationship between the two Governments would inevitably go against Hyderabad's interest, would rob her of whatever little independence and prestige she had and would make her still more subservient to the British Government. 'It would be too dear a price.'[77] In this context, Northbrook proved to be far more calculating and crafty than Salisbury. Northbrook, not Salisbury, shaped the course of the policy to be followed towards Berar in the next few years, and it may be said that the door to its restoration was finally closed by Northbrook.

Meanwhile, the Minister had not been relying only on the sense of justice of Salisbury or Northbrook. The need of some sort of pressure group had become obvious to him and he decided to bring his case before Parliament. He had earlier avoided this course as he had felt that it would only complicate matters and cause misunderstanding between the Government of India and his state.[78] Now he was highly suspicious of the bonafides of the British Government. All his representations, just and rightful, had met with the same answer, though couched in different languages. His only hope lay in activating the interest of the British people and Parliament in the cause of Hyderabad. He tried through friends, like George Yule and the Duke of Sutherland, and paid agents, like Palmer and Keay, to organize an agitation in England and in Parliament in favour of the restoration of Berar. 'As many supporters as possible should be secured in the House', was his instruction to his agents.[79]

The Government of India as well as the Home Government had long anticipated this move. Palmer once reported that the India Office had been in 'some trepidation' that the matter would create a 'profound sensation'.[80] 'He has powerful friends here', Salisbury wrote to Northbrook with obvious nervousness,—'the Queen had interfered and questioned me about him'. The Secretary of State was specially anxious to avoid any serious embarrassment in the House, and privately instructed Northbrook to keep all the facts ready for a Parliamentary discussion.[81] Northbrook, of course, was all the while aware that there were 'certainly some weak points' in British relations with Hyderabad. 'There are parts of the general case which, in the hands of an able man of character, will, I fear neither look well nor be very easy to answer.' He prepared lengthy documents on the subject and hoped that there was nothing that would be embarrassing to his chief when the inevitable Parliamentary discussion came up.[82] But the case finally generated very little interest, because the situation in Baroda instead made news. Alleged maladministration in that state, the attempted assassination of the Resident and the consequent removal of the Indian ruler—all these were quite understandably much more interesting to the British public than the question of the restoration of Berar. And Parliament did not have much interest in India anyway. India was, Salisbury aptly commented, 'like a bagged fox only turned out when there is no other.'[83]

As has been mentioned earlier, eventually Salar Jung decided to undertake a European tour himself with the object of gaining support for his cause. He did not wish the case to be brought up before Parliament during his stay in England—that would only 'embarrass' him—but he hoped that his agents had done the spadework, and that he would be able to settle the issue through discussion and negotiation with the men in power there. He had been encouraged by the Prince of Wales's 'kind and courteous' reception of him in Bombay.[84] The difficulty was, of course, Salisbury. He had reportedly said, 'If Sir Salar Jung comes here, I will show him every hospitality, but not one word shall he hear from me about business.'[85] He impressed upon the Prince of Wales the urgency of not giving Salar Jung any encouragement on political matters. Thus, though received everywhere with great civility and perfect courtesy, Salar Jung made no political progress. He dined with the Queen at Windsor, the Prince and Princess of Wales gave a dinner in his honour at Marlborough House, and the Honorary Degree of Doctor of Civil Law was conferred on him by the University of Oxford. But everywhere politics, not to mention Berar, were scrupulously avoided. The disappointed and slightly snubbed Minister complained to Salisbury that no one spoke to him of anything but the weather.[86] Yet, his presence in England gave rise to interesting speculations, and newspapers revived the Berar question. *Tinsley's Magazine*, *The World*, *The Times* and a few other British newspapers spoke in favour of Salar Jung's contention. In India, while *The Pioneer*, *The Bombay Gazette* and the *Deccan Herald* supported the Government stand, important papers like *The Times of India*, *The Statesman* and *The Hindoo Patriot* upheld Salar Jung's point of view.[87] To avoid any embarrassment to his Government, Salisbury conveyed a message to Salar Jung through Fitzgerald that, although he was unwilling to discuss Berar at that time, the Minister could, on his return to India, write a letter to the Government of India on the subject and this would be sympathetically considered. As Salar Jung discovered later, this message had been a 'mere blind' to prevent him from trying to revive the Berar issue during his stay in England.[88] Not realizing this at the moment, Salar Jung returned to Hyderabad, full of hope for the future, with encouragement from his personal friends, and with what he thought to be the support of the Secretary of State.

Lytton had by now replaced Northbrook. The story of Salar Jung's submission of a memorial on Berar before the Imperial Assemblage and of Lytton's strong reaction to it has already been described.[89] As a result of the Minister's defeat on the question of the Queen's suzerainty, Lytton consented, though grudgingly, to receive a fresh representation from the Minister, provided that the latter withdrew all his previous memorials.[90] Privately, the Viceroy assured his chief that he had only agreed to receive a proposal if respectfully worded, but 'it pledges us to nothing'.[91]

In all good faith, Salar Jung withdrew his earlier representations, and presented a new memorial on Berar. It was a repetition of the arguments set forth in the previous applications, ably supported by extracts from treaties and quotations from confidential exchanges. Here the Co-Regents pointed out that the people of Berar would not suffer at all on being transferred from British Government to the Nizam's Government, as the administration of Hyderabad had improved immensely and was recognized even by the British Residents to be excellent. It was also argued that the question of the Nizam's minority was not relevant. The Berar assignment was not a trust created during the minority of an heir, but a trust created by the state for the payment of the Contingent. Finally, they asked that the Contingent, which had not fired a shot (except on its own parade ground) since the suppression of the Mutiny, be disbanded and Berar restored to the Nizam.[92]

If Salar Jung had hoped that these arguments would induce Lytton to alter his policy, he was sadly mistaken. Lytton reacted sharply to the Co-Regents' letter. In his view, its form was 'decidedly objectionable' and it demanded 'stern treatment'.[93] He argued that the disbandment of the Contingent would contravene the terms of the treaty of 1853. He accepted Northbrook's stand, that any modification of the treaty involved other general questions and should not be undertaken during the Nizam's minority.[94] Lytton, as might be expected, was encouraged and fully supported by Salisbury. Apart from endorsing Lytton's arguments, the Secretary of State also observed that the fact that the lives of two million people would be affected by the transfer was a major point against it.[95]

Salar Jung deeply regretted the Secretary of State's decision, but he accepted it nevertheless.[96] Lytton was pleased and the elated Viceroy wrote to Col. Owen Burne, an old friend and erstwhile Secretary, that he had obtained his 'final triumph' over Salar Jung. The Minister had accepted the Secretary of State's decison 'as final' and 'pledged in writing' not to agitate the Berar issue during the Nizam's minority.[97] The Indian press, by and large, did not share the Viceroy's jubilation.

The Friend of India in particular voiced increasingly strong criticism of his policy. It was convinced of the substantial justice and reasonableness of Salar Jung's claims. 'We have ill-used this man, Salar Jung.' 'How is it that we have totally alienated him from us?' 'You [Lytton] are mean where you should have been magnanimous' were the paper's disparaging comments on the Viceroy.[98] Nor was *The Times of India* any more favourable towards Lytton. 'What is the Berar question', it asked, 'but a great illustration of the injustice of our relations with the Native Princes?'[99]

There were compelling reasons for Salar Jung's submission to this act of injustice. The story of the tremendous pressure exerted on him and the depth of his humiliation emerge from a study of the drafts of his letters to friends. The Co-Administrator of Hyderabad, the new Amir-i-Kabir—the former Vikar-ul-Umra—was an enemy of long standing. It was 'through the instrumentality' of this new colleague that the pledge was extracted from him. The Amir-i-Kabir conceived a Machiavellian plan to compel the Minister to give in. He began to interfere with the administration and intrigue against senior officials, men of enlightened views and drawn from other parts of India. Resident Meade, of course, gave the Amir-i-Kabir active support. Salar Jung realized that if this state of affairs continued he would be obliged to dismiss these officials. His whole administration would be ruined and his life's work destroyed. 'With a ready tool' in his colleague, the Resident could at any moment 'cause a mutiny, disorganize the administration or do any other mischief' to harass him or his Government. 'I had no alternative but to give in', he confided in a friend, 'or elect to see the State and the Government ruined'.[100]

Salar Jung's defeat completely changed his personality. The energetic and optimistic Minister of 1853 turned into a sour and bitterly disillusioned old man in 1877. He lost all interest in administration, all zest for life, all determination to fight. 'I have long ago given up', he wrote pungently to Yule, 'every hope not only of the restoration of Berar, but even of the possibility of our being able to improve and embellish the territory that is left still or of long preserving the internal autonomy of the State.'[101] As far as Salar Jung was concerned, the Berar question was definitely closed. It did come up before Parliament, though, as an upshot of the articles brought out in the London *Statesman* in 1881. They highlighted the unfair and humiliating treatment of the Minister on the co-regency as well as the Berar question, and caused an uproar in England. Sir George Balfour, a

Liberal M.P., asked for the Berar papers to be laid before the House, but the Secretary of State, Hartington, refused to do so on the ground that the papers were extremely confidential.[102]

By the end of 1881, when there was talk of the young Nizam visiting England along with his Minister, Bayley, Ripon's chief adviser on Hyderabad, proposed to see the Minister privately before his departure in order to gauge his views about reopening the Berar question. This would help Lord Hartington to learn exactly 'how the card lies and either avoid or enter on the subject as he pleases'.[103] Hartington himself was, however, convinced that it was best to take Northbrook's stance. 'We are under no plege', declared the Secretary of State, 'to do anything except to reopen the question in case the Nizam, coming of age, desired to bring the whole of the treaty arrangements between the two Governments under revision.'[104]

If Hartington was unconcerned about Salar Jung's visit, Salar Jung himself was unenthusiastic. He judged that should his visit give rise to discussions on Berar (as had the previous one) he would be accused of having encouraged them. Bayley at once suggested that it was quite easy for him to avoid all suspicion on this score by making definite public statements discouraging such discussion.[105] Salar Jung was still lukewarm and, reported Jones, the Resident, he was clearly trying to escape the English trip. To go to England and not agitate for Berar or possibly to have to put down agitation would be from his point of view a 'political mistake'. He was prepared to abstain from agitation, but to appear in England as a person who had no right to bring forward the Nizam's claim to Berar would mean placing himself at the mercy of the Government of India.[106]

In the meantime, unknown to Salar Jung, Viceroy Ripon had taken an important decision. He wished to begin a discussion with the Nizam's Government of the various questions regarding Berar *before* the Nizam came of age and soon after the return of the Nizam and his Minister from England. The issues involved in the question were so delicate, he pleaded with a reluctant Hartington, that it would be better to discuss them with an able and experienced Minister like Salar Jung than with a young Prince just come of age and surrounded by proud and ignorant nobles, and advised by other Indian Princes 'as hostile and as clever as Holkar'.[107] Had the discussions materialized, they would have marked a significant departure from the traditional Northbrook-Lytton-Salisbury policy. However, with Salar Jung's sudden death Ripon quickly dropped his plan.[108]

A critical review of the struggle for Berar makes it quite obvious that the British Government behaved very unfairly towards Hyderabad. There cannot be any doubt that Berar was taken from the Nizam unjustly, on a false pretence. Lord George Hamilton, who as Under-Secretary for India from 1874 to 1880 had to prepare the Indian Government's case for Parliamentary discussion, later said that, given a choice, he would sooner make a speech against the cession of Berar than in its favour. 'I never can look back upon the transactions which led to the transfer of that territory to us', he wrote, 'otherwise than with a feeling of shame.' The British had forced on the Nizam an enormous expenditure in respect of the Contingent in the most 'Shylockian manner'.[109] They had no right to maintain the Contingent at the expense of the Nizam, and yet when the Co-Regent demanded its disbandment they were curtly refused by Northbrook, Lytton and Salisbury. Nor was the British Government prepared to accept any form of financial security for its payment. Obviously, the Contingent or payment on its account was no more than an excuse with the British to keep Berar under any circumstances. On this matter almost every Secretary of State, Viceroy or Resident was of the same opinion. Salisbury put the matter in a nutshell: 'I don't think', he wrote to Lytton, 'we ought to tell him [Salar Jung] to believe that we shall do so [restore Berar] either now or at any future date.'[110] A Salisbury or a Lytton could not really give up Berar, nor could the more fair-minded Ripon. It was a matter of principle.

Berar had originally been taken for the cotton needs of Manchester and had subsequently to be kept for the imperial purposes of Britain. With the return of a steady supply of American cotton at the end of the Civil War and the growing realization that the poorer quality of Indian cotton was no substitute for the American long-stapled variety, the interest in and the price of Indian cotton in England had sagged. But, meanwhile, the imperial idea had become more sophisticated and developed wider dimensions. The restoration of Berar could be a signal for a general scramble in India, and consequently the breakdown of the British Indian Empire. Salisbury warned Lytton, 'If you once announce that you are going to inquire into the legality from the point of view of international law of the acquisition of the various possessions and rights we have in India, I do not see any other formula or principle we can lay hold of to prevent us sliding to the bottom. It is needless to say that there are claimants to Punjab, Oudh, Gwalior Fort, Sattara, Coorg, Pegu and probably many others. Indeed I do not see why the Prince of Arcot should not raise his head again.'[111] Here Salisbury, as yet only the Secretary for India but destined for three terms of Premiership that aggregated over thirteen years (beating Gladstone's record by one year), exhibited a true understanding of the relentless logic of imperialism.

The battle between Salar Jung and Northbrook or Lytton was not a personal one, as Lytton seemed to regard it. It was a battle of principles, a battle between the right of self-determination (in its nascent form) and ruthless imperialism (at its highest). And in the last quarter of the nineteenth century in India, during the high noon of the Empire, the historical forces were placed in such a way that the victory was bound to be on the side of the latter. Salar Jung nursed a rather naive faith in the British sense of justice. Yet, measured in terms of contemporary standards, he showed astonishing courage and determination to secure the rights of his state. The ultimate victory against imperialism was to be won only by the people. During Salar Jung's times, that force still lay in the womb of the future, although the first stir was already beginning to be felt.

II

The final act of the Berar drama was played out twenty-five years after Salar Jung's death, during Curzon's[112] viceroyalty. Curzon's motive was the same as Dalhousie's, viz., to win a permanent cession of Berar from the Nizam. His idea was to take a perpetual lease of Berar in return for a fixed annual rent of Rs 25 lakhs. At the same time, he wanted a solution to the military problem to get rid of the Hyderabad Contingent altogether. 'It will be a capital thing, if we can kill two birds with one stroke.'[113]

The Secretary of State, Hamilton, greeted Curzon's idea with a distinct lack of enthusiasm. In his opinion, a lease in perpetuity was little different from cession, and he knew that the Nizam would never agree.[114] Initially, the Nizam did, in fact, refuse to grant a permanent lease, and ended his discussion with Barr, the Resident at Hyderabad, 'with an absolute refusal unattended by any argument or reasons'. Curzon then paid a visit to Hyderabad to speak to the Nizam himself. Within twenty-four hours of his arrival in the state he succeeded in bringing about the settlement he desired. Curzon wrote to Hamilton, 'Nizam accepted my Berar proposals. ... As long as he thought that he had a chance of getting back Berar in complete restitution he said that he would naturally prefer not to consider any other solution. ... If I could tell him that the chance were so remote as to be unworthy of serious consideration, then he would not only accept my proposal with pleasure, but he was grateful for the generosity of its terms.'[115]

Curzon knew that so sudden and complete a *volte-face* on the part of the Nizam would generate universal criticism that undue pressure had been exerted on the helpless ruler of Hyderabad. In the hope of convincing the Secretary of State that all such suspicions were without foundation, the Viceroy placed on record his version of what had happened. The Nizam, it was claimed, had yielded not from weakness or alarm but because he was convinced by the Viceroy's arguments. 'I venture to assert', Curzon assured Hamilton, 'that at this moment, he [the Nizam] is the most contented man in Hyderabad.'[116] In his anxiety to prove this point, the Viceroy made the Nizam sign a document declaring voluntary cession. It is difficult to accept at face value these letters and official documents—reading between the lines and bearing in mind Curzon's attempts to convince posterity of the Nizam's 'contentment', it appears that Dalhousie's methods were ruthlessly repeated. The exact nature and extent of Curzon's so-called convincing arguments are unfortunately not known, but a contemporary political diary records that the Nizam surrendered under the threat of deposition and was so broken-hearted after the incident that he refused to eat for four days.[117]

By the treaty of 1902 Berar was leased in perpetuity to the Government of India for a permanent annual rental of Rs 25 lakhs. The Hyderabad Contingent lost its separate identity, was merged with, and recognized as an integral part of, the British Indian army. Its services were to be available to the Nizam, if necessary.[118] The 'garden' of the Nizam's state was annexed to the Central Provinces, a step which had been planned since Dalhousie's and Canning's days.

CHAPTER V

The Introduction of Railways

British business and manufacturing interests provided the motivation for building railways in India.[1] They tried to convince the East
India Company and the British Government that the railways would
be useful not only for the general development of trade but also for
imperial defence as well as internal security. The core of the pressure
seems to have come from the Lancashire textile interests. Lancashire
people, as we have seen, looked upon Indian cotton as a sort of
insurance against their excessive dependence on American cotton.[2]
For them, old-fashioned conveyance by bullock-carts was slow, expensive and uncertain, and was also not an efficient method of spreading
the consumption of factory-made cotton goods amongst the Indian
people.[3] The insistent demand from Manchester led the Home Government to take up railway projects and compelled the East India Company
to sign the first contracts with the East Indian Railway Company
and the Great Indian Peninsular Railway Company in London in 1849.[4]

Wood, the then President of the Board of Control, was sympathetic
to the wishes of Manchester and anxious to push the railroad from
Bombay into the cotton districts.[5] He also favoured the building of
good roads in India as feeders to the railways. Wood entrusted the
work of planning and starting India's railways to the ever-energetic
Dalhousie.[6] In a crisp, incisive letter, Wood expressed his own views
to the Governor-General:

> We ought in India to take care that they [the railways] are constructed upon
> a general plan. ... I assume that you will have one great line from Calcutta up
> the Ganges valley ... to some place in north-west India. I also assume that
> Bombay will always be the point of contact for India with England. ... If so,
> the main line of communication must centre at Bombay. This line would I
> suppose turn north-west somewhere and run into the Gangetic line ... and
> south also, getting down ultimately to Madras.[7]

This was Dalhousie's view as well. In his minute of 20 April 1853 he
laid down the blueprint of the general plan for the future Indian
railways. Three main trunk routes were proposed, one from Calcutta

to the north-west via the Gangetic valley, one from Bombay to the north and the third from Madras towards the western coast. To link the three Presidency towns, Dalhousie advised that from the Bombay line a junction should be effected with the Gangetic line by way of Baroda or the Narmada valley and that the Bombay and the Madras trunk lines should be joined through a line that would run via Cuddapah and Bellary.[8]

Wood applauded Dalhousie's very able minute and, at the same time, emphasized the need to open up Khandesh and Berar, the two cotton regions in India.[9] Consequently, the East India Company's previous agreements with the E.I.R. and the G.I.P.R. Companies were scrapped and a series of new contracts, the guaranteed interest railway contracts, were negotiated with them and several other companies for the construction of a few major lines as well as branch lines.[10]

II

During the construction of the Great Indian Peninsular Railway, the proposal for a railway to the city of Hyderabad was mooted for the first time before the Home Government. According to the original plan, the section of the G.I.P.R. connecting the Bombay and Madras lines was to run by way of Cuddapah and Bellary through Mudgul in the Raichur Doab. At the time of the transfer of the Doab to the Nizam in 1860 Salar Jung had been persuaded to agree to hand over (but not to cede) to the G.I.P.R. Company land required for the building of the line. He had also promised to grant magisterial powers to the British within the railway fence.[11]

In 1862 Sir Bartle Frere, the Governor of Bombay, came up with the suggestion that the line between Madras and Bombay should run from Sholapur to Cuddapah through Hyderabad instead of via Mudgul and Bellary. Frere seems to have looked at the problem purely from an economic and engineering angle. It was in his view 'a far easier and more useful extension' than the originally proposed line. 'Even if there are objections', Frere wrote to Wood, 'of which I am not aware, to going to Madras via Hyderabad, I think the completion of railway communication from Bombay to Hyderabad quite as important as that to Madras.' Frere was certain that the eastern line towards Hyderabad would be easy and cheap, on which every mile would add to the traffic likely to travel the whole distance to the sea at Bombay. On the other hand, the southern line towards Mudgul and Bellary, Frere felt, would be a difficult and expensive proposition. Besides the two enormous bridges required on the Bheema and Krishna, every mile would carry the railway further into a district the traffic of which had a natural tendency to find its own way to the sea by a shorter and more direct route to Vingola, Sedashegar and other ports.[12]

Wood was inclined to agree with Frere. Hyderabad appeared to be the proper meeting place for the Bombay and Madras lines. Unlike the Governor of Bombay, however, the Secretary of State's approach to the issue was entirely political. 'I think', he wrote to Frere, 'that the political object is great and there is no material difference in distance. The Nizam's Government will be more amenable when more accessible.'[13] Before finally making up his mind, Wood thought it prudent to sound his old friend Denison, the Governor of Madras, about the proposed change of route.[14]

Denison was unimpressed by both Wood's and Frere's arguments. To him Hyderabad was a dangerous place and its ruler a 'petty demi-savage'.[15] Denison was emphatic in his opposition to bringing the line from Bombay to Madras via Hyderabad. 'This I take to be a political question,' he wrote to Wood, 'and looking upon it in that light I should say by all means do anything which is likely to put light and life into a district occupied by a set of bigoted Mahomedens, with whom, before long, we shall most certainly come into collision. If however, you propose to continue in your cowardly policy towards the Nizam, if you are going to allow him to make the Resident, your ambassador, pull off his boots or shoes when he comes into his presence, then I say keep light and life out of his country till it becomes your own.' Denison's next letter was more sober. He conceded the Hyderabad route on political and military grounds but raised a few questions. The line was going to be forty miles longer and involving additional costs when a good deal of money had already been spent on the line between Cuddapah and Gooty on the Bellary route. A branch line would also be required to Bellary. Finally, Denison asked, 'Ought not the Nizam to pay a part of the interest?'[16]

Wood was clearly disappointed. The Government of India, too, seemed to support the Madras Governor. 'I hear', Wood asked Elgin, 'that you are in favour of carrying the Madras and Bombay railway in the old line by Mudgal and not by Hyderabad. Is that so? We rather incline to the line passing thro' Hyderabad as a means of bringing that place into better relations with us.'[17] On second thought, however, Wood changed his mind, doubtless because Denison's arguments weighed heavily with him. A few days later in an entirely different tone the Secretary of State wrote to Trevelyan, Denison's predecessor in Madras and now a member of the Viceroy's Council, 'I am not sure it is not better to have so essential a line of communication entirely in our own hand, i.e., in our own territory. There should be some line to Hyderabad, but it would hardly be safe to have our own line of communication exposed to the risk of being broken up and interrupted by a fanatical mob in the Nizam's unruly capital.'[18]

Totally unaware of the correspondence between the Secretary of State and his confidants in India, Yule at Hyderabad was expecting the Madras and Bombay railways to effect their meeting in Hyderabad. 'This would do more good', he wrote to Elgin, 'than all the advice of the Residents in the world.'[19] Yule was fully supported by Salar Jung (as yet a British ally), who at this stage was keen on bringing the railway to Hyderabad. His enthusiasm was doubtless inspired partly by his desire to enrich and modernize his state and partly by his anxiety to please the British Resident. He assured Yule—though not quite truthfully—that the Nizam himself approved of the idea and that there would be no difficulty about land, jurisdiction or duties.[20] None the less, Elgin was doubtful and evasive. He felt he needed some more information on the subject before coming to a final decision.[21] While Yule was painstakingly penning his minute for the perusal of his Government,[22] in England Wood had already taken his decision. Lawrence, Elgin's successor, although initially in favour of the Hyderabad line, later recommended the comparatively direct route through Raichur and Gooty as the safest and the most convenient[23]— and this was the route ultimately chosen. 1868 saw the meeting of the lines from Bombay and Madras at Raichur.

The value of a railway connection with the city of Hyderabad was, however, clearly recognized by Wood, who felt that the place could not be totally left out of the Indian railway system. 'I have no doubt,' he told Denison while giving in to the latter's advice, 'that if we make the Mudgul line as the principal line, Hyderabad will be ultimately made.'[24] Here again his calculation was political, and, more so, military. 'I should not be sorry,' he confided to Elgin, 'to have the power of sending 4000 or 5000 men down upon him [the Nizam] at once.'[25] This was Wood's principal motivation, although the incidental economic advantages of connecting Hyderabad with Bombay must have provided an added impetus.

By the time official instructions came from far-off London to Calcutta urging the construction of a branch line from Gullbarga on the G.I.P.R. to Hyderabad, Elgin had been succeeded by Lawrence. Wood explicitly ordered the new Viceroy not to resort to compulsion. 'I am against forcing the native princes', he wrote to Lawrence in the context of a railway in the Holkar's state 'to submit to a railroad. They will come to them soon enough and I prefer delay to forcing them.'[26] It was, therefore, necessary to secure the Nizam's willing consent to the railway plan. In the process it would also be extremely convenient if half of the guaranteed interest to the G.I.P. Company (which was to build the Hyderabad line) could be extracted from him.

The daunting task of persuading the Nizam to give his support to the enterprise fell on Richard Temple, Yule's successor at Hyderabad. From the Viceroy he received a telegram advising him to inquire whether the Nizam would agree to pay half the guaranteed interest on the capital required for the construction of the railway from Gulburga to Hyderabad. Sensing the certain hostility of the Nizam to the request, Temple, in an interesting letter to Salar Jung, not only defined the terms of the agreement but also suggested that the arguments be placed before the Nizam in order to make the scheme more palatable.

It was proposed that a railway line should be laid from Gulburga to Hyderabad at a rough estimated cost of Rs 120 or 140 lakhs. This money would come from England through the Railway Company, but the Government would have to pay to the Company a guaranteed interest at 5 per cent, which would amount to Rs 7 or 8 lakhs or, at the most Rs 10 lakhs per annum. The Government of India suggested that this interest money should be shared equally by the two Governments—the Government of India because it would gain in the convenience to its troops, and the Nizam because his country and people would benefit by the introduction of railways. The Nizam's share of money, it was clearly stated, would be paid from the surplus revenues of Berar, so that not a rupee had to be paid from the Hyderabad treasury. There would be 'no further demand nor liability beyond that above stated'. Jurisdiction of the Nizam's Government in police matters within the railway limits—a sensitive point with the Nizam—would remain unaffected.

While endorsing these terms, Temple hastened to enumerate the benefits that would automatically follow the introduction of railways. The *abadee* of Hyderabad would multiply tenfold, its people would prosper, the Nizam's revenues would increase, and his prestige enhanced. 'Put the arguments', Temple advised the Hyderabad Minister, 'with all fair advantage. But say that this is only asked as a question which His Highness can answer, according to his own pleasure and his own sense of what is proper.'[27]

It is significant that at this stage the proposal was not unfair to the Nizam, nor was any compulsion employed, at least openly. But Temple had an ally in Salar Jung. The Minister seems to have been over-enthusiastic about the railway enterprise. He even went to the length of suggesting that the Nizam should not be given any option, or else he would at once declare that he did not wish the railway to be brought to Hyderabad. Salar Jung proposed another modification in the terms as well. In case the Nizam sanctioned the proposal, the Minister would opt to pay the Nizam's share of the guaranteed interest directly from his treasury. It would not be necessary for the Government of India to pay it from the Berar surplus.[28] This was a serious miscalculation on Salar Jung's part. Little did he realize that in his anxiety to establish the Nizam's claim to Berar—almost an obsession with the Minister—and about the payment by the Indian Government of the Berar surplus to the Nizam, he was suggesting a scheme that might eventually cause the financial ruin of his state. His proposal was doubtless inspired partly by his belief that the Government of India would pay half the guaranteed interest for the construction of the line.

In any case, Temple stood his ground. The Government of India, he maintained, would prefer to pay the Nizam's share of money out of the Berar revenues, rather than receive money from the Durbar. The Viceroy would be happy if the Nizam approved of the railway plan, but the Resident was not in a position to say more than that. 'I am *not* instructed to press for, or insist on the point. I am directed to ask the question.'[29]

The Nizam's reaction to the question was expectedly unenthusiastic. He remained totally unconvinced by the Minister's apparently impressive arguments. And in this one instance, let it be said, the ruler, probably instinctively, proved wiser than his distinguished Minister. He doubted whether the revenues of the state would increase as a result of the building of the railways; he resented that his subjects would lose the land that would be taken up by the line; he was nervous that his relatives would jump into a train and leave the state without his previous permission and that their misconduct, when away from home, would bring disgrace on him and his family.[30] Lastly—this could easily be his real reason for opposition—he apprehended that the railways would give the British increased leverage

over him.[31] When Salar Jung urged him to give a quick answer to the
proposal before Temple left Hyderabad,[32] the Nizam was so annoyed
that he sarcastically commented that the Minister must have 'de-
scended from British ancestors'.[33] Even so, aware that he would
ultimately have to bow to the Viceroy's wishes, he brushed aside his
qualms and gave his reluctant consent to the railway project,[34] just
three days before Temple left Hyderabad.

Temple was delighted, and Lawrence more so.[35] The Nizam had
not only agreed to the building of a railway to his capital, but had
also promised to pay half the guaranteed interest. How the Nizam
was gradually trapped into bearing the entire expense of the railway
remains one of the most perfidious episodes of British political
manoeuvrings in India.

III

It was with the coming of Mayo that the scheme of the Hyderabad
railway was taken up in right earnest by the Government of India.
Immediately upon his arrival in Bombay, he wrote in his diary, 'The
cry, of course, is for Railways and means of communication with the
interior.'[36] 'Should there be a sudden demand of cotton,' he hurried
to assure Frere, Governor of Bombay, 'I will take care to make
every preparation that I can for facilitating communication and so
on.'[37] Mayo preferred the construction of railways not by
guaranteed companies but by the state itself. In this he was acting in
the spirit of the times.[38] By the late 1860s the guaranteed-interest
contracts had been discredited. 'Private enterprise at public risk'
had proved to be too expensive for the Government. The 1870s were
the decade of state railways, before the switch-over in the 1880s to
the policy of encouraging private companies to construct or manage
railways in India.[39] In this new setting it was necessary to negotiate
fresh terms with the Nizam's Government for the building of the
Hyderabad railway. The initiative here seems to have been taken by
Mayo himself. He chalked out the details of the scheme, making
radical changes in Lawrence's original proposal. In the first place,
Mayo decided that the junction of the Hyderabad line with the
G.I.P. line would be at a place south of Caugnee, instead of at
Gulbarga.[40] Second, the construction of the projected railway would
rest entirely with the Indian Government. And third, and most
important, the Nizam's Government must pay wholly for it. There
was now no question of the Government of India bearing half the

cost. 'I hope', Mayo wrote to Secretary of State Argyll as early as October 1869, 'we shall get all the money we want for the Hyderabad railway from Sir Salar Jung.'[41]

Salar Jung was in a tight corner. He had all along been enthusiastic about the railway, but had not bargained for bearing the whole of its cost. The dismayed Minister rushed two alternative proposals for the Viceroy's consideration. He suggested in the first place that the Nizam's Government would provide, either from its own funds or with the help of private capital, all the money required for the railway, interest being paid at the rate of 4 per cent from the revenues of Berar. Alternatively, he proposed participation in the capital by the Government of India. The sum subscribed by the Government of India would, however, be provided by the Nizam's Government against promissory notes bearing interest at 4½ per cent to be paid from the revenues of India. A part of the capital, up to £500,000, would be provided by the Nizam's Government at its own risk. But for any sum beyond £500,000, interest would be paid from the Berar revenues.

Mayo totally rejected Salar Jung's first proposal, and pretended to accept the second, modifying it in such a way as to alter its entire character. The Viceroy insisted that the interest on the British share of the capital would be paid not from the imperial revenues, but from the revenues of Berar.[42] Clearly, his object was to throw the whole burden of the transaction on the Nizam's Government. A contribution from the revenues of Berar was not the same as payment from British imperial revenues. As the Berar surplus belonged to the Nizam, the payment of interest from the revenues of Berar would necessarily affect his financial interests. This was Mayo's design. If his proposal was accepted, he admitted to Saunders, the Resident at Hyderabad, the entire fund for the construction of the railway would in effect be actually provided by the Nizam's Government. The Government of India's participation would be limited only to the regular payment of interest on a portion of the capital out of the revenues of Berar. The Viceroy judged it 'convenient and desirable' that the Hyderabad state should have 'the credit of the whole enterprise'.[43] Mayo insisted that one point, however, must be made clear to the Minister. It was essential 'that the construction and working of the Railway must be kept entirely under the control of the British Government'.

Mayo followed up these broad proposals with a suggestion that they come from the Nizam's Government itself rather than appear as an imposition on it. 'I think', he privately instructed Saunders, 'it would be very desirable if the proposal in the terms in which I have now suggested could come from Sir Salar Jung himself. It should be in an official form and framed in such a manner that it would appear upon the proceedings of the Government of India and be published.'[44] This was in essence a demand from the Viceroy. Nevertheless, it was only after 'a good deal of demi-official correspondence' and many interviews with the Resident, that a resentful and reluctant Minister was persuaded to acquiesce in it.[45] In the process, a few other alterations were made in the scheme.

Eventually the Minister agreed that the Nizam's Government would provide all the capital required for the railway, partly from Hyderabad's own resources and partly by raising funds from local capital. It would also pay the whole interest thereon as long as the capital remained unpaid. Money was to be raised from local capital in two ways: by (i) loan, bearing interest at 6 per cent per annum without participation in profits, and (ii) loan, bearing interest at 5 per cent per annum but with participation in profits. The subscribers to the loan would be precluded from all interference with the working and construction of the railway.[46]

Mayo was now impatient to have the scheme sealed through a treaty. In a hypocritical speech delivered on the occasion of the opening of the Khamgaon Railway in Berar on 4 March 1870, the Viceroy applauded Salar Jung as a staunch friend of the British, fighting hand in hand with them against ignorance, prejudice and idleness. Mayo declared:

> At his recommendation, the Government of the Nizam has within the last few days, made a specific proposal for constructing, at its own expense, a Hyderabad State Railway .... this is very encouraging, and if the Government of India have had the satisfaction of constructing within the assigned districts of Berar our first State Railway, Sir Salar Jung will enjoy the proud honour of being the first representative of a native Government that has made a State Railway for itself. Though our first object in coming here is to celebrate the opening of this little line, we are here also to do all honour to one who has set so willing an example to his countrymen in India.[47]

Ironically, whilst an unsuspecting crowd cheered the noble sentiments in all good faith, the object of all these panegyrics sat silent and unhappy throughout the proceedings. The Minister was courteously invited to visit the Viceroy in Calcutta. Mayo planned 'to make as much of him as possible'. Ringing in confidence and satisfaction, he reported to his chief, 'I hope while he is here the whole affair of the Hyderabad Railway will be finally settled.'[48] And it was.

In terms of the final agreement concluded on 19 May 1870, the Nizam's Government was to provide, with the aid of shareholders, all the capital required for the construction, maintenance and working of the railway, the cost of which was estimated at about one crore of British Indian rupees. The Government of India was to construct and manage the railway through the Resident at Hyderabad. The railway, to be called the Nizam's State Railway, would be the property of the Nizam's Government. Troops, military stores and police of both the Governments would be carried on the railway at a concessional rate. The mails of both the Governments would be carried free. The General Railway Act applicable to British India was to be made applicable to the Nizam's State Railway and its management. The Government of India would be free to construct a telegraph line along the railway route.[49]

A first glance at this contract leaves little doubt as to who got the better share of the bargain. The railway was oriented to British needs, but was entirely financed by the Nizam's Government without any financial commitment from the Government of India. Small wonder, Mayo gloated over his success. He was able to tell Argyll— as he had earlier hoped to do—'that for the first time in the history of India a native Government has embarked a million of money in a State Railway of its own.' Highly pleased at the manner in which Salar Jung had behaved, he praised the Minister eloquently before the Home Government and recommended rewarding him with the G.C.S.I.[50]

Understandably, the recipient of the honour and applause was most unhappy.[51] In signing the railway agreement, he had accepted an enormous financial burden for his state. The construction of the line, without any control by the Government which financed it, was bound to prove very expensive (a primary reason, it may be recalled, that had induced the Government of India to discourage guaranteed-interest contracts for the building of railways in India). Nor was the Hyderabad line ever likely to pay its way. The route of the railway was faulty; large towns were by-passed; the line traversed unproductive and sparsely populated areas.[52] Instead of Gulbarga, a large city with a big population and considerable trade, Wadi, a relatively unimportant place, was chosen as the junction between the Great Indian Peninsular Railway and the Nizam's State Railway, depriving the Nizam's capital of the commercial and other benefits of a connection with a flourishing city. Salar Jung was opposed to this route and wished altogether a different line. But a military line, taking the shortest route to the military cantonment at Secunderabad, appeared to Calcutta to be 'the one thing needful'.[53] Dubbs, a director of the line, attributed to the selection of this route its commercially non-viable character.[54]

Instead of being taken straight to the Nizam's capital, the line was brought to a point about six miles away, viz., Begampet on Husain Sagar, presumably to avoid the risk of trains being exposed to the guns of the Nizam's fortress at Golconda.[55] At Begampet the line forked off in two directions, one branch going to Hyderabad, the other to Secunderabad. The two branches were connected with a loop-line which formed a triangle and enabled trains to proceed, if necessary, direct between Wadi and Secunderabad.[56] A short branch line ran to the cantonment at Trimulgherry for the exclusive use of the army. The almost excessive concern of the Government of India with the scheme and the route leaves no doubt that the whole project was a military one.

Because of the railway's primarily military character, Mayo did not accede to Salar Jung's request for a narrow gauge line, notwithstanding his own advocacy on grounds of economy of the narrow gauge in other parts of India.[57] It is pertinent to point out here that the famous Battle of the Gauges was being bitterly fought in official minutes, pamphlets, and newspapers throughout the early 1870s. Mayo and the Secretary of State, Argyll, were both in favour of the metre gauge in India because a broad gauge was a much more expensive operation. Defence needs and the fear of Russia eventually triumphed over economy, and, under pressure from the military authorities, the broad gauge was sanctioned for the major railways in British India, although the building of a few metre gauge lines was also permitted.[58] The Hyderabad Railway was a vital part of the British military railways. A narrow gauge would isolate it.[59] 'In branch lines of short dimension,' Mayo gave his orders to Saunders, 'convenience points to unbroken gauge.... Hyderabad is a very

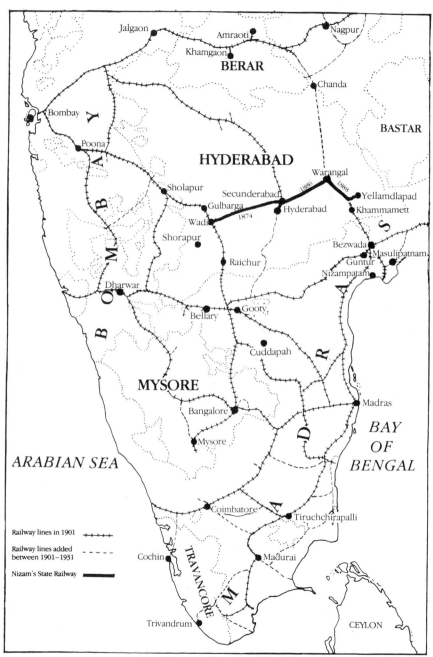

Railways in the Nizam's Dominion

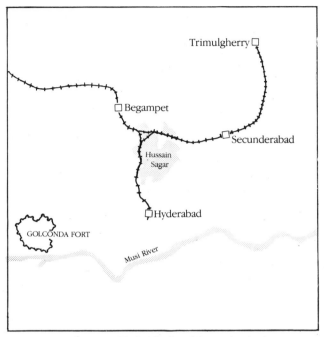

Railways at Hyderabad and Secunderabad

important place. . . . I cannot but think that the additional money which the Broad Gauge would cost would be well spent in this case. . . . I own I should much regret if the original intention is ultimately departed from, and the line does not fulfil all that was expected from it.'[60] Salar Jung had no alternative but to give in,[61] and Mayo now urged speedy construction of the line. 'It would be a matter of great satisfaction to me,' he wrote to Saunders, 'if before I leave India, I could be present at the opening of the first Indian Railway that has ever been constructed from the unaided resources of a Native State.'[62]

IV

Construction work on the Nizam's State Railway began in 1871, and as the work progressed it became increasingly obvious that the Nizam's state was incapable of coping with the mounting financial burden that had been placed on it. Builders of the line had no need to economize since they were not bearing the costs for it. Money was being spent recklessly but funds were not flowing in. Till 1872 no public issue of shares had been made; the shares, at any rate, were unsaleable except at a very heavy discount. The local capitalists, used only to quick returns by the sale of *hundies*, were reluctant to invest in the State Railway, presumably because they were unable to comprehend the nature of such investment. Against this dismal background, Salar Jung offered employment to one Seymour Keay as his confidential agent for raising money.[63] Keay had been engaged as the agent of the Bank of Bengal at Hyderabad and was consequently known to the local financiers.

Saunders, who seems to have been sympathetic to Salar Jung's financial problems, did not object to Keay's appointment.[64] Even so, Northbrook, who came out as Viceroy in 1872, refused to sanction it. Though his ostensible excuse was that Keay's appointment was inconsistent with the spirit of Act 37 Geo III Chap. 142 Sec. 28, he privately admitted that this ground did 'not hold water'. The Viceroy's opposition stemmed from the fact that Sir Richard Temple (now Financial Member of his Council), who knew both Salar Jung and Keay well, opposed the appointment in the strongest manner. Northbrook's own private investigations, too, had satisfied him that Keay would not be 'a proper appointment' from the Indian Government's standpoint.[65] There was much truth in

Temple's and Northbrook's assessment. There can be no question that Salar Jung also had a political object in appointing Keay, namely, to use him to promote his own Berar plans.

Annoyed with Saunders for allowing Salar Jung a free hand in the matter, Northbrook temporarily replaced Saunders with Lumsden, who was believed to be 'a good and safe man'. Despite Saunders's resentment and threat to resign if the negotiations were taken out of his hands, Northbrook refused to alter his decision, and Saunders had to proceed on leave. Hyderabad, in Northbrook's opinion, needed 'a stronger man', and he could rely on Lumsden to carry out his orders with greater zeal.[66] Lumsden justified his master's confidence. He lost no time in inducing Salar Jung to withdraw the appointment offered to Keay.[67] Northbrook was relieved, and reported home the satisfactory settlement of the 'troublesome business' at Hyderabad.[68]

However, the incident fuelled Salar Jung's pent-up resentment against the Government of India. He had appointed Keay after consultation with the Resident and felt that the withdrawal of the offer undermined the prestige of his Government. Nor did he see why he should be denied the assistance of a competent man in mobilizing local capital. He feared it would now be more difficult to procure capital, since the episode would leave the unfortunate impression that the Government of India had no sympathy for the enterprise.[69] While Salar Jung was embarrassed and enraged, Keay, the key figure of the controversy, proved to be completely understanding, despite his disappointment. He declared before his departure from Hyderabad that his regard and attachment to Salar Jung and his Government remained 'unalterable' and that he would always be ready to serve the interests of both.[70] Interestingly, Keay was back again within two months, in September 1872, as manager of the mercantile agency firm of Messrs Nicol & Company of Bombay. Privately Keay became one of Salar Jung's close confidants and trusted agents for operating in the English money-market and influencing people in Britain concerning the restoration of Berar to the Nizam.

Meanwhile, a significant development in Hyderabad had added a new dimension to the railway question. This was the discovery of coal. In 1871 coal was found in the Madhavaram field on the Godavari, and in April 1872 the Singareni coalfield, the richest and most important coalfield in the Nizam's dominion, was discovered by W. King, the Deputy Superintendent of the Geological Survey of India. A field-report by him indicated that the coal area was extensive and favourably situated for the export of coal. It was only fifty-two miles from the town of Nagunpole, which was close to the right bank of the Godavari and, fortunately, below all the barriers that obstructed its navigation. The locality was reported to be eminently suitable for the construction of a railroad.[71]

The demand for coal in India was rising fast with the expansion of the network of railways. The G.I.P. Railway Company and the South Indian Railway Company, however, had to depend solely on imported English coal. As yet only the coalfield in eastern India was being worked, and the cost of transporting coal from there to Bombay and Madras proved to be prohibitive. In this setting, the value of the extension of the Nizam's State Railway through the Singareni mines up to the Godavari in the south and Chanda in the north, thereby connecting the coalfield with the network of British Indian railways, was clearly recognized by Salar Jung. Apart from giving access to a vast supply of cheap fuel, the projected extension had the added advantage that the expectedly large coal traffic for the G.I.P. and the South Indian Railways would transform the unremunerative Hyderabad railroad into a paying one.[72] Not unnaturally, he wished to plan and carry out this new line without the assistance or interference of the Government of India.

On an earlier occasion, while assenting to Mayo's proposal for a broad gauge for the Nizam's State Railway, Salar Jung had broached the subject with the Viceroy. The Minister had stipulated that he would construct a narrow gauge railway wherever he pleased in the state under the immediate control and management of the Nizam's Government. Mayo had made no promises. He had merely agreed that any future line in Hyderabad approved by the Government of India might be narrow gauge.[73] Keay had at once pointed out to Bowen, Salar Jung's Private Secretary, that this did not necessarily mean any commitment from Mayo that the Minister would be allowed to construct and manage the new line. 'On the contrary I believe,' warned Keay, 'if H.E. trusted to any such idea, he would find he was bitterly mistaken and if he allowed the matter to fall into the cognizance of the Government of India at all in its initial stage, he would have the State Railway fight all over again and in the end would lose both the construction and the management of the new line, as he lost the old.' Keay's advice was to keep

the matter secret from the Government of India and to do everything through English friends who would manage to procure the
sanction of the Secretary of State himself to the scheme.[74] In accordance with this advice, Salar Jung quietly and unobtrusively had the
projected line surveyed and mapped out and plans drawn up for the
future extension of the Nizam's State Railway.[75]

Of greater immediate concern to Salar Jung at the time was
finding money for the Nizam's State Railway (which was opened in
October 1874). To his dismay he found that the final estimate for
the Nizam's State Railway was *Halli Sicca* (Hyderabad rupees)
1,30,92,775 or British Indian rupees 1,11,99,380. While the Nizam's
Government had already paid *Halli Sicca* rupees 1,11,50,000, it had
raised less than half of this large amount, *Halli Sicca* rupees 54,29,000
from the local financiers. The state treasury had paid the balance and
had still to pay *Halli Sicca* rupees 19,42,775.[76]

In search of money, Salar Jung hit upon a new plan. He gave up the
idea of borrowing from local financiers, who were anyway unwilling
to lend. Nor would he take a loan from the Government of India
which would thereby gain greater control over the state. He wished to
raise the money in the London market. Apprehending that the
Government of India would not sanction this method of raising
funds, he decided to take a roundabout way. It would be better to
raise the fund by issuing shares in the name of a company. In 1873, by
the Nizam's edict, a joint-stock company, the Nizam's State Railway
Company, was formed to provide capital for the construction of the
railway and to purchase or acquire all rights (not sovereignty) and
liabilities of the Nizam's Government under the agreement of 1870.
The capital of the Company was to be Rs 1 crore and could be
increased by a further crore. The Company was also empowered to
make and maintain all necessary and convenient accessory extensions, branches, etc., with the approval of the Nizam's
Government.[77]

In early 1874 Salar Jung informed the Directors of the State
Railway Company that, since very few of the Company's shares had
been subscribed, his Government had to advance money on the
Company's account for the construction of the railway. He wanted
the Directors to now make special efforts to sell the remaining shares
to the public and repay the Government advances.[78] This
letter was followed up by an agreement between the Nizam's State
Railway Company and the Nizam's Government in October 1874.

The Company was authorized to sell its shares outside the Nizam's territory to the extent of Rs 50 lakhs. The Nizam's Government agreed to pay a dividend on them at the rate of 6 per cent per annum. To render the scheme fool-proof against all doubts as regards the risk involved, it was decided that a fixed investment in Government of India securities would be made and held by trustees as security.[79]

The Railway Company arranged—in actual fact Salar Jung arranged it for the Company[80]—through the agency of the Hyderabad firm of Lakhmidas Lachmondas to have the shares floated in the London market. On behalf of this firm, Smith, Fleming and Company, the London financiers, approached the Secretary of State, for permission to offer the shares in London, although it would be *ultra vires* of the Act of 1797. It was clearly pointed out by the London firm that the issue of the shares was by the Nizam's State Railway Company and not by the Nizam's Government.[81]

The exact terms of the railway agreement of 1870 were not known to the India Office, except that it had been agreed that the Nizam would provide the required capital for the railway with the help of shareholders.[82] Salisbury telegraphed the Government of India inquiring whether the agreement mentioned that the shareholders were to be strictly local capitalists or whether it authorized raising funds in England as well. In its answer the Government of India stated somewhat vaguely that only local capitalists were contemplated, and that it had not sanctioned the raising of money in England under the guarantee of the Hyderabad Government.[83]

To the Secretary of State, however, the agreement of 1870 seemed to have sacrificed the policy of the Statute of 1797 by its silence on this point. In his view the pledge in Mayo's agreement to allow 'shareholders' could not be narrowed down by an afterthought into 'shareholders at Hyderabad'. He and his Council, therefore, felt 'compelled' to allow the raising of money by the Nizam's State Railway Company in England.[84] A jubilant John Fleming, head of the House of Smith, Fleming and Company telegraphed to Messrs Nicol and Company in Bombay that the Secretary of State had sanctioned the loan. On 4 June 1875 a telegram dispatched by Reuter from England announced that subscriptions were invited for a loan of half a million rupees for the Nizam's State Railway at 6 per cent interest guaranteed by the Hyderabad Government. The shares were immediately issued and subscribed.[85]

Northbrook was outraged. He came to know about Salisbury's

final decision only from Reuter's telegram. He felt himself slighted by the Home Government and by-passed by Salar Jung. The Home Government had done what the Indian Government had refused. 'The effect has been unfortunate' fumed the Viceroy, 'and damaging to the position of the Resident and the Government of India.' The communication from England would encourage Salar Jung in the belief that the Government of India might be set aside and that he could get what he wanted through his agents in England. Further, Northbrook pointed out—and this was his trump card— that Salar Jung was a born intriguer. The British Government's position on the Berar question would not be strengthened by yielding to him on the railway loan. 'I am quite sure', wrote Northbrook bitterly to Salisbury, 'you will not willingly do anything to strengthen Salar Jung's hands, for after all, you will have more trouble with him than we shall.'[86]

These words had the desired effect. 'I will do nothing willingly to make him more powerful', promised Salisbury. Almost half apologetically he explained that he had declined to fight Salar Jung because he believed that the British Government had 'no case' and would lose if the question came up before the House.[87] The Secretary of State also hastened to placate the Viceroy by stating unequivocally that this transaction would not be allowed to form a precedent.[88] A similar view was expressed publicly by Lord George Hamilton, Under-Secretary of State for India, in the House of Commons, that this single permission to the Nizam's State Railway Company did not indicate any intention on the part of the British Government to depart from the Statute of 1797.[89] None the less, Salar Jung must have relished his victory. He had, it has to be said, won it in a slightly devious manner. The Nizam's State Railway Company, for all practical purposes a defunct body, was undoubtedly created by him only for the purpose of raising funds in England. Short of legal technicalities, the transaction was basically a loan to the Nizam's Government.

Encouraged by the success of this experiment, Salar Jung made a serious miscalculation—he repeated it. He was anxious, as we have seen, to implement the extension of the Nizam's State Railway up to the Godavari and Chanda. In 1876–7 the construction of the extension appeared to be even more imperative because of a famine threatening the state. The new railroad, apart from opening up the coalfield and the rice-country, would considerably help the work of

famine relief.[90] Salar Jung authorized the State Railway Company
to increase its capital to the extent of Rs 1 crore (already permitted
by the Nizam's edict of 1873), and to renew negotiations with
foreign capitalists through Keay to raise the money in England.[91]

While the Minister was in Europe on his way to England, Smith,
Fleming and Company again approached Salisbury for permission
to raise money in England through a further issue of shares on
behalf of the Nizam's State Railway Company. It was argued that,
unlike the earlier occasion, when shares had been floated to repay
the advances of the Nizam's Government, this time the fund was
meant for an extension of the railroad to the coal-districts. John
Fleming amassed statistical data to prove to Salisbury the value of
the projected line to the G.I.P. Railway Company as well.[92] This
Company had to use only English coal and the cost was on an
average Rs 20 per ton in Bombay.[93] If Singareni coal was available
even at Rs 15, a large saving would be effected.

The claim was thoroughly justified. Coincidentally, Lord George
Hamilton stated in the Commons that the cost of fuel per mile upon
the G.I.P. Railway was six times than that on the East Indian Rail-
way, which was able to work the Indian coalfields.[94] The Railway
Report for 1875–6 also showed that while the East India Main Line
paid only 6s 10d per ton of coal, being near the Raniganj coalfield, the
G.I.P. Railway paid £1 18s 11d and the Madras Railway £2 18s 8d.[95]
The G.I.P. Railway Company and the Madras Railway Company
would naturally benefit by the extension of the Hyderabad-
Singareni-Godavari Line.

Nevertheless, Salisbury, grown wiser from past experience, refused to give any answer to Fleming's pleading without referring the
matter to the Government of India. His own view was that it was not
desirable that any more of the Nizam's stock should be offered in
the London market.[96] In the mean time, undaunted by Salisbury's
evasive reply, John Fleming was persevering in what was obviously
an 'uphill work'. The following year, he again begged Salisbury for
permission to float the Nizam's State Railway Company's share in
the London market.[97]

By this time Salisbury had revised his earlier opinion. His
reasons, however, were not altruistic or philanthropic, but
pragmatic and diplomatic. He did not see any serious evil in allowing the Minister to raise money in Britain. It would encourage him
to pledge, by way of interest, all his surplus revenue and prevent

him from spending money in either armaments or agitation. 'His spare cash may quite as profitably be used for the benefit of the British industrialists as for the purpose of setting up more factories in Hyderabad.' Besides, the loan would provide the Nizam with a host of inexorable creditors in Britain, who would back up the Government of India, if ever it should become necessary to bring his administration under more direct control. Nor would this transaction give Salar Jung any hold over the House of Commons. 'People will not wish to increase the Nizam's independence because the Nizam owes them money.' Finally, Salisbury judged that since Salar Jung's plea for the restoration of Berar had been rejected, this small request might well be granted. Salar Jung might stop his intrigues if allowed to have his own way once in a while. It would be good 'to stop his mouth' by concessions of this kind.[98]

Initially, Lytton concurred with his chief, and Sir John Strachey, a prominent member of his Council, shared the same view.[99] Strong opposition, however, came from Meade, the Resident at Hyderabad. He carefully called attention to the fact that the loan was thriftless in nature. Since one-third of the money subscribed was proposed to be deposited in London in the hands of trustees as a guarantee for the payment of 6 per cent interest, the nominal rate of 6 per cent interest would be increased. If Salar Jung ceased to be the Minister, Meade argued, the Nizam might resent paying so large an interest. The powerful body of British shareholders would then press home their case for protection against any breach of contract, and the Government of India would willy-nilly have to intervene in the affairs of Hyderabad. It was not wise, Meade stressed, to allow Indian chiefs, particularly a great chief like the Nizam, to raise money in England on any ground whatsoever. It would be far better if the Government of India encouraged other princes to lend the money or offered to advance the money itself on the security of the Berar surplus.[100]

Here Lytton differed with Meade. In a private letter to the Resident, he elaborated his reasons for recommending a concession to Salar Jung on this particular point. Salar Jung was doubtless the most dangerous man in India and British relations with him could never be really satisfactory. That would be no cause for concern if the British could suppress him altogether. Unfortunately, he could not be got rid of. It would be good policy, therefore, 'to humour the man' on matters of small consequence. The Government of India was prepared to advance a loan, but he would not accept it. Allowing the Indian chiefs to lend money to the Nizam was, however, a dangerous plan because it would give them a direct pecuniary interest in Hyderabad. 'Although Machiavellian as such a policy would appear if openly avowed,' the Viceroy further explained, 'I am inclined to think we should benefit more by weakening than by strengthening the Hyderabad state and thriftless loans by Salar Jung would effect the object for us.'[101]

Meade remained unmoved. While pretending to appreciate Lytton's concern to gratify Salar Jung on small issues, if possible, Meade added another reason for refusing the present request. The astute Minister was sure to use the subscribers in England to open the Berar question again. His agents might make it appear to them that the restoration of Berar was necessary to enable the Nizam's Government to meet its obligation in connection with the loan.[102] This argument converted both Lytton and Strachey to Meade's views. Lytton submitted the case to his Council, and the Viceroy-in-Council unanimously decided against any suspension of the statutory prohibition in favour of Hyderabad.[103]

Salisbury was frankly disappointed, and regretted the Calcutta Council's decision. In his view, the British people generally looked on with dislike at Indian states which borrowed money from them. That would have given the British Government 'much more elbow-room' in dealing with states like Hyderabad, towards which some strong measures would have to be taken sooner or later. 'If you publicly stand forward', Salisbury complained to Lytton, 'and say that you will not allow them to improve, that you will exclude them from the great panacea of prosperity in British eyes—a new Railway—and that to a fine coalfield, you will excite for them an amount of sympathy.' Nor did the Secretary of State see how the case for refusal was arguable before Parliament.[104]

Salisbury was no match for Lytton who, once he had made up his mind, liked to have his own way. Further, the Secretary of State's Council did not back him and its members went almost unanimously with Lytton, presumably because Meade's arguments weighed heavily with them as well. Salisbury yielded to his Council and to Lytton, and conceded half-heartedly that their arguments were 'probably valid'.[105] Armed with the support of the Home Government, the India Government informed Salar Jung that it would not sanction the application to raise the loan in England. It was, how-

ever, prepared to lend the money itself or to construct the line on
behalf of the Hyderabad state on a guarantee of interest by the
latter. Salar Jung politely thanked the Indian Government and
refused to accept either offer.[106] The depth of his frustration and
annoyance was powerfully expressed by John Bright[107] in an interesting speech in Parliament. While advocating the interest of
British capitalists, Bright nevertheless had genuine sympathy for
Salar Jung, and severely criticized the Government of India for its
resistance to the investment in India of any English money which
was not under its control. Observed Bright:

> I suppose Sir Salar Jung would say, if he said exactly what he thought, no,
> I have not the funds to make it [the railway] myself or for my Government
> and I do not wish you to make it and get more absolute possession of my
> country than you have now .... but I can go to London, and there find
> plenty of people who will trust the Government of Hyderabad, and I can
> raise a million sterling for the purpose of making this railway 200 miles
> long ... which will enable me to communicate from Hyderabad with the
> line that runs from Bombay to Calcutta, and at the same time to carry a
> branch railway through an extensive coalfield that promises to be of the
> greatest value.

The refusal of the Government of India to grant him this liberty,
Bright insisted, was a sample of the 'narrow, jealous and miserable
spirit' in which the Government acted.[108] It is significant that the
money for the railway extension did come eventually, as we shall see,
from Britain itself—but on far worse terms than Salar Jung had
visualized for his state.

V

The Nizam's State Railway was making no money. The entire expenditure on the line up to the end of 1877–8 was, according to
Salar Jung *Halli Sicca* Rs 1,90,00,075 and the entire receipts
amounted to *Halli Sicca* Rs 26,39,187. A net liability of *Halli
Sicca* Rs 1,63,40,888 had been incurred by the Nizam's Government. Of this large amount, *Halli Sicca* Rs 1,10,72,977 had been
obtained by the issue of shares (on which dividend had to be paid
irrespective of profit or loss) and *Halli Sicca* Rs 52,67,911 had been
paid from the state treasury.[109] Not unnaturally, Salar Jung was
desperate to find an escape from this situation. Meanwhile, Ripon
had come out as Viceroy and Bayley had taken over from Meade.
Since better relations were restored between Salar Jung and the

Government of India, the Minister again decided to raise a loan from the English market.

In 1881, Abdul Hak, Sirdar Diler Jung,[110] brought the Minister a proposal from a friend in Bombay and an agent of a syndicate of capitalists in England for the extension of the existing railroad. The syndicate proposed to form a company in London which would pay the Hyderabad Government Rs 2 crores to buy the Nizam's State Railway, and would find capital for the construction of a new broad gauge line from Hyderabad to Chanda in the north as well as to the Godavari in the south. The estimated cost would be Rs 2.40 crores, and the Nizam's Government would have to guarantee the payment of 4 per cent interest for five years.[111] *Prima facie* the proposal appeared to be extraordinarily favourable to Hyderabad. But there was a catch: in return for their services, the syndicate expected to receive a concession of mining rights, namely, an absolute monopoly for ninety-nine years of all mines, known and unknown, in Hyderabad.[112]

Initially, Salar Jung gave his unqualified support to the plan, so anxious was he to sell the State Railway and get rid of the financial liability. On further thought, however, he appears to have changed his mind. He needed a little time, he told the Resident, to go more deeply into the whole project, presumably because he realized that the mining concessions asked for were extravagant and that the real motive of the promoters was not the Railway but a monopoly of the precious mines.[113] He found support in Jones who was officiating as Resident while Bayley had gone on leave for six weeks. Jones questioned the *bona fides* of the promoters and the genuineness of their proposal. He disapproved of the extreme haste with which things were being done and the fact that the promoters of the company had not thought it necessary to consult the Government of India. It is significant that Jones, at first so strongly opposed to the scheme, quickly changed his mind. After a long interview with Abdul Hak, during which he was presumably won over, he telegraphed the Foreign Office withdrawing his objection to both the railway and the mining schemes.[114]

When Bayley came back to Hyderabad he opposed the mining scheme, which in his view mentioned far too vaguely the powers of the concessionaires. If they failed in their business, the Nizam's Government could do nothing and for ninety-nine years the mineral wealth of the state would be unused. Bayley, however, gave his whole-hearted approval to the railway proposal. It would relieve the Nizam's Government of a perpetual liability and, besides, provide the state at a nominal cost with a valuable line that would immensely improve the resources of the country. This line had a great strategic value for the Indian Government as well. There was every possibility, Bayley explained, of the Nagpur line being extended to the East Indian Railway near Calcutta. In that case it would be a matter of extreme importance to the Government of India to extend the Hyderabad line to join the Wardha line. This would considerably shorten the through communication between Calcutta, Chotanagpur and the Central Provinces on the one hand and the Deccan and Madras Presidency on the other. Bayley had come back to India from his furlough, perhaps with instructions to urge the Minister to take up the scheme (1) as a link in the most important line of through communication, (2) as a means of opening out the mineral wealth of Hyderabad, and (3) as likely to improve the prospects of the present unremunerative line to Wadi.

Bayley's point was accepted by the Foreign Department. The Foreign Secretary, Grant, clearly recognized that ∙the new Hyderabad railway would, upon the completion of the Nagpur-Calcutta line, become the main line of communication between Calcutta and Madras and an important means of moving troops from and to the large military cantonment at Secunderabad. Ever sensitive to British needs, the Foreign Secretary took care to suggest that suitable arrangements must be made for carrying British troops and mails on the new railroad.[115] Opposition came from Sir Evelyn Baring, the Finance Member of the Viceroy's Council. He had misgivings regarding the financial position of the promoters and the genuineness of their scheme. Why, he asked, should anyone pay Rs 2 crores for an undertaking which had originally cost only a crore and a half, and which was not a paying one at that? He would have nothing to do with the matter unless he had better evidence of the standing of the promoters and their ability to float the undertaking with a good chance of success.[116] Baring was not opposing the extention scheme, but only objected to the promoters who sought to implement it.

Ripon agreed with Baring. In his view there were two distinct issues involved. First, the general one of the attitude that the Government of India should adopt towards the construction of railways in Hyderabad by a private English Company. Second, and more important, was the nature of the offer now made and the character of the persons making it. Ripon had no hesitation on the first issue; supported by his Council he felt that employment of private capital and construction of new railways in Hyderabad should not be barred—at any rate, such prohibition would not be within the purview of the Act of 1797. However, Ripon had strong views on the second issue. He judged that the people involved in the transaction were untrustworthy and that it would not be right to allow the Government of Hyderabad 'to be pigeoned by a set of speculators'.[117] The proposal of the Bombay syndicate was, therefore, rejected by the Government of India, but it informed the Resident at Hyderabad that it would 'view with pleasure' the extension of the railway system in the Nizam's state. Nor would it have any objection to the employment, as agents, of a private company composed of persons whose financial position ensured that they would be able to fulfil their engagement.[118]

Abdul Hak was then deputed to England to arrange matters there for the formation of a suitable company to undertake the two schemes. He was given strict instructions to put himself in communication with the Secretary of State and not conclude any final agreement without consulting the Minister. Salar Jung no longer wanted to sanction such a general monopoly as the Bombay Syndicate had asked for, but was prepared to make a concession with regard to the mines already known. The mining scheme had to be kept separate from the railway scheme in accordance with the suggestion of the India Government. Abdul Hak first negotiated with the Rothschilds, who were the Nizam's agents in London, and on their refusal to entertain the project, he approached Messrs Morton, Rose and Company to underwrite the new Hyderabad railway.[119] On 16 June 1882 they submitted a proposal covering both the construction of the new line and the take-over of the existing one. The total investment required was to carry an interest guaranteed by the Nizam at 5 per cent per annum for twenty-five years. Salar Jung straightaway rejected the terms on the ground that they were not favourable to Hyderabad.[120] The Company then put forward another proposal. This may be summarized as follows: a joint stock company was to be formed with a share capital of £3,000,000 and debenture powers to the extent of £1,500,000. It would construct a broad gauge railway from Hyderabad to Warangal and from there to a place near Chanda in the north and to the banks of the Godavari or the Krishna in the south-east. It would purchase and work the existing line and pay the purchase money thus—(i) £500,000 in fully paid-up shares of the new company, (ii) £1,091,666 in cash, and (iii) £75,000 to be deposited in the Bank of England to form a security for interest. The Nizam's Government would pay 5 per cent interest for twenty years on all money paid towards the capital, as well as the purchase money for the existing line. The Nizam's Government would also grant land for railway construction and allow all materials for the railway to enter Hyderabad duty-free. The line would become the property of the Nizam's Government after ninety-nine years.[121]

Connected with this scheme—although kept apart from it—was another proposal mooted by Messrs Watson and Stewart of London[122] for concessions of mining rights throughout the state of Hyderabad. They deposited £100,000 as caution money in the National and Provincial Bank of England and undertook to form a company with a share capital of £1,000,000 with powers to increase it, to work all the mines in the Nizam's territory already registered or that might be registered within five years, provided they were granted the concession before 30 April 1883 and the proposed company for the extension of railways was floated by that date. The company, when incorporated, was to undertake to spend immediately £100,000 in the development of the mines. On the completion of the proposed railway, the company would guarantee a minimum mineral traffic equivalent to 1 per cent on the capital of the railway company. The terms of the concession were as follows: (i) all known mines were included, (ii) the concession was to run for ninety-nine years, (iii) during this period the concessionaires were to be put in possession of all land required by them for working the mines on payment of the usual land assessment, (iv) a royalty of 5 per cent on net profits was to be paid to the Nizam's Government on gold and silver, and six *Halli Sicca* annas on each ton of coal sold, and one *Halli Sicca* rupee on each ton of iron sold, (v) all accounts were to be subjected to inspection by the Nizam's Government, and (vi) if the concessionaires failed to fulfil their obligations, the concession would become null and void.[123] Salar Jung approved of the mining proposal.[124]

The railway proposal mooted by Morton and Rose was, on the other hand, clearly worse than that of the Bombay syndicate. In addition to a guaranteed interest for twenty years, it also required the payment of interest on the amount of the capital as well as on the purchase money of the existing line. Besides, the actual cash that the Nizam's Government would receive was only £1,091,666, with which it would have to buy off all existing shareholders before handing over the old line to the new company.

Bayley, who had by now left Hyderabad, could not bring himself to support the scheme, the terms of which had been telegraphed to him by Owen Burne from London. He was not prepared to accept Burne's view that the proposal was free from risk for the Nizam's Government. On the contrary, it bound the Nizam for twenty years to pay an interest which was beyond the resources of his state. 'Interested as I am in the project,' Bayley wrote privately to Ripon, '...I should hesitate as a private adviser to urge Sir Salar Jung to accept the terms.' Nevertheless, as a member of the Government of India, he thought that it should abstain altogether from giving Salar Jung any advice on the financial aspects which concerned the Nizam's Government alone. It was for Salar Jung to say what price he could afford to pay for the benefits which the line was likely to give him. 'And though we are interested in seeing', continued Bayley, 'that he thoroughly understands what its price amounts to and what these benefits are likely to be, this is quite as far as we can go and we should hesitate to put any pressure upon him in either direction of acceptance or refusing the term, unless indeed the former should obviously involve bankruptcy.'[125]

Salar Jung must have seen the possibility of financial bankruptcy which the proposal would bring upon his state; nevertheless, he accepted it.[126] He was reportedly under relentless pressure from Abdul Hak and Major Trevor, the First Assistant Resident, who was in practice virtually the Resident. Salar Jung's fighting spirit, too, appears to have left him by now and he quietly surrendered this time and 'affected' to approve the scheme.[127] It would be unfair to put the entire blame on Trevor or Abdul Hak, responsible as they were for forcing the scheme on the Minister, for the real pressure came from London with the Secretary of State himself playing the tune.

Hartington seems to have taken an unusual interest in the Hyderabad Railway extension scheme. He was annoyed when he heard that Salar Jung had refused to agree to the first proposal of Morton, Rose and Company and had directed Abdul Hak to return home. Abdul Hak had made 'a very favourable impression' on all who had seen him and 'watched his proceedings here', Hartington wrote to Ripon, and he expressed his unhappiness that Hak's

labours had ended in failure. Hartington added with acerbity,
'There is an impression here that the whole thing has been too
honest, and that if certain parties at Hyderabad had been conciliated in the way which has been customary in negotiating between
European capitalists and Asiatic Ministers, the thing would have
gone through.' In an unprecendented move, the Secretary of State
decided to see Abdul Hak before his departure from London so that
he could ascertain Salar Jung's reasons for refusing the terms. He
would also like to find out whether the objection was final or whether
it would be worthwhile sending the papers to India for Baring's
information, in case he paid a visit to Hyderabad in the winter.[128]

Ripon found it difficult to agree with Hartington. The first proposal of Morton, Rose and Company did not appear to him to be as
advantageous to the Nizam as Hartington seemed to think it was. 'We
are not surprised', Ripon wrote firmly to Hartington, 'at Salar
Jung's rejection of it. There was, I think, plenty of ground for that
rejection without resorting to the supposition alluded to by you,
that the failure to conciliate certain parties at Hyderabad prevented
the acceptance of the Morton, Rose and Company's proposal.'[129]
Hartington's next letter to Ripon, written obviously after his interview with Abdul Hak and before receiving the reply from Ripon
quoted above, laid the blame squarely on Salar Jung. The Secretary
of State subtly suggested that the Government of India and the
Resident might do well to persuade the Minister to accept the
second proposal of Morton, Rose and Company. Abdul Hak had
told Hartington about Salar Jung's reservations to take any important step without the distinct approval and encouragement of
the Government of India. The Minister must have considered the
refusal of the Resident to give him any advice in favour of the
scheme as tantamount to disapproval of it. 'I do not suppose',
Hartington wrote to Ripon, 'that you will think it advisable to take
any action in regard to it; or even if you should agree with the
opinion held here, that the terms are very favourable, that you will
now think it expedient that Baring should pay the visit to
Hyderabad ... I quite understand that you do not wish to take the
responsibility of advising the Government of the Nizam to enter
into new financial arrangements, but at the same time if you think
that without incurring undue responsibility, Baring could still go,
and explain to him what the scheme really is, I do not think that we

should have any objection here.'[130] Shorn of the verbosity and
euphemism of diplomatic language, it was clear enough an order to
the Viceroy that Salar Jung should be made to accept the scheme,
and that Baring should visit Hyderabad (which he did). Not surprisingly, when Morton, Rose and Company eventually forwarded their
second proposal, Salar Jung accepted it.

One can only speculate about Hartington's motive and the rather
unusual interest he took in this matter. It is hard to believe that he
was totally charmed and deceived by Abdul Hak, a desperate
intriguer who, as later investigations proved, was involved in shady
pecuniary transactions with the promoters of the railway and mining schemes. On the contrary, the Secretary of State's sympathetic
references to 'all' who met Abdul Hak and the 'impression here'
seem to suggest that he was influenced by a section of people in
England. It is well known that British houses of trade and finance
had long influenced Indian administration both through Parliament
and by direct correspondence with the India Office. Considering
that a substantial amount of British capital was still seeking investment abroad—mainly in South America, in the Dominions, in the
United States and the Far East—after the depression of the mid-
1870s was over,[131] it appears that Hartington was acting under
pressure from a group whom Leland Jenks describes as 'the people
of the stocks-and-bonds' and 'the people who earned them divi-
dends'.[132] In the 1880s British enterprise and capital were again
drawn to Indian railway investment (conditional, of course, on the
guaranteed interest), and it is known that 'financially, the railways
represent the greatest single injection of British capital into India's
economic life'.[133]

If it is unfortunate that Hartington was won over by English
capitalists and middlemen, it is no less a sad comment on Ripon that
he, despite his misgivings, allowed the proposal to pass. He judged
that the Government of India should confine itself to explaining
facts and supplying information, but should not give advice.[134]
Clearly, Ripon had changed his stand since the days of his rejection
of the Bombay Syndicate's proposal. It is also possible that he was far
too busy with his own schemes for local self-government and the
spread of education in British India to spare much time for
Hyderabad.[135]

VI

Salar Jung died suddenly before the conclusion of the railway settlement. On his death, the papers moved with incredible speed. Jones, now the Resident at Hyderabad, unable to give his approval to the railway and mining schemes, pleaded that he had no time to read through the papers. Charles Grant, too, passed them on with a 'somewhat hasty' note. No one seemed to be able to go into the details of the projects, and yet the Government of India approved them.[136]

The railway scheme, of course, was of primary concern. A telegraph message was sent to the Resident that the Government of India hoped the Council of Regency in Hyderabad would accept the scheme which Salar Jung himself had thought to be beneficial to his state.[137] Notwithstanding its initial unwillingness,[138] the Council of Regency was eventually persuaded to accept the railway proposal mooted by Morton, Rose and Company.[139] The Government of India hurried to give its sanction, but disclaimed any responsibility for general results. In its view, the matter was primarily a concern of the Hyderabad Government and the decision was its own.[140]

If the members of the Council of Regency were easily won over, the people of Hyderabad proved to be difficult. For the first time in the history of Hyderabad, they started an organized popular agitation against the railway scheme. A contemporary newspaper, *The Times of India*, reported on 13 May 1883 that the scheme was 'exercising the minds of all classes very sorely', and the consensus of opinion was very much against it. 'It is a common thing to hear people of the city saying that if the late Minister's uncle lost silver to this Government by the assignment of Berar, he [Salar Jung] may be said to have lost gold.' It was alleged by the Hyderabadis that the aim of the scheme was to impoverish the state and pave the way for a future cession of territory. Meetings of a semi-public nature were held and largely attended. A committee to consider the railway scheme was formed. It was reportedly composed of many noblemen, most of the leading bankers and merchants, and a large number of government officials. About fourteen thousand people 'representing all classes of interests' joined the committee. Public feeling ran so high that the leaders of the agitation, Dastur Hashang, one of the secretaries of the committee, and Dr Aghorenath Chatterjee, Principal of Hyderabad College, had to be arrested and deported to British India.[141]

It is significant that the intensity of the agitation attracted the attention of the British Parliament. In answer to a question in the House, J.K. Cross, Under Secretary for India, admitted that there had been 'considerable feeling' shown in Hyderabad against the railway scheme. A week later, O'Donnell, a member of the House, again asked whether the local people had protested against the proposed extension of the railway on the ground that the guaranteed interest for it would unduly tax the resources of Hyderabad, and whether persons interested in the success of the London Company had induced the Resident to forcibly remove the leaders of the agitation from the state. Answering O'Donnell's question as to why British officials at Hyderabad had intervened on behalf of a Company of English railway promoters, J.K. Cross somewhat lamely said that negotiations with the Company were still pending, and that the proposal had been sanctioned by Salar Jung himself before his death.[142]

Meanwhile, Morton, Rose and Company withdrew from the scheme. They decided, according to Abdul Hak, that it would not be possible to induce the public to subscribe to the capital necessary for the extension of the Hyderabad railway on the terms offered by him. It is also possible that they withdrew because the time limit set by them, viz., 1 April 1883, had expired before the final approval of the Hyderabad Government and the Indian Government reached them.[143] Abdul Hak then negotiated with other people in England and ultimately persuaded W.C. Watson who was, significantly, a promoter of the mining scheme as well, to float the railway company, known as the Nizam's Guaranteed State Railway Company. Watson's proposal was powerfully supported by Jones's successor, Cordery, who was doubtless in league with Abdul Hak. Cordery reported to Ripon that the scheme was 'sound' and could be 'financially floated', and that all the changes which Abdul Hak had further introduced in the scheme were 'pecuniarily beneficial to the Nizam's Government'.[144] Under relentless pressure from Cordery, the Council of Regency accepted the new scheme,[145] and the agreement was concluded between the Nizam's Government and the Nizam's Guaranteed State Railway Company Limited on 27 December 1883. Calcutta and London gave their sanction to the deal.[146]

The Company was to take over the Nizam's State Railway and build a new line to the south-eastern frontier of Hyderabad near

Bezwada and to the northern frontier of the state near Chanda. The
Nizam's Government was to deliver over to the Company through
the Government of India the existing railway 'freed and discharged
of and from all claims' on its part under its agreement of 1874 with
the Nizam's State Railway Company. The capital of the new Company was to be issued as follows: £2,000,000 in shares and
£2,000,000 in redeemable mortgage debentures, and any sum of
additional capital, not exceeding £500,000, as the Company would
require. It would pay £1,666,666 as the purchase money in the
following manner: (i) issue to the Nizam's Government fully paid
up shares of the Company to the amount of £500,000; (ii) deposit
£625,000 in the National Provisional Bank of England on the
Nizam's account for acquiring the interest of the English shareholders of the existing line; (iii) deposit £200,000 in cash with the
same bank as a Guarantee Fund in security for the payment of
interest by the Nizam's Government; (iv) pay £341,666 in cash to the
Nizam's Government. The Nizam's Government was to pay for
twenty years to the Company in London in sterling 'an annuity
equal to 5 per cent per annum' on all sums not exceeding £4,500,000
issued in shares and debentures by the Company.[147]

   Clearly, the terms were even less favourable to Hyderabad than
the Morton and Rose proposal. The new Company paid only
£341,666 in cash for the old line and left the Nizam to buy off the
shareholders in India. Out of this deal the Nizam got nothing apart
from a stupendous financial liability to pay 5 per cent on four and a
half million pounds for twenty years. This was equal to no less than
31 to 32 lakhs of Hyderabad rupees, a sum vastly in excess of any
surplus realized by the Hyderabad Government.[148] The swindling
of the state by a few adventurous and determined men with the
connivance of the British Government seems an outrageous business. Small wonder, the scheme continued to excite 'the most lively
opposition' from the people. All sorts of pressure were brought
upon the young Nizam after his installation in 1884, reported the
then Resident, 'to get the concession quashed by fair means or
foul'.[149] That was not to be. The first section of the new line was
completed by 1886.[150] The same year witnessed the final mining
agreement between the Nizam's Government and the Hyderabad
Deccan Mining Company, floated by Messrs Watson and Stewart.[151]

   It is evident that railway development in Hyderabad constitutes
one of those episodes in which political manipulation, selfishness

and profiteering are inextricably intermingled. The first railway in Hyderabad was built to meet the political and military needs of the Government of India. The principle followed was simple enough. Let Hyderabad make the railway and let the Government of India reap its benefits. Nor can it be denied that it was in the immediate interest of the Indian Government that the Hyderabad railway was extended and linked with the British Indian railway system to the north as well as the south. The political interest of the Government of India in this respect seems to have 'coincided happily with the pecuniary interests' of a section of the Queen's British subjects.[152]

The impact of the railway on Hyderabad is best judged in the context of the Indian railway system in general. The railways are universally acknowledged to be the harbinger of modern civilization, and there is no question that nothing that was done in India by the British more powerfully affected the country's economic, social and cultural life than the railways. 'It is the one service', Elgin wrote to Wood, 'rendered by the English to India which natives of all classes appreciate'.[153] There was much truth in this assessment. The railways broke down barriers of caste and class, stimulated population movements, increased the volume of trade and opened up the interior of the country. And yet, while in other leading railway powers, like the U.S.A., Germany and Japan, the railway was 'the veritable dynamo of the Industrial Revolution', in India it had no such effects. The truth is that the railways will not have the same impact on a country that is free and on one that is colonized. Writing about the Indian railways in general, Daniel Thorner observes: 'The economic changes which the railways made possible in India were retarded by the way in which the railways were built and the way they were run.'[154] What is true of the Indian railways in general appears to have been even truer of the Hyderabad railway in particular. Those who made it and managed it did not have to pay for it, and there was no incentive to economize. The Nizam's Government had to pay far too high a price for the advantages which the railway conferred on the state. A different type of railway, one built and managed by its own Government, oriented towards the satisfaction of the state's needs, and run along a route conducive to its progress and prosperity, on a gauge that the treasury could afford to pay for, would doubtless have brought Hyderabad much further along the path of modernization, enlightenment and advancement.

Conclusion

If there was any one motif running through the twenty-five years of Hyderabad's history from 1858 onwards, it was the consolidation of British paramountcy over the state. The process was begun during Wellesley's day, but in the course of the fifty years that followed, British power vis-á-vis Hyderabad passed from the stage of ascendancy to that of paramountcy. After the take over of direct Indian administration by the Crown, the concept of paramountcy assumed wider dimensions and was given a new orientation. The post-1858 British policy towards the princely states was pioneered by Canning and powerfully supported by Wood in the India Office. It was decided that these states would be maintained as separate entities. If treated kindly and diplomatically, they would be useful tools in upholding the British Indian Empire in times of crisis. 'What a gain it would be, in case of disturbances...to have the states...entirely with us', Canning wrote to Wood.[1] The Indian princes and chiefs were to be infused with loyalty to the Crown and were to enjoy a clearly defined position, intermediate between the suzerain and the local nobility in the British Indian provinces. Canning and Wood, between themselves, transformed the character and position of the princes, at the time semi-independent allies of the Company, into those of feudatories of the Crown.

When Elgin came out to India in 1862, he felt that the Indian field 'no longer contained any laurels to be reaped' by Canning's successor, and consequently devoted himself to the 'humble' discharge of the task to which he succeeded.[2] Nor could the mediocre Lawrence, an agent of the masterful Wood, break new ground. It was left to the energetic, imaginative and personally charming Mayo to develop further the Canning doctrine by cultivating political friendship with the princes. He managed to impress upon them the fact that they had a far from passive role to play in the Empire and that they had to be trained for their new position of responsibility and the important duties which they would later be called upon to discharge. Northbrook continued his predecessor's policy, though less ably, while his successor, Lytton, added an element of drama and pageantry to the hard reality of imperialism. The idea was to impress the Indian populace and princes with the magnitude of British power. The Indian princes were now to become the tributary vassals of an empress and (to borrow the words of Michael Edwardes) 'to bask in the warm glow of the Victorian sun and acquire new dignity in its reflected glory'[3]. It was with Ripon that British policy wore a more liberal look, a look of 'sunburnt Gladstonianism', though he, too, no less than his preceding Viceroys, was firm in asserting British paramountcy over the Indian states.

It must be remembered, however, that the gradual evolution of paramountcy was not the handiwork of the individual Viceroys only. This was the general policy of the British Government, Conservative or Liberal, the guidelines of which were indicated by a Wood or a Salisbury from the India Office. None the less, each Viceroy, the man on the spot, could and did give specific orientations to the general policy according to his own temperament and ability. Canning or Lytton certainly contributed more towards shaping the contours of Indian policy than did Elgin or Lawrence. Wood and Salisbury, on the other hand, wielded a much more effective voice in the Indian administration than Northcote or Argyll. By the end of the nineteenth century the pattern of British relationships with the Indian states had emerged clearly. The latter became integral parts of the British imperial fabric and subservient to its major policy decisions that governed the rest of British India.

Hyderabad, the principal state, did not prove any exception to this general rule. Afzal-ud-Daula, the ruling Nizam in 1858 became, in the new setting, virtually a feudatory of the Crown. Despite his reluctance, he was now a Grand Commander of the Star of India, wearing the Queen's effigy as a symbol of his loyalty to her, and he had to accept the Adoption Sanad (signed by Canning and sent to him during Elgin's viceroyalty) as a mark of favour from the suzerain. In actual fact, the Nizam was not allowed to govern his state. Adorned in his princely attire, he held gorgeous durbars, while his as-yet Anglophile Minister Salar Jung ran the administration. The age-old British policy of controlling the state indirectly through a Minister acting in close cooperation with the Resident was superbly executed during the first decade after the Great Revolt.

The warm friendship between Salar Jung and the British, as we have seen, was short-lived. On Afzal-ud-Daula's death the Minister, who governed the country as Co-Regent, developed ambitions for his state as well as his master. To reinstate the Nizam to the status he had enjoyed at the beginning of the century and to restore Berar to Hyderabad became the consuming passions of his life. The assignment of Berar had been an injustice done to his state, and he was determined to see the wrong redressed.

Here lay the root of the conflict. Salar Jung's ambitions were the perfect antithesis of British aims and policies. During Mayo's time the first seeds of discord germinated, although not visibly. An avid propagator of British paramountcy, Mayo accepted the permanence of British rule in India as an article of faith. 'I am here only for a time', he declared in a famous speech at the Ajmer Durbar. 'The able and earnest officers who surround me will, at no distant period, return to English homes, but the Power which we represent will endure for ages.'4 The infancy of the Nizam afforded Mayo an opportunity too good to be missed. He immediately decided to control the Nizam's education, presumably with a view to Europeanizing him, and he imposed on Hyderabad, much to the resentment of its Minister, an expensive and unremunerative railway built for the military needs of the British.

If Salar Jung had hoped that Mayo's Liberal successor Northbrook would treat Hyderabad more sympathetically, he was soon to be disillusioned. A nominal Liberal, Northbrook was no less an imperialist than the Conservative Mayo; but he lacked the latter's charm and genial manners. He judged that trouble in India might come one day from its greatest Muslim state; its Minister was a born intriguer and should, if possible, be removed. The question of Berar, he insisted, could be discussed only when the Nizam would come of age, and that, too, on condition of a revision of all the Nizam-British treaties, a revision that could only result in the extension of British power over the state. Northbrook, behind a calm and cold exterior, was the shrewdest and most implacable opponent of Salar Jung's ambitions. It was he who engineered the policy that culminated during Lytton's viceroyalty.

In Lytton's view, and in that of his chief, Salisbury, who almost unfailingly endorsed the Lytton standpoint, Salar Jung's ambition and power were a constant source of embarrassment and danger to the British; more so because of the looming threat of a general Muslim uprising inspired by Sher Ali of Kabul and the Sultan of Turkey. In this setting Salar Jung's statements in England representing Hyderabad as a semi-independent ally of the Crown and his insistence on the

Nizam's claim to Berar appeared to Lytton to be impudent and dangerous. The Viceroy seems to have taken an exaggerated view of the
situation and in Delhi he blew up what would have been an insignific-
ant affair into a matter of serious importance. Not content with snub-
bing the Minister, he imposed on him, as we have seen, a colleague
whom the Minister detested. The result was a disaster for the state, and
equally harmful to the British. It widened the gulf between them and
the Minister and implanted in the minds of the people of Hyderabad a
deep distrust of the British.

Ripon, to his credit, chose a different policy and was the one Viceroy
who meant to give Hyderabad a fair deal. Doubtless he believed, no
less than Northbrook (a close friend) or Lytton (a much disliked
predecessor), in British paramountcy. But he realized that it was
better to work towards British aims with a more or less pacified Salar
Jung than to alienate and antagonize a worthy Minister. This stance
proved successful. The Minister returned to his old policy of subordinate co-operation with the British, and mutual confidence and friendship between the two Governments were restored. Unfortunately,
Salar Jung died suddenly and with his death the slender possibility of
any opposition to the tightening British grip over the state was lost.
'The question of British suzerainty in India', remarked a British official, 'was buried (we hope for ever) in Salar Jung's grave.'[5]

One must not ignore the fact that during Salar Jung's days (despite
his determined challenge in the later years) British paramountcy was
repeatedly asserted over Hyderabad. In the political arena it meant the
complete subjection of the Nizam and his Minister to the British, and
continual British interference in its administration, professedly in the
name of good government. No less significant was the impact in the
economic field. The paramount power, itself under pressure from the
manufacturing and trading interests in Britain, particularly those of
Lancashire, was motivated to further their advancement. It stood for
laissez faire in Hyderabad, a convenient slogan for the expansion of
British capitalism in the overseas market. Free trade, it has been said,
was England's best policy, because 'England, having a great advantage
in her production of manufactures, gained by exchanging them with
others countries.'[6] This was by no means an inflexible principle, and
the British departed from it whenever they needed to. 'Pragmatic
considerations counter-balanced and neutralized the *laissez faire*
bias.'[7] The British upheld, and receded from, *laissez faire* as and when
it suited them. Salt and opium, for example, were treated as excep-

tions, not out of any altruistic considerations, but the former in the interest of imperial revenue and of Chesire salt, and the latter to meet the demands of the China trade. Consequently, salt of any variety (Hyderabad manufactured earth-salt of a kind) was not allowed to be exported from Hyderabad, while the export of grain was permitted. Whereas opium was not to be grown in the state (the formal convention was concluded after Salar Jung's death),[8] the cultivation of cotton was encouraged. With the abolition of transit duties and the reduction of customs duties on all imports and exports, British manufactured products poured into Hyderabad. The advantages of selective free trade were supplemented by building the railways and constructing feeder roads. British interests reigned supreme.

This is not to suggest that the British impact on Hyderabad was totally destructive or that it lacked any redeeming feature. The paramount power, it should be said, fostered good government in the protected state, primarily in its own interest, but for a principle as well. Carrying 'civilization' to India was at once an imperial necessity as well as a mission of pride to the British of the nineteenth century. Good administration became a matter of the first importance after the change over to the Crown's rule. The Queen herself emphasized through her Proclamation the value of good government and Canning, her first Viceroy, proclaimed in no uncertain terms the absolute authority of the British Government to right abuses or maladministration in an Indian state. To all the succeeding Viceroys, Mayo and Ripon in particular, good government was the *sine qua non* for British rule in India. 'If we respect your rights and privileges, you should also respect the rights and privileges of those who are placed under your care'— these words of Mayo at Ajmer highlight the attitude of the British rulers to the Indian princes and chiefs. Hyderabad, commanding a strategic and central position in the Indian sub-continent, deserved special attention. An efficient administration there was essential, as Ripon neatly put it, 'not only in the interest of the inhabitants, but because the preservation of order and tranquillity in so large a native state has a very direct connection with the general peace of India.'[9]

Here Salar Jung unfailingly co-operated with the British, regardless of his opposition to their political hegemony. At a very young age he became the Minister of what was described as the 'most misgoverned state of India'. The treasury was bankrupt, the army unpaid, the police inefficient, the judiciary corrupt, and the land farmed out to creditors. It became the mission of the young Minister to restore order in the state and 'to extricate the Government from its embarrassment'. The details of the nature of his reforms have been ably described by Cherag Ali in four volumes of *Hyderabad Under Salar Jung*. There is no need to repeat them here, but it is interesting that, in all he did, British influence preponderated. Having been educated from his earliest years under European supervision and imbued with a liberal education, he honestly believed in the superiority of the British mode of administration. 'No rule can be established', he pleaded with the Nizam, 'which will not bear some resemblance to those of the British Government', because Britain unquestionably possessed superior ability and was 'at unity with all other nations.'[10] Salar Jung adopted the fundamentals of British principles of administration; he came into contact with them in the Restored Districts and extended them to other parts of his state. In this task he was encouraged, given support and advice, and sometimes even prodded, by successive British Residents.

So long as Afzal-ud-Daula was on the *musnud*, Salar Jung had to depend entirely on the Resident's co-operation for carrying out his reforms. Yule gave him effective support and came to his rescue whenever the Nizam wanted to get rid of him. It was, however, with the coming of Temple that Salar Jung took up with vigour and determination his schemes of reform. Outwardly, Temple kept quiet and aloof; he preferred to advise the Minister privately. 'I shall be happy...to give you counsel quietly', he wrote to the Minister, 'without appearing to interfere. I am willing to take any amount of personal trouble in order to help you to make your administration good for the interests of the Nizam and his dominions.' The advice was for the Minister's own ears, 'none need to know about it'.[11] It was only after consulting Temple, and obtaining his approval, that Salar Jung introduced the *zillabandi* system in 1867. The country was divided into five *simts* and seventeen zillas, each zilla being divided into taluks. Over each *simt* was placed a *Sadr Talukdar* with revenue and judicial powers corresponding very nearly to those of the Divisional Commissioner and Sessions Judge in British territories. Over each zilla was appointed a *talukdar*, who was magistrate, collector and civil judge, in power and position corresponding as nearly as possible to the district officers of the non-regulation provinces of British territory.[12]

Temple was particularly concerned with the unhealthy municipal conditions in the state. He knew of the prejudices and difficulties which stood in the way of any thorough renovation of the capital city, but there were many improvements that might be effected without offending anyone. 'Nobody', Temple pointed out, 'would object to carts being sent round to carry away rubbish and refuse from the streets, nor to holes full of nasty water being filled up, nor the drains being kept a little cleaner than at present, nor in fact to any improvement which are good to all without troubling or hurting any individual.'[13] Salar Jung thanked Temple for his suggestions and took up the scheme enthusiastically. Progress was gradually made, streets were widened and lit, drains laid out and the accumulated rubbish cleared. A system of municipal administration on the lines of that in British India was introduced in 1869, a year after Temple's departure from Hyderabad.

On Afzal-ud-Daula's death, with a young Nizam on the *musnud* and the administration in his hands, Salar Jung was free to go ahead with his schemes of reform. He made various changes in the administrative infrastructure after consulting Resident Saunders on every minor detail.[14] Western concepts of centralized administration dominated these changes. The influence of English ideas was revealed in his land revenue reforms as well. The pernicious system of revenue farming was abolished; graded revenue authorities collected revenue throughout the dewani districts and the principles of survey and assessment adopted were, except for a few trivial changes to suit local circumstances, identical with those prevalent in Bombay Presidency. As a result of these reforms land revenue went up from *H.S.* Rs 58,95,544 in 1853–4 to *H.S.* Rs 1,94,76,801 in 1878–9—an increase of more than 230 per cent in twenty-five years. Trade patterns revealed a similar trend. The reduction of customs duties, made at the insistence of the British Resident, operated chiefly in favour of the British manufacturing interests. None the less, it contributed to the growth of Hyderabad's own commerce. Trade statistics indicate an upward swing; income from customs duties rose from *H.S.* Rs 42,362 in 1853–4 to *H.S.* Rs 30,05,638 in 1878–9.[15] The extension of cotton cultivation—under the encouragement of the Resident as well as the Minister—acted as an incentive to the foundation of textile mills. The Hyderabad Deccan Spinning and Weaving Company was established in 1877, the Gulburga Mahbub Shahi Mill in 1886 and the Aurangabad Spinning and Manufacturing Company in 1889. All this was facilitated by the building of railways and the construction of roads which allowed easier movement of goods and labour.

The British connection, the influence of Christian missionaries as well as Salar Jung's personal interest in the spread of education, stimulated the desire for learning among all classes in Hyderabad. Both the western and oriental systems of education were encouraged. In 1856 the Dar-ul-Ulm or Oriental College affiliated to the Punjab University was established. Here English was taught along with the oriental languages. In 1873 the Madrassa-i-Aliya was founded to give western education to the sons of the nobles. While two schools, one Persian and the other vernacular, were established in each taluk, the City Anglo-Vernacular School, which later became known as Hyderabad College and was affiliated to Madras University, was founded in the capital. The promotion of some knowledge of western sciences among the people was greatly encouraged. A medical school for transmitting western medical knowledge to the local people had been established as early as 1846, on the initiative of the Residency Surgeon, Dr Maclean. In 1869 a civil engineering college was founded on Temple's suggestion. 'Could you not set up a small school of engineering', he had asked the Minister, 'like your medical school?'[16] The courses of study here were the same as those prescribed for the Roorkee School in British India. These schools and colleges, where the study of English naturally involved acquaintance with English ideas and thought, acted as westernizing influences in the state.

Since experienced local men were not available to carry out all these reforms, Salar Jung rose above parochial considerations and invited enlightened and efficient men from British India. These men, the most notable among whom was Syed Hossain Bilgrami,[17] contributed greatly to the growth of an enlightened outlook in the state. They were placed in high posts and enjoyed Salar Jung's confidence. This was, of course, resented by the local people, but Salar Jung never intended this to be a permanent arrangement. He planned to give educated young Hyderabadis administrative training in British provinces and to send a few promising youths to suitable colleges in British India.[18] This clearly indicates the source from which Salar Jung derived his inspiration for reforms and the model on which they were based.

Consequent to these innovations, western ideas and values poured into Hyderabad. As in British India, they transformed the world of thought and made a powerful impact on Hyderabad society. Old customs were often identified with conservatism and old modes of living became obsolete. In certain areas western ideas were synthesized with traditional ones, whereas in other fields they were superimposed on existing customs and laws. The interaction of these forces inevitably culminated in the emergence of a hybrid culture. At the same time, cosmopolitanism emerged, a new enthusiasm was released and a new consciousness born. *The Times of India* correspondent on 21 May 1883 wrote:

> The Hyderabadi proper, as I have seen him for years past takes but little interest in the affairs of the state—he piously abstains from interfering, directing or questioning the acts of the Sircar...but what a change had come over these very Hyderabadis within the past three or four years... Associated as they have been with native foreigners, atheists and several other ists, they have blossomed into a very extraordinary character, wearing as they do half European and half native clothes. Be they Hindu or Mahomaden, with few exceptions, they all wear English boots and shoes, while the highly fashionable Persian cloth cap is indispensable, sometimes the Turkish fez. Almost every second native you meet on the streets of the city and Chudderghat is dressed in this peculiarly mixed costume. Can it be at all a matter of surprise, therefore, when they readily lay aside their ancient and graceful costume, to imitate these strangers, that they should get talked over and become apt pupils of theirs and adopt their notions in politics, etc.?[19]

The people of Hyderabad—the elite took the lead—began to exhibit an active interest in public affairs, which had hitherto been regarded with indifference. The magnitude of this change was revealed in the public agitation against the Chanda Railway Scheme. The movement was led by Dr Aghorenath Chatterjee, Mulla Abdul Qayum and Dastur Hassang. They mobilized a force of 50,000 people representing all sections of society and publicized a unique demand for placing all the relevant papers regarding the proposed railway before the general public. This was the first instance of organized constitutional opposition in Hyderabad. A movement of this nature would not have been conceived, much less attempted, during the early years of Salar Jung's dewanship. This was the direct impact of the new awakening in Hyderabad.

The movement was suppressed; nevertheless, initiation in a new doctrine had been made. The seeds of a new Hyderabad had been sown, and they were nurtured by the press. The *Deccan Times* had come out in 1864, the *Hyderabad Telegraph* appeared in 1882 and the *Hyderabad Records* in 1885. The Urdu press followed suit and adopted a more or less bold and independent attitude. Although the Government of the state was denied political intercourse with foreign countries, the people were aware of the major incidents that shaped the contours of the political and cultural world outside the state.

There was doubtless a multi-dimensional transformation in Hyderabad in the late nineteenth century. Many features of modern civilization, like the electric telegraph, railways, a public works department, improved postal communication, state-patronized education, and scientific medical knowledge emerged in the state. The inspiration for most of the changes was British and, while some were introduced with the approval of the great Minister, others were imposed. And yet, the contribution of Salar Jung towards this development should not be overlooked. The transformation was primarily brought about by the leaven of western ideas and British influence, but Salar Jung intensified the process by encouraging the flow of liberal and progressive ideas associated with the West. By the time of his death the dawn of a new era had arrived in Hyderabad. It was probably not what Wellesley or Dalhousie had worked or hoped for, or had even foreseen, but was what English liberalism would come gracefully to accept as its own progeny.

One final question can now be posed. If British paramountcy had not been established in Hyderabad, would the state have remained still within its medieval shell? In the logic of historical development, each civilization finds its own way towards progress and advancement, and adjusts itself to changing times in its own characteristic way. Scientific inventions are made under compulsions of human needs and can hardly be confined within the territorial limits of the country of their origin. The railway or the telegraph would have reached Hyderabad without Mayo or Dalhousie, or, for that matter, even without Salar Jung, as it did other parts of the world that never witnessed British paramountcy. The process of modernization was doubtless accelerated by the policy of the paramount power, but Hyderabad had to pay for it. 'I do not believe', Northbrook once wrote to Gladstone, exhibiting rare insight, 'we have conciliated the affection of the people, excepting perhaps at Bombay where the Parsees are as good as English.... Unless one is to ignore the opinion of those who know the people here, there is considerable discontent.'[20] What was true of British India was equally true of Hyderabad. The main consideration of the British in all the modernization they encouraged was to ensure the continuity of their rule in India, and the welfare of the protected state was at best a secondary consideration. The long-term benefits to the people of the state came as a by-product and even then, paid for dearly. British statesmen and administrators from Wood and Canning to Salisbury and Lytton, Conservative and Liberal alike, put imperial progress before the progress of the state they were supposed to be allies of. The fact that the process of transformation of Hyderabad was started by the British, or at least done under their guidance, is but a poor apology for the ruthless domination that characterized their paramountcy. A railway oriented to the promotion of the interests of the state, an educational policy to enrich the indigenous culture and an administrative set-up primarily concerned with the people's welfare, might have taken the state along the path of modernization more slowly, but it would have been a natural growth, not a foreign graft.

Appendices

Appendix I

SECRETARIES OF STATE FOR INDIA, 1853–85

Lord Stanley (afterwards 15th Earl of Derby)	1858–9
Sir Charles Wood (afterwards Viscount Halifax)	1859–65
Earl de Grey and Ripon	1866
Viscount Cranborne (afterwards Marquess of Salisbury)	1866–7
Sir Stafford Northcote (afterwards Earl of Iddesleigh)	1867–8
Duke of Argyll	1868–74
Marquess of Salisbury	1874–8
Viscount Cranbrook	1878-80
Marquess of Hartington (afterwards 8th Duke of Devonshire)	1880–2
Earl of Kimberley	1882–5

Appendix II

VICEROYS AND GOVERNORS-GENERAL OF INDIA, 1858–84

Earl Canning	1858–62
Eighth Earl of Elgin	1862–3
Sir Robert Napier (Baron Napier of Magdala)	1863
Sir William T. Denison	1863
Sir John Lawrence (afterwards Lord Lawrence)	1864–8
Earl of Mayo	1869–72
Sir John Strachey	1872
Lord Napier of Merchistoun	1872
Earl of Northbrook	1872–6
Earl of Lytton	1876–80
Marquess of Ripon	1880–4

Appendix III

RESIDENTS AT HYDERABAD, 1858–84

Col C. Davidson	1857–62
Major A.H. Thornhill	1862–3
Sir George Yule	1863–7
Sir Richard Temple	1867–8
Mr J.G. Cordery	1868
Mr A.A. Roberts	1868
Mr J.G. Cordery	1868

Mr C.B. Saunders	1868–72
Col P.S. Lumsden	1872
Mr C.B. Saunders	1872–5
General Sir Richard J. Meade	1875–81
Sir Steuart C. Bayley	1881–2
Major G.H. Trevor	1882
Mr W.B. Jones	1882–3
Mr J.G. Cordery	1883–4

Appendix IV

RULERS OF THE ASUPHEA DYNASTY

Nawab Mir Qamruddin Nizam-ul-Mulk Asaf Jah I, appointed *Subahdar* of the Deccan in 1713; established his supremacy there in 1724	1724–48
Nawab Mir Ahmed Khan Nasir Jung	1748–50
Nawab Hidayatt Mahiuddin Khan Muzaffar Jung	1750–1
Nawab Sayyid Muhammad Khan Salabat Jung	1751–61
Nawab Mir Nizam Ali Khan Asaf Jah II	1761–1803
Nawab Sikander Jah, Asaf Jah III	1803–29
Nawab Farkhunda Ali Khan Nasir-ud-Daula Asaf Jah IV	1829–57
Nawab Mir Tahniat Ali Khan Afzal-ud-Daula Asaf Jah V	1857–69
Nawab Mir Mahub Ali Khan Asaf Jah VI	1869–1911
Nawab Mir Osman Ali Khan Bahadur Asaf Jah VII	1911–50

when he retired

Notes and References

PROLOGUE

1. Mir Osman Ali Khan became Nizam in 1911, and retired on 26 January 1950. He died in 1967.
2. After the independence of India, Hyderabad became an Indian state in 1948 as a result of Sardar Patel's 'police action' against the Nizam, who was trying to maintain an independent position for himself. After the re-organization of the Indian states in 1956, various regions of the old state of Hyderabad became parts of Andhra Pradesh and Maharashtra in the Republic of India.
3. W. W. Hunter, *Imperial Gazetteer of India* (London, 1811), vol. 3, p. 500. The estimate, however, seems to be only approximate and not accurate. Without Berar the area of the state was 82,698 square miles. *Census of India, 1891, His Highness the Nizam's Dominions* (Bombay, 1893), vol. 23, part 1, p. 1.
4. Yusuf Husain Khan, *Nizamu'l-Mulk Asaf Jah I* (Bombay, 1963), p. 66. This is a useful biography of the first Nizam.
5. For the composition of the East India Company, see C. H. Philips, *The East India Company, 1784–1834* (Manchester, 1940), chap. I. For the story of the foundation and composition of the French Company, see S. P. Sen, *The French in India* (Calcutta, 1958), pp. 15–32.
6. C. U. Aitchison, *A Collection of Treaties, Engagements and Sanads* (Calcutta, 1909), vol. 9, p. 20.
7. Ibid., pp. 22–3, 31.
8. Although Nizam Ali solicited the co-operation of his British allies against the Marathas, Cornwallis refused 'to gratify this expectation' or to encourage Maratha–Nizam rivalry. Cornwallis to Kennaway, 28 Jan. 1791 and to Secret Committee, 8 Sept. 1791, C. Ross (ed.), *Correspondence of Charles, First Marquis Cornwallis* (London, 1850), vol. 1, pp. 82, 120–1.
9. Shore said that he was 'disinclined' 'to run the risk of a war with the Peshwa for the purpose of supporting the tottering fabric of the Nizam's Government'. Shore to Dundas, 21 Aug. 1794 & 7 Feb. 1795, H. Furber (ed.), *The Private Record of an Indian Governor-Generalship* (Cambridge, 1933), pp. 56, 64–5.
10. For a more detailed account see V. K. Bawa, 'The French in India: The Case of Hyderabad', in P. M. Joshi & N. A. Nayeem (eds.), *Studies in the Foreign Relations of India; Prof. H. K. Sherwani Felicitation Volume* (Hyderabad, 1975)), pp. 257–91.
11. C. U. Aitchison, op. cit., pp. 52–3.
12. Mornington to Kirkpatrick, 30 June 1799, R. M. Martin, *The Despatches, Minutes and Correspondence of the Marquess Wellesley* (London, 1836), vol. 2, p. 68.
13. C. U. Aitchison, op. cit., pp. 67–73.
14. Ibid., pp. 78–81.
15. The first British Resident was appointed at Hyderabad in 1779. *Some Notes on the Residency Office* (Hyderabad Residency, n.d.), p. 1.

16. Sarojini Regani, 'The Appointment of Diwan in Hyderabad', *Andhra Pradesh Research Society Journal*, vol. 25 (1958–60).

17. Palmer established a mercantile firm at Hyderabad, ostensibly speculating in timber and shipbuilding, but really conducting monetary transactions with the Nizam. See Messrs Palmer & Co. to Henry Russell, 30 March 1814, *Hyderabad Papers* (Resident's Office, Hyderabad, 1819), pp. 3–4.

18. For Metcalfe's role in the affair, see. J. W. Kaye, *The Life and Correspondence of Charles, Lord Metcalfe* (London, 1858), vol. 1, pp. 402–34. The Nizam, entered into an agreement with the East India Company by which he agreed to give up his claim to the annual *peshkash* for the Northern Sarkars. In return, the Company paid him a lumpsum of Rs 1,16,66,660, with which he extricated himself from financial difficulties.

19. H. G. Briggs, *The Nizam. His History and Relations with the British Government* (London, 1861), vol. 2, p. 55. R. G. Burton, *A History of the Hyderabad Contingent* (Calcutta, 1908) gives a detailed account of the organization, development and achievements of the Contingent.

20. Anonymous, 'Hyderabad—The Nizam's Contingent', *Calcutta Review* (1849), vol. 11, p. 175.

21. Col. H. Fraser, *Memoir and Correspondence of General James Stuart Fraser* (London, 1885), p. 291.

22. Dalhousie to Fraser, 26 Dec. 1851, Dalhousie Papers (microfilm, National Archives of India), reel 21.

23. Fraser to Secy., Govt. of India, 4 Feb. 1851, and Dalhousie to Nizam, 6 June 1851, *P.P. 418 of 1854*, pp. 13 & 40.

24. Sarojini Regani, *Nizam–British Relations, 1724–1857* (Secunderabad, 1963), p. 289. Regani shows how Dalhousie foiled the Nizam's attempt to raise money with the help of *sahukars*.

25. Dalhousie to Fraser, 5 May & 16 Sept. 1852, Dalhousie Papers, reel 22.

26. Dalhousie's detailed instructions were given to Low in a confidential letter, 17 Feb. 1853, Dalhousie Papers, reel 22.

27. Res. to Offg. For. Secy., 10 May 1853, *P.P. 418 of 1854*, p. 127. For the painful story of how the Nizam was bullied and coerced, see also Briggs, op. cit., vol. 1.

28. Footnote to para 26, Salar Jung to Res., 19 Sept. 1872, For. Sec. Progs., Jan. 1874, no. 60.

29. A newspaper later commented in its editorial that the Nizam had consented to the treaty 'by considerations similar to those which have led many a poor gentleman to put into alien hands his watch and purse'. *The Friend of India*, 12 Aug. 1876.

30. Annual payment due from the Nizam was as follows:

Average annual pay of the Contingent	Rs	37,89,240
Yearly cost of Military stores	Rs	59,500
Appa Dessaye's Chouth	Rs	1,20,000
Allowance to Mohiput Ram's family	Rs	5,600
On account of Thuggee Department	Rs	7,971
Total	Rs	39,82,311

which came to about 34 lakhs in the Company's rupees. Nandan Prasad, *Paramountcy Under Dalhousie* (Delhi, 1964), footnote, p. 150.

31. The *surf-i-khas* taluks in these territories were left to the revenue management of the Nizam's officers.

32. C. U. Aitchison, op. cit., pp. 93–7.

33. Wood to Dalhousie, 8 & 24 May, 19 Aug., 5 Sept., 21 Oct., & 24 Nov. 1853; & 24 Jan. & 8 March 1854, Wood Papers (India Office Library), (IB) LB III & IV. That Wood was a strong annexationist is evident from his letters to Dalhousie. He not only wanted Berar, but also Oudh and was only waiting for the 'opportunity and pretext' to grab it. Wood to Dalhousie, 5 Sept. 1853, ibid.

34. Wood to F. Dorin, 8 Feb. 1854, ibid., LB IV.

35. Dalhousie to Low, 28 and 30 May, 1853, Dalhousie Papers, reel 22.

36. Arthur Silver, *Manchestermen and Indian Cotton, 1847–72* (Manchester, 1965) gives an excellent analysis of the motives and attitudes of the people of Manchester and the pressure-tactics of the cotton interest groups.

37. Minute of Dalhousie, 28 Feb. 1856, *P.P. 245 of 1856*, p. 9.

38. Italics mine.

39. Dalhousie to Low, 30 May 1853, Dalhousie Papers, reel 22.

40. Minute of Dalhousie, 28 Feb. 1856, *P.P. 245 of 1856*, p. 71.

41. Dalhousie to Fraser, 16 Sept. 1852, Dalhousie Papers, reel 22.

42. Nawab Mir Turab Ali Khan Bahadur, Salar Jung, Shuja-ud-Daula, Mukhtar-ul-Mulk, G.C.S.I., D.C.L. (1829–83), great grandson of Mir Alam, grandson of Munir-ul-Mulk, nephew of Siraj-ul-Mulk; appointed talukdar of Khammam, 1847; Dewan of Hyderabad, 1853–83. For a contemporary account of the life and works of Salar Jung, see Syed Hossain Bilgrami, *A Memoir of Sir Salar Jung* (Bombay, 1883).

43. For the causes and the nature of the Rising of 1857, see Sir J. W. Kaye and G. B. Malleson, *History of the Indian Mutiny* (London, 1878–80), 3 vols., G. W. Forrest, *A History of the Indian Mutiny* (London, 1904–12), 3 vols., S. N. Sen, *Eighteen Fifty-Seven* (Delhi, 1957), R. C. Majumdar, *The Sepoy Mutiny and the Revolt of 1857* (Calcutta, 1957), and S. B. Chaudhuri, *Civil Rebellion in the Indian Mutinies 1857–59* (Calcutta, 1957).

44. St. Nihal Singh, *The Nizam and the British Empire* (printed privately for the author, 1923), p. 1.

45. *The Freedom Struggle in Hyderabad* (Hyderabad, 1956), vol. 2, p. 1.

46. Mahdi Ali (complied), *Hyderabad Affairs* (Bombay, 1883), vol. 3, p. 213. Hereafter this book will be referred to as *Hyderabad Affairs*, with volume number indicated.

47. *Bombay Telegraph and Courier*, 21 July 1960.

48. Res. to For. Secy., 19 May 1859, For. Pol. Consult., 15 April 1859, no. 351; Res. to Secy., Govt. of India, 15 June 1858, For. Sec. Consult, 29 Oct. 1858, no. 17.

49. *Freedom Struggle*, vol. 2, p. 34.

50. Hyderabad Residency Records (National Archives of India), vol. 102, p. 291.

51. The state of Shorapur was a tributary of the Nizam. During the minority of Raja Venkatappa Naik, Capt. Meadows Taylor was appointed his guardian and administrator of the state. The Nizam's legal authority remained unimpaired. In 1853, when the Raja became a major, the state was handed over to him.

52. Col. Meadows Taylor, *The Story of My Life* (London, 1877), vol. 2, pp. 258–63.

Chapter I   THE NIZAM'S 'REWARD'

1. Mangles to Canning, 26 Oct. 1857, Canning Papers (Central Library, Leeds), vol. 3.
2. The panic is reflected in numerous communications that passed between Calcutta and London. See, for instance, Canning to Mangles, 4 & 20 June 1857, ibid., vol. 31; Mangles and Sykes to V. Smith, 4 Feb. 1857; Mangles and Currie to V. Smith, 29 June & 14 July 1857, General Correspondence, Letters from E. I. Co. to I. B. (India Office Library, London), vols. 24-5; V. Smith to Chairman and Dy. Chairman, E. I. Co., 5 & 7 Aug. 1857, General Correspondence, Letters from I. B. to E. I. Co., vol. 49.
3. Palmerston to V. Smith, 18 Jan. 1857 & to Canning, 21 Nov. 1857, Palmerston Papers (British Museum, London), Add. MSS. 48580. Palmerston warned Canning about a possible attempt by the rebels to blow up the magazine at Fort William in Calcutta. He even considered sending over West Indian Regiments to India.
4. For a lucid description of Canning's policy during this period, see M. Maclagan, *Clemency Canning* (London, 1962).
5. Palmerston to Canning, 9 Feb. 1858, Canning Papers, vol. 2. Gladstone, too, expressed great pleasure that the Mutiny, whether a rebellion, a civil war or whatever it might be called, was at an end. 'I heartily congratulate you as well as ourselves and the Empire at large ... upon this long desired happy and providential intelligence.' Gladstone to Canning, 23 July 1859, ibid.
6. See Chap. II for a fuller discussion.
7. V. Smith to Canning, 8 Jan. 1858, Canning Papers, vol. 4.
8. Mangles to Canning, 26 Oct., 25 Nov. & 9 Dec. 1857, & 30 March 1858, ibid., vol. 3. Mangles toyed with the idea of the Crown creating a special order of distinction with which to reward the princes. He believed this would be greatly appreciated by them and 'a very politic measure'.
9. Canning to Mangles, 22 Oct. & 11 Dec. 1857, Canning Papers, vol. 31.
10. Canning to V. Smith, 20 Feb. 1858, ibid., vol. 34.
11. Stanley to Canning, 26 July & 2 Aug. 1858, ibid., vol. 6
12. Canning to Wood, 17 Nov. 1859, ibid., vol. 38.
13. Canning was unwilling to reward Holkar with land. 'I do not think it at all imperative upon us to give him any, if we treat him handsomely in other ways', Canning wrote to Wood. Ibid.
14. Speech by V. Smith, 11 Feb. 1859, Hansard, *Parliamentary Debates Third Series* (hereafter *Hansard*), vol. 152. Interestingly, in this speech Smith advocated a good understanding with the princes as 'the safest defence against recurrence of such disasters' as the Mutiny. The loyal princes should be rewarded 'not only from motives of gratitude', but 'in order to secure the future well-being and tranquillity in India'.
15. Stanley to Canning, 29 Jan. 1859, Canning Papers, vol. 6.
16. Canning to Stanley, 30 Nov. 1858 & 29 Jan. 1859, ibid., vol. 36.
17. Stanley to Canning, 10 March 1859, ibid., vol. 6.
18. Oliphant to Salar Jung, 9 Aug. & 17 Dec. 1858, 17 March, 3 May & 3 June 1859, Salar Jung Papers (State Archives, Andhra Pradesh), packet no. 292.
19. Granville to Canning, 27 June 1859, cited in M. Maclagan, op. cit., p. 246.
20. Oliphant to Salar Jung, 17 June 1859, Salar Jung Papers.
21. Wood to Dalhousie, 19 Aug., 21 Oct. & 24 Nov. 1853, Wood Papers (IB), LB IV.

'Administering and paying over surplus to a roi faneant', Wood had said, 'is absurd.'

22. Arthur Silver, op. cit., pp. 58-98; see also R. J. Moore, *Sir Charles Wood's Indian Policy, 1853-66* (Manchester, 1966), pp. 138-40.
23. Speech by J.B. Smith, 19 July 1866, *Hansard*, vol. 184, p. 1123. J.B. Smith, the chief spokesman for Manchester in the House of Commons, had acquired the nickname of 'Godavari Smith.'
24. P.W.D. Desp., Court of Directors to Gov. in Council, Madras, no. 8, 29 June 1858.
25. Speech by Shaftesbury, 1 Aug. 1862, *Hansard*, vol. 168. J.B. Smith powerfully argued that cotton was not merely a Manchester question but of national importance as its manufacture amounted in value to over £600,000 per annum. Speech by J.B. Smith, 3 Feb. 1860, ibid., vol. 156.
26. Wood to Dalhousie, 8 Feb. & 10 July 1854; to Harris, 24 May & 8 June 1854, Wood Papers (IB), LB IV & V.
27. Wood to Denison, 18 Aug. 1861, ibid. (IO), LB 8.
28. Wood to Pottinger, 24 March 1853; & to Harris, 24 July 1854, ibid. (IB), LB III & IV.
29. Wood to Denison, 18 Aug. 1861, ibid. (IO), LB 8. Wood's annoyance with Manchester is also expressed in letters to Canning. Wood once related an interesting episode to Canning. A deputation of 'cotton gentlemen' from Manchester 'assured me that we knew nothing of India, and that it was impossible to get any crop, sugar or anything else, without some fresh legislation. Arbuthnot was standing beside me, and replied, "I found no difficulty from that or indeed any other cause". "What did you do?" said my Manchestermen, to which Arbuthnot simply replied, "I paid a fair price, and in ready money, and had always as much sugarcane as I wanted".' Wood to Canning, 18 Feb. 1861, ibid., LB 6.
30. Wood to Trevelyan, 26 Jan. & 25 May 1860, ibid., LB 2. Later, Wood admitted to Lawrence 'that we have over-estimated the advantage' of the Godavari works. Wood to Lawrence, 18 Oct. 1865, ibid., vol. 22. 'These works were all ordered from Home, by Sir Charles Wood', Lawrence told Northcote, 'at the instance of the House of Commons. J.B. Smith, the member for Stockport, supported by the Manchestermen were the moving parties'. Lawrence to Northcote, 18 July 1867, Iddesleigh Papers (British Museum, London), Add. MSS. 50023.
31. Speech by Wood, 3 Feb. & 9 Aug. 1860, *Hansard*, vols. 156 & 160.
32. Wood to Trevelyan, 8 Nov. 1859 & 26 April 1860, Wood Papers (IO), LB 1 & 3.
33. As early as 1858 the Govt. of Madras had urged the abolition of these duties. Actg. Secy., Madras Govt. to Res., 5 Nov. 1858, For. Pol. Progs., 14 Jan, 1859, no. 140.
34. They, of course, receded from this principle whenever it suited them. For a fuller discussion, see S. Bhattacharya, '*Laissez Faire* in India', *The Indian Economic and Social History Review*, vol. 2, no. 1.
35. Wood to Harris, 24 Sept. 1854, Wood Papers (IB), LB VI.
36. Wood to Trevelyan, 8 Nov. & 10 Dec. 1859, ibid., (IO) LB 1 & 2.
37. Wood to Canning, 18 Jan., 3 Feb. & 3 April 1860, ibid., LB 2 & 3.
38. Canning to Wood, 8 Sept. 1860, Canning Papers, vol. 40.
39. Canning to Davidson, 30 July 1859, ibid., vol. 61.
40. Canning to Wood, 6 Jan. 1861, ibid., vol. 42.
41. Salar Jung to Res., 25 May 1860, For. Part A Consult., Nov. 1860, K.W. Nos. 508-15; See also *Bombay Telegraph and Courier*, 18 Sept. 1860.
42. Secy. Govt. of India to Res., 6 July 1860, For. Part A Progs., Nov. 1860, no. 500; For.

Dy. Secy. to Res., 5 Sept. 1860, For. Part A Consult., Nov. 1860, no. 514.

43.   Beadon to Davidson, D.O., 7 May 1860, ibid., K.W. Nos. 508-15.

44.   Draft of agreement, ibid.

45.   Davidson to Beadon, D.O., 22 May 1860 & D.O. (n.d.), ibid.

46.   Salar Jung to Res., 25 May 1860, ibid.

47.   The estimate for Rs 32½ lakhs was arrived at as follows:

Payment provided under the treaty of 1853

Contingent	Rs 26,75,000
Miscellaneous	Rs 3,75,000
Total	Rs 30,50,000
Cost of Berar administration	Rs 4,50,000
	Rs 35,00,000
Less interest due on the Nizam's loan	Rs 2,50,000
	Rs 32,50,000

48.   For. Dept. to Res., 7 July 1860; Davidson to For. Dept., tel., & Beadon to Davidson, tel., 4 Aug. 1860, For. Part A Progs., Nov. 1860, nos. 500, 504 & 505.

49.   Salar Jung to Res., 11 Aug. 1860; & Res. to For. Secy., 12 Aug. 1860, *P.P. 338 of 1867*, pp. 14 & 18.

50.   Canning to Wood, 8 Sept. 1860, Canning Papers, vol. 40.

51.   For. Dy. Secy. to Res., 5 Sept. 1860, For. Part A Consult., Nov. 1860, no. 514.

52.   Davidson to Beadon, tel., 26 Sept. & Beadon to Davidson, tel., 29 Sept. 1860, Hyderabad Residency Records, vol. 102, p. 113 (E).

53.   Canning to Wood, 4 Nov. 1860, Canning Papers, vol. 40.

54.   Res. to Salar Jung, 30 Sept. 1860, For. Part A Progs., Nov. 1860, K.W.E. Nos. 516-26.

55.   Res. to Secy., Govt. of India, 12 Oct. 1860, Hyderabad Residency Records, vol. 102, p. 11.

56.   For. Secy. to Res., 19 Nov. 1860, encl. draft of letter to Nizam, For. Part A Consult., Nov. 1860, nos. 525-6.

57.   Canning to Wood, 4 Nov. 1860, Canning Papers, vol. 40.

58.   C.U. Aitchison, op. cit., pp. 105-6.

59.   Canning to Wood, 21 Dec. 1860, Canning Papers, vol. 40 & Wood to Canning, 23 Jan. 1861, Wood Papers (IO), LB 6.

60.   For. Secy. to Res., 17 Dec. 1860; Salar Jung to Res., 26 Dec. 1860, For. Part A Progs., Jan. 1861, nos. 77 & 83 A.

61.   Wood to Morehead, 10 Oct. 1860, & to Canning, 18 Oct. 1860, Wood Papers (IO), LB 4 & 5.

62.   Canning to Wood, 8 Sept. & 4 Nov. 1860 & 6 Jan. 1861, Canning Papers, vols. 40 & 42.

63.   Res. to Commissioner of Nagpur, 10 Oct. 1860, Hyderabad Residency Records, vol. 213, p. 259. A Glasford, Asst., Agent to the G.G. took possession of the Godavari districts on behalf of the Govt. of India and made them over to Nagpur.

64.   Davidson to Beadon, D.O., 22 May 1860, For. Part A Consult., Nov. 1860, K.W. Nos. 508-15.

65.   Salar Jung to Res., 25 May 1860, ibid.

66. Salar Jung to Res., 13 Aug. 1860, C.U. Aitchison, op. cit., p. 107.
67. Canning to Wood, 8 Sept. 1860, Canning Papers, vol. 40.
68. G.G.'s *khureeta* to Nizam, 26 July 1861, For. Pol. A Progs., Dec. 1861, no. 60; Res. to Offg. For. Secy., 5 Oct. 1861; & Offg. For. Secy. to Res., 25 Nov. 1861, For. Pol. A Progs., Nov. 1861, nos. 82, 83.
69. Statement of Revenue and Receipts of East and West Berar and *surf-i-khas* taluks; Res. to Offg. For. Secy. & to Commissioner of the Assigned Districts, 6 April 1861; Offg. For. Secy. to Res., 8 May 1861, For. Part A Progs., May 1861, nos. 29, 34, 37 & 39.
70. Asst. Commissioner, Assigned Districts to Ist Asst. Res., 23 Oct. 1861; Res. to Offg. For. Secy., 31 Dec. 1861; Offg. For. Secy. to Res., 30 Nov. 1861, For. Pol. A Progs., Nov. 1861, Nos. 110, 111 & 114.

Chapter II   PARAMOUNTCY AND SUBORDINATE CO-OPERATION

1. Palmerston to Canning, 9 Oct. 1857, Canning Papers, vol. 2.
2. Clanricarde to Canning, 10 Feb. 1858, ibid.
3. Argyll to Canning, 9 Feb. 1858, ibid.
4. Mangles to Canning, 25 Jan. 1858, ibid., vol. 3; Mangles & Currie to V. Smith, 31 Dec. 1857 & 9 Feb. 1858, Letters from E.I. Co. to I.B., vol. 26. A memorandum, 'Improvement in the administration of India during the last thirty years', was also forwarded to Smith, describing in detail the principal measures lately adopted by the Company to improve the administration of India and the condition of its people.
5. See *Hansard*, vol. 148, appendix. Independent of the cause, this presents the arguments with admirable clarity.
6. Mangles to Canning, 8 Feb. 1858, Canning Papers, vol. 3; Canning to Clarendon, 23 Jan. 1858, ibid., vol. 30.
7. Mangles to Canning, 9 April 1858, ibid., vol. 3.
8. Even Stanley admitted that the India Council was 'really the Court revived under a new name'. Stanley to Canning, 5 Oct. 1858, ibid., vol. 6. Palmerston's comment on the bill was crisp: 'We have passed an abominably bad India Bill', Palmerston to Canning, 20 July 1858, ibid., vol. 2.
9. Bernard S. Cohn, 'Representing Authority in Victorian India' in E. Hobsbawm and Terence Ranger (eds.), *The Invention of Tradition* (Cambridge, 1983), p. 180.
10. Stanley to Canning, 26 July, 2 Aug. & 8 Sept. 1858, and Canning to Stanley, 19 Oct. 1858, Canning Papers, vols. 6 & 36. Canning said that had he any choice, he would have preferred hardly any show so as to attract as little notice and raise expectations as little as possible. But he was afraid that this would create much dissatisfaction in Calcutta.
11. Canning to Stanley, 2 Nov. 1858, ibid.
12. Copy of Proclamation, encl. with Secret letter from Court, 9 Sept. 1858, For. Sec. Consult., Sept. 1 '58, no. 1.
13. Queen to Canning, 2 Dec. 1858, Canning Papers, vol. 1.
14. K.M. Panikkar, *Indian States* (London, 1942), p. 14. The British evolved the doctrine of paramountcy, it was not defined in any treaty. Barbara Ramusack

writes, 'Paramountcy was used to legitimatize whatever action the British, as paramount power, deemed necessary or desirable to secure the objectives outlined in the treaty.' Barbara N. Ramusack, *The Princes of India in the Twilight of Empire* (Cincinnati, 1978), p. xvii. They used it, however, to achieve goals not outlined in the treaty as well.

15. Pol. Desp., G.G. to S.S., 30 April 1860, For. Consult., 30 April 1860, no. 43A.
16. Canning to Granville, 24 Dec. 1859 & to Wood, 28 Jan. 1860, Canning Papers, vols. 30 & 40.
17. Pol. Desp., G.G. to S.S., 30 April 1860, For. Consult., 30 April 1860, no. 43A.
18. Canning to Low, 13 Aug. 1860, Canning Papers, vol. 64.
19. Canning to Wood, 5 May, 13 & 18 June 1860, ibid., vol. 40.
20. Wood to Canning, 26 June & 26 July 1860, Wood Papers (IO), LB 3.
21. Wood to Bartle Frere, 10 Aug. 1860, ibid., LB 4. Wood was influenced by Frere's very able minute in support of Canning's policy. See Confidential Minute by Frere, 19 June 1860, ibid., vol. 55(4). The Queen herself was, of course, Canning's patron. She wanted Wood to approve Canning's adoption despatch, believing that it would be equally beneficial to the Indian chiefs and the British Government. Queen to Wood, 19 June 1860, ibid., vol. 60(1).
22. Wood to Elgin, 17 Oct. 1862, ibid., LB 11.
23. The most apt comment on Canning's policy came from his successor Elgin: 'My own opinion is that Canning never intended to let the chiefs get the bit into their mouths, or to lose his hold over them .... His policy of deference to the authority of native chiefs was a means to an end—the end being the establishment of the British Raj in India, and when the means and the end came into conflict, or seemed likely to do so, the former went to the wall.' Elgin to Wood, 9 Sept. 1862, Elgin Papers (India Office Library, London), vol. 2.
24. Pol. Letter, S.S. to G.G., 21 April 1859, no. 18.
25. This inscription was kindly translated for me by Mr Zakir Hussain, Asst. Archivist, National Archives of India.
26. Res. to For. Secy., 21 Dec. 1858, For. Pol. Consult., 31 Dec. 1858, no. 3367. A copy of Persian inscriptions on the seals was enclosed with the letter.
27. Canning to V. Smith, 20 Feb. 1858, Canning Papers, vol. 34.
28. Res. to Secy., Govt. of India, 6 March 1858; & Secy., Govt. of India to Res., 29 July 1858, For. Consult., 6 Aug. 1858, nos. 96-7. As early as 1836 the Court of Directors had advocated the introduction in the Indian states of a coinage uniform with that of British India. Letter from Court, 30 March 1836, Hyderabad Residency Records, vol. 72, p. 208. In 1843, Resident Fraser unsuccessfully pressed the Nizam to adopt a currency of the same intrinsic value as that of the Company. Res. to Secy., Govt. of India, 19 Sept. 1843, ibid., vol. 79, pp. 156-7. In 1856-7 Salar Jung introduced a new standard rupee called the *Halli Sicca* (i.e., the modern coin). Although made by primitive methods and worth less in intrinsic value than the British Indian rupee, it was a decided improvement on the previous Hyderabadi currency. See John Law, *Modern Hyderabad* (Calcutta, 1914), pp. 141-2.
29. Hastings Fraser, *Our Faithful Ally, the Nizam* (London, 1865), p. 305.
30. Res. to For. Secy., tel., 24 Oct. 1859, For. Pol. Consult., 28 Oct. 1859, no. 29.
31. Queen to Canning, 18 May 1859, Canning Papers, vol. 1.
32. Canning to Queen, 4 July 1859; to Wood, 24 Dec. 1859, ibid., vols. 1 & 38.
33. Queen to Wood, 25 Feb. 1860, Wood Papers, vol. 60(1).

34. Wood to Canning, 25 May, 18 June, 2 Sept. & 10 Dec. 1860; & 3 Jan., 4 Feb., 25 June & 3 July 1861, ibid., (IO) LB 3, 4, 5 & 6; Canning to Wood, 17 June, 19 July, 31 Oct. & 3 Nov. 1860, Canning Papers, vol. 40.

35. I owe this idea as well as the words to B. S. Cohn, op. cit., pp. 181–2.

36. Canning to Queen, 17 Dec. 1861, Canning Papers, vol. 1, and Wood to Canning, 9 Jan. 1861, Wood Papers (IO), LB 6.

37. For. Secy. to Res., 5 July 1861 & Res. to For. Secy., 31 Aug. 1861, Hyderabad Residency Records, vol. 102, pp. 280-91; Wood to Canning, 18 Oct. 1861, Wood Papers (IO), LB 9 & Canning to Davidson, 19 Oct. 1861, Canning Papers, vol. 63.

38. Salar Jung to Res., 1 Nov. 1861, For. Pol. A Progs., Nov. 1861, no. 51. Sindhia, too, had created difficulties for the Govt. of India before agreeing to accept the knighthood. Bartle Frere had to persuade Sindhia to enter the Order. Bhupen Qanungo, 'A Study of British Relations with the Native States of India, 1858-62', *Journal of Asian Studies*, vol. 26, 1967, p. 263.

39. Canning to Queen, 17 Dec. 1861, Canning Papers, vol. 1.

40. Canning to Davidson, 19 Oct. 1861, ibid., vol. 63.

41. Res. to Offg. For. Secy., 25 Nov. 1861, Hyderabad Residency Records, vol. 102, p. 243.

42. Translation of placards, ibid., p. 346.

43. Res. to For. Secy., 19 March 1859, For. Pol. Consult., 15 April 1859, no. 351. Davidson told Fraser, who had thrown himself with an open sword between Davidson and the assassin, that it was fortunate he had not cut down the latter, for the crowd would then have fallen on all the Residency staff. Hastings Fraser, op. cit., p. 302.

44. Canning to Stanley, 2 April 1859 & Stanley to Canning, 8 May 1859, Canning Papers, vols 6 and 36; For. Under Secy. to Res., 2 April 1859, For. Pol. Consult., 15 April 1859, no. 354.

45. Res. to Offg. For. Secy., 10 March 1862, For. Pol. A Progs., March 1862, no. 225; For. Secy. to Res., 10 May 1862, For. Pol. A Progs., May 1862, no. 72.

46. Pol. diary of Richard Temple, 22 April (1867), Temple Collection (India Office Library, London), vol. 81.

47. Stanley to Canning, 26 July & 30 Sept. 1858, Canning Papers, vol. 6.

48. Canning to Stanley, 30 Nov. 1858, ibid., vol. 36.

49. Res. to For. Secy., 9 Jan. & 9 Feb. 1860; translation of Salar Jung's letter to Nizam, 5 Feb. 1860, For. Part A Progs., May 1860, nos. 10, 17 & 19.

50. Res. to Offg. For. Secy., tel., 27 May 1861; Res. to For. Secy., 28 May; to Nizam, 27 May, 1861; Salar Jung to Nizam & Res., 30 May; For. Secy., to Res., 4 July 1861, For. Part A Progs., Aug. 1861, K.W. nos. 42-51, & nos. 42-3, 47-8.

51. Res. to For. Secy., 26 June 1861, ibid., no. 51. At the time of the restoration of these districts the Resident requested the Nizam to place them under Salar Jung's personal control. The Nizam delayed making over the districts to the Minister and kept them for his own private use. Salar Jung to Res., 29 May 1861, ibid., no. 49.

52. Wood to Canning, 18 Oct. 1860, Wood Papers (IO), LB 5.

53. C.U. Aitchison, op. cit., p. 108.

54. Res. to For. Secy., 15 April 1861, Hyderabad Residency Records, vol. 106, p. 44.

55. Res. to For. Secy., 5 Oct. 1860, ibid., vol. 102, p. 107; see also For. Pol. A Consult., March 1862, no. 420.

56. J.L. Morrison, *The Eighth Earl of Elgin. A Chapter in the Nineteenth-Century*

Imperial History (London, 1928), p. 276.

57. Canning to Elgin, 9 Sept. 1861, Canning Papers, vol. 30.
58. Wood to Elgin, 17 Oct. 1862, Wood Papers (IO), LB 11. Elgin had once protested with some annoyance and said that it was not advisable for Wood to communicate with the Indian chiefs other than through the Govt. of India. Elgin to Wood, 9 May 1862, Elgin Papers, vol. 1.
59. Wood to Canning, 10 Jan. 1862, Wood Papers (IO), LB 9.
60. Elgin to Canning, 2 Aug. 1861, Canning Papers, vol. 2.
61. Elgin to Queen, 20 Jan. 1863, Elgin Papers, Section 1, Part IV; and to Wood, 8 & 19 March & 2 Aug. 1862, ibid., Section 1, Part I, vols. 1 & 2.
62. Wood to Elgin, 26 June 1862, Wood Papers (IO), LB 10.
63. Elgin to Wood, 9 Sept. 1862, Elgin Papers, vol. 2.
64. Wood to Elgin, 10 Oct. 1862, Wood Papers (IO), LB 11.
65. Yule to Elgin, 18 May 1863, Elgin Papers, vol. 24; Note by Palmer, 3 July 1862, ibid; and Elgin to Yule, 11 July 1863, ibid., vol. 17. For details of these reforms, see M. Fathulla Khan, *A History of Administrative Reforms in Hyderabad State* (Secunderabad 1935), pp. 58-61.
66. Wood to Durand, 17 & 25 Dec., to Maine, 3 Dec. 1863, Wood Papers (IO), LB 15.
67. A. West, *Recollections, 1832 to 1886* (London, 1899), p. 213.
68. R.B. Smith, *Life of Lord Lawrence* (London, 1883), vol. 2, p. 411.
69. Res. to For. Secy., 8 March 1864; For. Secy. to Res., 27 May & 7 June 1864, For. Pol. Progs., June 1867, nos. 66-68.
70. Wood to Lawrence, 2 Aug. 1864, Wood Papers (IO), LB 17; Pol. Desp., S.S. to G.G., 3 Aug. 1864, no. 8.
71. Actg.-Secy., Bombay Govt. to Offg. Secy., Govt. of India, 22 Feb. 1862, For. Pol. A Progs., April 1862, no. 138; Secy., Madras Govt. to Res., 13 April 1860, For. Part A Progs., Nov. 1860, no. 463; Res. to Actg. Collector, Krishna District, 15 Oct. & 30 Nov. 1860, Hyderabad Residency Records, vol. 514, pp. 38 & 81.
72. Salar Jung to Res., 27 Nov. 1861, For. Genl. B Progs., Jan. 1862, no. 140; Res. to For. Secy., 14 Dec. 1861, For. Genl. A Progs., Dec. 1861, no. 99; Offg. Res. to For. Secy., 17 Sept. 1862, Hyderabad Residency Records, vol. 106, p. 242.
73. Yule to Elgin, 18 May 1863, Elgin Papers, vol. 24; and Elgin to Yule, 11 July 1863, ibid, vol. 17.
74. Res. to For. Secy., 14 Dec. 1863, For. Rev. A Progs., Jan. 1864, no. 24.
75. For. Secy. to Res., 12 Jan. 1864, ibid., no. 26; & S.S. to G.G., 16 April 1864, referred to in Fin. Progs., 26 May 1864, For. Rev. A Progs., June 1864, no. 50.
76. Res. to Chief Secy., Bombay Govt., 23 Feb. 1864, For. Genl. A Progs., June 1864, no. 2.
77. Salar Jung to Res., 25 Jan. 1867, For. Pol. A Progs., Feb. 1867, no. 138 (ix).
78. For a detailed list of the rates on different articles and a list of articles exempted from import and export duties, see For. Rev. A Progs., Dec. 1864, nos. 93 & 94; see also Res. to For. Secy., 8 Dec. 1864, Hyderabad Residency Records, vol. 107, pp. 16-17.
79. See Table I.
80. Extracts from For. Dept. Progs., 11 Sept. 1865, For. Genl. A Progs., Sept. 1865, no. 28.
81. Res. to For. Secy., 26 Oct. 1865, For. Genl. A Progs., July 1866, no. 37.
82. Extracts from For. Dept. Progs., 18 July 1866, ibid., no. 56.

83. Salar Jung to Res., D.O., 6 Sept. 1866, and For. Secy. to Res., 13 Oct. 1866, For. Genl. A Progs., Oct. 1866, nos. 27 & 28.

84. Cranborne to Lawrence, 19 Nov. 1866, Lawrence Papers, reel 1.

85. Lawrence to Cranborne, 19 Dec. 1866, ibid., reel 2.

86. Pol. Desp., S.S. to G.G., 29 June 1867, no. 118.

87. C.U. Aitchison, op. cit., p. 53

88. Salar Jung to Res., 25 Feb. 1862; Actg. Secy., Bombay Govt. to Res., 6 May 1862; For. Secy. to Res., 15 May 1862, For. Pol. A Progs., May 1862, nos. 162, 164 & 167.

89. Translation of the Nizam's Proclamation, 7 July 1862, For. Pol. A Progs., Aug. 1862, no. 179; Res. to Secy., Bombay Govt., 11 Dec. 1863, For. Pol. A Progs., Aug. 1866, no. 134.

90. Salar Jung to Res., D.O., 25 Jan. 1867; Res. to For. Secy., 2 Feb. 1867, For. Pol. A Progs., Feb. 1867, nos. 138 (ix) & 137; Res. to For. Secy., 28 March 1867, For. Pol. A Progs., April 1867, no. 132.

91. Salar Jung to Temple, 8 May 1867, Temple Collection, vol. 77; For. Under Secy. to Res., 31 May 1867, For. Pol. A Progs., June 1867, no. 23.

92. This list of criminals was incorporated in Article 4 and included all the offences mentioned in Section 21 of Act VII 1854 of the Govt. of India.

93. C.U. Aitchison, op. cit., vol. IX, pp. 108-9. The Govt. of India soon felt that it should be guided in this matter by its own municipal laws and not by treaties. A new arrangement was accordingly made in 1887 with the Nizam's government. Cases of extradition from British India to Hyderabad were to be regulated henceforth by the procedure prescribed by the existing law in British India. Ibid., p. 110.

94. Pol. Desp., S.S. to G.G. For. Consult., 31 Aug. 1867, no. 148.

95. Karen Leonard, 'The Hyderabad Political System and Its Participants', *Journal of Asian Studies*, vol. 30 (1971), p. 572. In this interesting article Leonard gives an overview of patrons, clients and intermediaries in the eighteenth-century Hyderabadi political system.

96. Salar Jung to Temple, 27 April 1867, Temple Collection, vol. 77; Yule to Salar Jung, D.O., 22 Jan. & Salar Jung to Yule, D.O., 24 Jan. 1867; Res. to For. Secy., 2 Feb. 1867, For. Pol. A Progs., Feb. 1867, nos. 137, 138(2) and 138(7). See also *Times of India*, 2 March 1867.

97. Rafi-ud-din Khan, Umdut-ul-Mulk, Nawab Shums-ul-Umra Amir-i-Kabir (d. 1877), Co-Regent of Hyderabad, 1869-77. The Amir-i-Kabir was the hereditary head of the *Paigah* or household forces. The most important noble family in Hyderabad, the *Paigah* family was Sunni, like the Nizam himself, and was allied to him by matrimony. For the history of the *Paigah* see K. Krishnaswamy Mudiraj, *Pictorial Hyderabad* (Hyderabad, 1934), vol. 2, pp. 45-89.

98. Salar Jung to Temple, 27 April 1867, Temple Collection, vol. 77.

99. Service Message, Res. to For. Secy., 18 Feb. 1867, For. Pol. A Progs., Feb. 1867, no. 141; Res. to For. Secy., 15 March 1867, Hyderabad Residency Records, vol. 107, p. 156. In 1866 the Order of the Star of India was enlarged into three grades— G.C.S.I., K.C.S.I., & C.S.I.

100. Salar Jung to Temple, 16 April 1867, Temple Collection, vol. 77; Pol. diary of Richard Temple, 17 April (1867), ibid., vol. 81.

101. Salar Jung to Temple, 27 April 1867, ibid., vol. 77.

102. Richard Temple, *Men and Events of My Time in India* (London, 1882), p. 289, and *The Story of My Life* (London, 1896), vol. 1, p. 183.

103. Lawrence to Cranborne, 14 Feb. 1867, Lawrence Papers, reel 3.
104. Offg. For. Secy. to Res., 20 Feb. 1867, For. Pol. A Progs., Feb. 1867, no. 142.
105. Lawrence to Cranborne, 19 Dec. 1866, Lawrence Papers, reel 7. See Chap. IV for a fuller discussion.
106. Salar Jung to Temple, 29 April 1867, Temple Collection, vol. 77.
107. Ibid.
108. Nizam's *khureeta* to G.G., 29 April 1867, For. Pol. A Progs., May 1867, no. 173.
109. Northcote to Lawrence, 26 May 1867, Lawrence Papers, reel 1.
110. Lawrence to Cranborne, 14 Feb. 1867, ibid., reel 3.
111. Elgin to Wood, 1 June 1863, Elgin Papers, vol. 4.
112. R.B. Smith, op. cit., vol. 1, p. 437.
113. Pol. diary of Richard Temple, 17 April (1867), Temple Collection, vol. 81.
114. Salar Jung to Temple, 28 April 1867, ibid., vol. 77
115. Richard Temple, *The Story of My Life*, vol. 1, p. 170.
116. Pol. diary of Richard Temple, 23 April (1867), Temple Collection, vol. 81.
117. Ibid., 21 & 25 April (1867).
118. Richard Temple, *The Story of My Life*, vol. 1, p. 174.
119. Richard Temple, *Men and Events of My Time in India*, p. 288.
120. Salar Jung to Temple, 28 April, 8 & 20 May, 20 & 22 July, 22 Aug., 3 Sept., 8 & 19 Oct., 21 Nov. 1874; to Cordery, 26 Sept. 1867, Temple Collection, vol. 77. Although Salar Jung took Temple's advice concerning plans to modernize the state, he disapproved of the Resident's attempts to communicate with local people and sought to restrict social contact between the Residency staff and his own bureaucracy or the nobility. After Temple's departure, Salar Jung sent a lengthy memorandum to his successor, explaining the prevalent custom and telling him that Temple's moves to sponsor social gatherings were impediments to the implementation of Govt. policy. Karen Leonard, 'British Impact on Hyderabad: Cultural Change and Bureaucratic Modernization in 19th Century Hyderabad', P.M. Joshi & M.A. Nayeem (eds.), op. cit., p. 449.
121. Res. to For. Secy., 22 May 1867, Hyderabad Residency Records, vol. 107, pp. 200-2.
122. Asst. Res. to For. Secy., tel., 28 Jan. 1868, For. Pol. A Progs., Feb. 1868, no. 29.
123. Asst. Res. to For. Secy., 10 Feb. 1868; Res. to Salar Jung & For. Secy. to Ist Asst. Res., 21 Feb. 1868, For. Pol. A Progs., March 1868, nos. 1, 3 & 4.
124. A.C. Campbell, *Glimpses of the Nizam's Dominions* (Bombay, 1898), p. 109.
125. There are voluminous records on the subject. Of special interest are Pol. Desp., S.S. to G.G. 24 June 1861, For. Consult., 24 June 1861, no. 85; G.G. to Res., 22 March 1869, For. Pol. A Progs., March 1869, no. 284.
126. Salar Jung to Res., 11 May 1866, For. Mily. A Progs., June 1866, no. 11.
127. Pol. diary of Temple, 27 May (1867), Temple Collection, vol. 81.
128. Salar Jung to Temple, 27 May 1867, ibid., vol. 77.
129. Pol. diary of Temple, 30 May (1867), ibid., vol. 81.
130. Lawrence to Denison, 21 May 1865, enclosed with Denison to Wood, 31 May 1865, Wood Papers, 87/5.
131. Salar Jung to Temple, 2 June 1867, Temple Collection, vol. 77 It is doubtful that Salar Jung really relished Temple viewing the Reformed Troops, particularly as he probably knew that Temple did not like what he had seen.
132. Wood to Frere, 9 April 1865, Wood Papers (IO), LB 22.
133. Argyll, Secy. of State, 1868-74, consulted Wood whenever he could. Argyll to

Gladstone, 20 Oct. 1870, Gladstone Papers (British Museum, London), Add. MSS. 44100.

134. Cited in A. West, op. cit., p. 224.

135. Northcote himself was interested in the Indian viceroyalty, and requested Disraeli to nominate him. Northcote to Disraeli, 7 & 9 June 1868, Iddesleigh Papers, Add. MSS. 50016.

136. Argyll to Gladstone, 5 Dec. 1868, Gladstone Papers, Add. MSS. 44100.

137. Argyll to Mayo, 18 Dec. 1868 & 12 Feb. 1869, Mayo Papers, reel 7.

138. Lawrence to Northcote, 14 & 27 July & 5 Aug. 1868, Iddesleigh Papers, Add. MSS. 50026.

139. Speech by Mayo, quoted in G.B. Mullick (ed.), *Speeches in England and India by Earl of Mayo* (Calcutta, 1873), p. 75.

140. Res. to G.G., tel., 26 Feb. 1869, For. Pol. A Progs., March 1869, nos. 258 & 259.

141. Pol. diary of Richard Temple, 20 April (1867), Temple Collection, vol. 81.

142. Res. to G.G., tel., 26 Feb. 1869, and to For. Secy., 27 Feb. 1869, For. Pol. A progs., March 1869, nos. 260 & 270.

143. Anonymous, 'The Nizam's Dominions', *Calcutta Review*, vol. 52 (1871), p. 121; see also 'The Shoe Question' in *Friend of India and Statesman*, 10 June 1879.

144. Res. to For. Secy., 4 March 1869; For. Secy. to Res., 15 March 1869; For. Pol. A Progs., March 1869, nos. 274 & 273.

145. Mayo to Fitzgerald, 4 March 1869, Mayo Papers, reel 1.

146. Mayo to Argyll, 2 & 10 March 1869, Argyll Papers (microfilm copy, National Archives of India), reel 1.

147. Salar Jung, who was considered as 'representing English influence at court', was associated with 'the leader of the opposition'. The Amir-i-Kabir's association with the administration was expected to prevent intrigues against it by the less enlightened members of the Hyderabad community. See Anonymous, 'The Nizam's Dominions', pp. 122-3.

148. Nawab Sir Khursheed Jah Bahadur (1841-1902), nephew of Amir-i-Kabir and eldest son of Vikar-ul-Umra, became Amir-i-Kabir in 1881; member, Council of Regency, 1883; member, Council of State, 1884.

149. Res. to For. Secy., 6 March 1869; Salar Jung to Res., 2 March 1869; For. Pol. A Progs., March 1869, nos. 279 & 279A.

150. For. Secy. to Res., 22 March 1869, ibid., no. 284.

151. Mayo to Argyll, 23 March 1869, Argyll Papers, reel 1.

152. Mayo to Fitzgerald, 4 March; to Argyll, 2 March 1869, Mayo Papers, reel 1.

153. Mayo to Argyll, 12 Aug. 1869, ibid.

154. Salar Jung to Res., 2 March 1869, For. Pol. A Progs., March 1869, no. 279B.

Chapter III   PARAMOUNTCY CHALLENGED

1. Richard Temple, *Men and Events of My Life*, p. 288, and Pol. diary of Temple, 8 Dec. (1867), Temple Collection, vol. 81.

2. For a detailed description of Salar Jung's reforms, see Maulavi Cherag Ali, *Hyderabad (Deccan) under Sir Salar Jung* (Bombay, 1886) 4 vols., Syed Hossain Bilgrami and C. Willmott, *Historical and Descriptive Sketch of His Highness the Nizam's Dominions* (Bombay, 1883), vol. 2, and M. Fathulla Khan, op. cit.

190   *Hyderabad and British Paramountcy*

3. For an analysis of the Telengana rebellion in the 1940s see Carolyn M. Elliott, 'Decline in a Patrimonial Regime: The Telengana Rebellion in India 1946-51', *Journal of Asian Studies*, vol. 34 (1974), pp. 27-47. Elliott argues that had the reforms been successful, they would have transformed the Hyderabadi administration into a modern bureaucracy. But they were not completed. 'The effect of modernization in Hyderabad was to isolate the regime from its Hindu population.'
4. I am indebted for this paragraph to Karen Leonard's excellent article, 'Hyderabad: The Mulki–Non-Mulki Conflict', in Robin Jeffrey (ed.), *People, Princes and Paramount Power* (Delhi, 1978), pp. 65–73.
5. Mayo to Argyll, 1 Sept. 1871, Argyll Papers, reel 4.
6. This concept is developed in Francis G. Hutchins, *The Illusion of Permanence: British Imperialism in India* (Princeton, 1967). Hutchins analyses how 'a new frame of mind which had as its governing idea the justness of the permanent subjection of India to British rule' dominated British policy inIndia after 1857.
7. Northbrook to Salisbury, 19 Nov. & 18 Dec. 1874; to Ripon, 17 June 1881, Northbrook Papers (microfilm copy, National Archives of India), reels 4 & 1.
8. Salisbury to Northbrook, 1 & 28 May & 2. Sept. 1874, Salisbury Northbrook Papers (microfilm copy, National Archives of India), reel 7; Salisbury to Lytton, 11 May 1877, Lytton Papers (microfilm copy, National Archives of India), reel 4.
9. Sher Ali was the *Amir* of Kabul, 1868-79.
10. Lytton to Meade and to Salisbury, 11 May 1876; to Queen, 6 Aug. 1877, Lytton Papers, reels 5 & 6.
11. For. Secy. to Res., 22 March 1869, For. Pol. A Progs., March 1869, no. 284.
12. Salar Jung to Res., 20 April, to Offg. Res., 29 April, 1869; For. Secy. to Res., 31 May 1869, For. Pol. A Progs., June 1869, nos. 47, 48 & 51.
13. For details, see Chap. V.
14. Sir O.T. Burne, *Memoirs* (London, 1907), pp. 131-4, gives a moving description of Mayo's assassination.
15. Strachey to Argyll, 16 Feb. 1872, Argyll Papers, reel 4.
16. Cited in G.B. Mullick, op. cit., pp. 49-50, 57-8.
17. Halifax to Gladstone, 13 Feb. 1872, Gladstone Papers, Add. MSS. 44185.
18. Argyll to Gladstone, 14 & 19 Feb. 1872, ibid., Add. MSS. 44102.
19. B. Mallet, *Thomas George, Earl of Northbrook* (London, 1908), p. 53.
20. Northbrook to Dufferin, 8 Sept. 1884, quoted in ibid., p. 122.
21. For. Secy. to Res., 19 June 1873, For. Pol. A Consult., June 1873, no. 256.
22. Pol. Desp., S.S. to G.G., 20 March 1873, ibid., no. 255; Res. to For. Secy., 21 July 1873, For Pol. A Consult, Sept. 1873, no. 148.
23. Draft of letter, Salar Jung to Palmer, 11 Aug. 1873, Salar Jung Papers.
24. Capt. John Clerk, served in the Crimea, 1854–5; ADC to his father as Governor of Bombay, 1860; Captain in the 4th Dragoon Guards; Nizam's tutor, 1874–6.
25. G.G. to Res., tel., 15 Sept. 1874, For. Genl. B Progs., oct. 1874, no. 26.
26. Capt. Claude Clerk (1832-1905), joined Madras Cavalry, 1850; Nizam's tutor, 1876; resigned, 1887. He maintained a brisk correspondence with his brother John who, even after retirement, retained interest in Hyderabad. These letters, available in the Claude Clerk Collection (India Office Library), give a glimpse of contemporary power-politics in Hyderabad.
27. Res. to For. Secy., 3 June 1876; G.G. to S.S., 26 June 1876; G.G. to S.S. tel., 30 June & 10 July 1876, For. Pol. A Progs., March 1877, nos. 697, 699, 703 & 705.

Notes and References

191

28. Northbrook to Argyll, 10 April 1874, Argyll Papers, reel 8.

29. On Northbrook's resignation, see E.C. Moulton, *Lord Northbrook's Indian Administration, 1872-1876* (Bombay, 1968), pp. 257-80.

30. Northbrook to Gladstone, 9 Aug. 1875, Gladstone Papers, Add. MSS. 44266. In March 1875 it had been announced that the Prince of Wales was intending to visit India. Affairs in India were quiet at that time, and Northbrook was enthusiastic about the visit: 'Although the suggestion did not come from me (as seems to be supposed at home)' he informed Gladstone in a letter, 'I think the visit may do good'. For details of the visit, see *H.R.H. The Prince of Wales' Visit to India* (London, n.d.). Cohn aptly comments that these royal visits were significant in terms of the representation of the bond between the princes and people of India and their monarch. B.S.Cohn, op. cit., p. 152.

31. See Chap. IV.

32. Northbrook to Salisbury, 24 Nov. 1875, Northbrook Papers, reel 4.

33. Interestingly, Salar Jung invoked the aid of both the *Paigahs* and the Nizam's grandmother in the attempt to prevent the Nizam from going to Calcutta or Bombay. By consulting the ladies of the zenana and using their names, he often tried 'to protect himself from unreasonable interference of the Resident'. Karen Leonard, 'British Impact on Hyderabad', p. 40, and Server-ul-Mulk, *My Life* (London, 1932), p. 98. Server-ul-Mulk also relates how Saunders tried to influence the Nizam to go to Bombay and how unwilling Salar Jung was to send him. See pp. 144-5.

34. Northbrook to Queen, 13 Sept. 1875, ibid., reel 3.

35. Clerk to Northbrook, 10 Sept. 1875, ibid., reel 7.

36. Northbrook to Salisbury, 23 Aug. & 20 Sept. 1875, Northbrook Papers, reel 4.

37. Clerk to Northbrook, 10 Sept. 1875, ibid., reel 7.

38. Northbrook to Queen, 13 Sept. 1875, ibid., reel 3.

39. Northbrook to Salisbury, 20 Sept. 1875, ibid., reel 4.

40. Northbrook to Salisbury, 7 Oct. & 24 Nov. 1875, ibid.

41. Salisbury to Northbrook, 29 Sept. 1875, ibid.

42. Northbrook to Salisbury, 13 Sept. 1875, ibid.

43. Salisbury to Northbrook, 15 Oct. 1875, ibid.

44. Northbrook to Salisbury, 25 Feb. 1875; Salisbury to Northbrook, 20 Sept. 1875, ibid.

45. Res. to For. Secy., 31 Oct. 1875, For Pol. B Progs., Feb. 1877, no. 91.

46. Sir Henry Norman (1826-1904), member, G.G.'s Council, 1870-7; member, India Council, 1878-83.

47. Norman to Northbrook, 19 Oct. 1875, Northbrook Papers, reel 7.

48. Northbrook to Salisbury, 25 Oct. 1875, ibid., reel 4.

49. Rashid-ud-din Khan, Nawab Vikar-ul-Umra (d. 1881), an eminent nobleman in Hyderabad; half-brother of Rafi-ud-din Khan, Shums-ul-Umra II, Amir-i-Kabir; became Shums-ul-Umra Amir-i-Kabir and Co-Administrator of Hyderabad on Rafi-ud-din Khan's death in 1877.

50. Nawab Bashir-ud-Daula, Umdut-ul-Mulk, Azum-ul-Umra, Sir Asman Jah Bahadur (1839-98), nephew of Rafi-ud-din Khan, Amir-i-Kabir and Rashid-ud-din Khan, Vikar-ul-Umra; member, Council of Regency, 1883; Dewan, 1887-93.

51. Mohtashim-ud-Daula, brother of Bashir-ud-Daula; an important nobleman in Hyderabad.

52. Maharaja Narayan Pershad Narendar Bahadur (d. 1888), Peshkar, 1853; senior member of the Council of Regency, 1883–4.
53. Northbrook to Salisbury, 20 Oct. 1875, Northbrook Papers, reel 4.
54. Saunders to Northbrook, 8 Nov. 1875, ibid., reel 7.
55. Northbrook to Saunders, 5 & 12 Nov. 1875, ibid.
56. Northbrook to Salisbury, 24 Nov. 1875, ibid., reel 4.
57. Northbrook to Salisbury, 31 Dec. 1875, ibid.
58. *Friend of India*, 25 Sept. 1875 & 29 Jan. 1876.
59. Salisbury to Northbrook, 5 Nov., 10, 17 and 23 Dec. 1875, & 7 Jan. 1876; and Northbrook to Salisbury, 24 Nov. & 31 Dec. 1875, Northbrook Papers, reel 4.
60. Salisbury to Northbrook, 18 Feb. 1876, ibid.
61. B. Mallet, op. cit., p. 123.
62. Meade to For. Secy., D.O., 3 April 1876, For. Pol. A Progs., March 1877, K.W. Nos. 697-709.
63. Meade to Northbrook, 14 Feb. 1876 and Northbrook to Salisbury, 25 Feb. 1876, Northbrook Papers, reels 8 & 4.
64. Meade to Northbrook, 14 Feb. 1876; & Northbrook to Meade, 22 Feb. 1876, ibid., reel 8.
65. Mookaram-ud-Daula was the nephew and son-in-law of Salar Jung.
66. Res. to For. Secy., 23 Feb. 1876; & For. Secy. to Res., 11 March 1876, For. Pol. A Progs., April 1876, nos. 3 & 8.
67. Lytton to Salisbury, 14 April 1876, Lytton Papers, reel 5.
68. Lytton to Disraeli, 30 April 1876, ibid.
69. Lytton to Salisbury, 11 & 25 May 1876, ibid.
70. Lytton to Meade, 2 April 1877, ibid., reel 6.
71. Lytton to Salisbury, 11, 14 April & 11 May 1876; to Meade, 11 May 1876, ibid., reel 5.
72. Lytton to Queen, & to Salisbury, 20 Aug. 1876; to Prince of Wales, 21 April 1876, ibid.
73. Salisbury to Lytton, 18 Sept. 1876, ibid., reel 3.
74. Lytton to Meade, & to Salisbury, 2 May 1876, ibid., reel 5.
75. Meade to Lytton, 9 May 1876, ibid., reel 9.
76. Salisbury to Lytton, 16 June 1876, ibid., reel 3.
77. *The Friend of India*, 5, 12 & 19 Aug. 1876.
78. S. Gopal, *British Policy in India 1858-1905* (Cambridge, 1965), p. 113; *Friend of India*, 6 May, 3 June & 30 Dec. 1876.
79. Lytton to Queen, 4 May 1876; to Disraeli, 30 April 1876, Lytton Papers, reel 5.
80. Lytton to Queen, 21 April & 15 Nov. 1876; to Salisbury, 11 & 25 May 1876; Lytton's confidential note, 25.7.1877, ibid., reels 5 & 19.
81. Salisbury to Lytton, 9 June 1876, ibid., reel 1. Salisbury had earlier expressed similar views to Northbrook. See Salisbury to Northbrook, 25 Aug. 1875, Salisbury Papers, reel 7.
82. Lytton to Queen, 15 Nov. 1876; to Salisbury, 30 Oct. 1876, Lytton Papers, reel 6.
83. Lytton to Salisbury, 30 July 1876; to Queen, 12 Aug. 1876, ibid.
84. Queen to Lytton, 8 Dec. 1876; Salisbury to Lytton, 11 Aug. 1876, ibid., reels 33 & 1
85. Lytton to Disraeli, 30 April 1876, ibid., reel 5.
86. For details, see S. Gopal, op. cit., pp. 115-16.
87. Lytton to Salisbury, 20 Aug. 1876; to Meade, 21 Aug. 1876, Lytton Papers, reel 6.

88. ·Meade to Northbrook, 13 Jan. 1877, Northbrook Papers, reel 8; Meade to Lytton, 4 Sept. 1876; Lytton to Queen, 11 Sept. & 15 Nov. 1876, Lytton Papers, reels 6 & 10; Nizam's *khureeta* to G.G., For. Pol. A Consult., Dec. 1877, no. 499A.
89. Lytton to Salisbury, 18 Dec. 1876, Lytton Papers, reel 6.
90. Lytton to Meade, D.O., 24 Dec. 1876; note of a communications between Salar Jung and Meade from 24 to 27 Dec. 1876 & note of a private interview between Salar Jung and Lytton on 2 Jan. 1877, For. Sec. Progs. Dec. 1879, nos. 421, 423 & 429; Meade to Northbrook, 13 Jan. & 6 May 1877, Northbrook Papers, reel 8.
91. Notification by For. Dept. 30 Dec. 1876, For. Pol. A Progs., Dec. 1877, no. 579.
92. Extract from Financial Statement for 1877, published in Gazette of India Extraordinary, 15 March 1877, ibid., no. 495.
93. For a vivid description of the Durbar, see J.T. Wheeler, *The History of the Imperial Assemblage at Delhi* (London, n.d.), pp. 70-89, & *The Friend of India* and *Statesman*, 5 Jan. 1877.
94. H.T. Thornton, *General Sir Richard Meade and the Feudatory States of Central and Southern India* (London, 1898), p. 311.
95. Strictly Confidential memo of Euan Smith, 23 June 1877, For. Sec. Progs., Dec. 1879, K.W. 4, nos. 32-60, p. 44.
96. Lytton to Salisbury, 11 Jan. 1877, Lytton Papers, reel 6.
97. Salisbury to Lytton, 9 March 1877, ibid., reel 2; Meade to Northbrook, 13 Jan. 1877, Northbrook Papers, reel 8; drafts of letters, Salar Jung to Bright, 10 Feb., & to Bartle Frere, Lord Elcho & Henry Russell, 17 Feb. 1877, with copies of memorandum of conversation, Salar Jung Papers; Res. to Offg. For. Secy., 30 June & Offg. For. Secy. to Res., 10 Aug. 1877, For. Sec. Progs., Dec. 1879, nos. 334 & 338.
98. Meade to Lytton, 23 June & 23 July; Lytton to Meade, 12 July 1877, Lytton Papers, reels 6 & 12.
99. Lytton to Queen, 6 Aug. 1877, ibid., reel 6.
100. Lytton to Salisbury, 12 April 1877, ibid.
101. Salisbury to Lytton, 9 March & 11 May 1877, ibid., reel 4.
102. The titles of Amir-i-Kabir and Shums-ul-Umra were granted by the Nizam to Fakhr-ud-din Khan, who left two families, the senior branch headed by Rafi-ud-din Khan, and the junior one headed by Rashid-ud-din Khan. After Fakhr-ud-din Khan's death Rafi-ud-din got the titles. The head of the junior branch, Rashid-ud-din, whose title was Iktidar-ul-Mulk, was then given the title of Vikar-ul-Umra. On Afzal-ud-Daula's death, Rafi-ud-din, the Amir-i-Kabir, became Co-Regent. He adopted the sons of his brother, Sultan-ud-din Khan, viz., Bashir-ud-Daula and Mohtashim-ud-Daula and named them his successors.
103. Salar Jung to Res., D.O., 13 April 1877; & Res. to Offg. For. Secy., 22 June, 3 & 9 July 1877, For. Sec. Progs., Dec. 1879, K.W.4, nos. 328-60 & nos. 339 & 348.
104. Salar Jung to Res., 14 April 1877, ibid.
105. Res. to Salar Jung, 3 May 1877, ibid.; Meade to Northbrook, 6 Oct. 1877, Northbrook Papers, reel 8.
106. Lytton to Northbrook, 5 Aug. 1877, ibid.; to Salisbury, 14 July 1877, Lytton Papers, reel 6.
107. Salar Jung had told Euan Smith, the First Asst. Resident, that he would resign if the Vikar-ul-Umra was appointed Co-Regent. Apart from differences over policy, the two had a personal animosity. (This is clearly revealed in the Vikar-ul-Umra's letter of 3 Aug. 1877 to Euan Smith; For. Sec. Progs., Dec. 1879, no. 351. See also

Salar Jung to Richard Temple, 22 & 29 July 1867, Temple Collection, vol. 77.)

108.   Res. to For. Secy., Confidential, 28 May 1877, para 19, For. Sec. Progs., Dec. 1879, no. 328. Paras 17 to 23 of this letter were recast and a new letter substituted for the original one. This letter is to be read with For. Sec. Progs., Feb. 1882, nos. 410-18, where the whole story is told.

109.   Meade to Lytton, 23 June & 21 July 1877, Lytton Papers, reel 12.

110.   Lytton to Salisbury, 2 & 14 July, to Northbrook, 5 Aug. 1877, ibid., reel 6.

111.   Lytton to Meade, 12 July 1877, ibid.

112.   Meade to Lytton, 23 July 1877, ibid., reel 12.

113.   Lytton to Salisbury, 2 July 1877, ibid., reel 6.

114.   Lytton to Buckingham, 6 July 1877, ibid. The reference here is to a series of agreements concluded by the Govt. of India in 1877-9 with the princely states of Rajputana and Central India for controlling the manufacture of salt. The Govt. wanted to equalize salt duties throughout India. In the process, the duties were raised. For the official version of the policy, see John and Richard Stratchey, *The Finances and Public Works of India from 1869 to 1881* (London, 1882), pp. 217-25. For the Indian point of view, see Romesh Dutt, *The Economic History of India in the Victorian Age* (London, 1908), pp. 144-9, 524-5.

115.   Lytton to Salisbury, 9 July & 24 Sept. 1877, Lytton Papers, reeels 6 & 7.

116.   Salisbury to Lytton, 3 & 10 Aug. 1877, ibid., reel 4.

117.   For. Secy. to Res., 19 Aug. 1877, For. Sec. Progs., Dec. 1879, no. 332.

118.   Lytton to Salisbury, 5 Sept. 1877, Lytton Papers, reel 7.

119.   Meade to Northbrook, 6 Oct. 1877, Northbrook Papers, reel 8.

120.   Lytton to Salisbury, 23 Sept. 1877, Lytton Papers, reel 7. It is clear from these private letters that the principal actor on the British side was not Meade, but Lytton. The entire plan was Lytton's and he made careful arrangements for its successful execution.

121.   Salar Jung to Res., 22 Sept. 1877, For. Sec. Progs., Dec. 1879, no. 370.

122.   Meade to Northbrook, 6 Oct. 1877, Northbrook Papers, reel 8; Lytton to Salisbury, 24 Sept. 1877, Lytton Papers, reel 7; Res. to Salar Jung, 23 Sept. & note of interview between Salar Jung and Smith on 23 Sept. 1877, For. Sec. Progs., Dec. 1879, nos. 373 & 374.

123.   Salar Jung to Res., 24 Sept. 1877, ibid., no. 375.

124.   'Restitution of Berar-III', *London Statesman*, July 1881.

125.   Dinkar Rao, chief minister of Gwalior, 1851-9, rendered invaluable service to the British during the Revolt of 1857.

126.   Madhav Rao, chief minister of Travancore, became Dewan of Baroda after the Gaikwar's deposition.

127.   Res. to For. Secy., 10 Sept. 1881, For. Sec. Progs., Feb. 1882, no. 393.

128.   Draft of letter, Salar Jung to John Fleming, 20 Aug. 1878, Salar Jung Papers.

129.   Notification, 24 Sept. 1877, For. Sec. Progs., Dec. 1879, encl. no. 276; Meade to Lytton, 26 Sept. 1877, Lytton Papers, reel 13.

130.   Meade to Northbrook, 6 Oct. 1877, Northbrook Papers, reel 8.

131.   For a detailed description of the durbar & for the Resident's speech on the occasion, see supplement to *The Friend of India and Statesman*, 19 Oct. 1877. See also *London Statesman*, Oct. 1880, no. 5.

132.   Meade to Lytton, 26 Sept. 1877, Lytton Papers, reel 13.

133.   Lytton to Meade, 19 Aug. 1877, to Salisbury, 24 Sept. 1877, ibid., reel 7.

134. Salisbury to Lytton, 25 Oct. & 9 Nov. 1877, ibid., reel 2.

135. Ripon to Hartington, 21 Dec. 1881, Ripon Papers (British Museum), BP7/3, vol. 2.

136. *The Friend of India and Statesman*, 27 Oct. 1880 & *London Statesman*, Oct. 1880, no. 5.

137. The Vikar-ul-Umra had been found guilty in 1861 of trying to bribe Davidson's wife in order to obtain Salar Jung's removal from office. In consequence, he was forbidden to attend any durbar at which the Resident was present. This ban was removed by Mayo in 1869. See Salar Jung to Res., 17 Nov. 1862, Hyderabad Residency Records, vol. 106, p. 249; & Viceroy to Resident, tel., 27 Feb. 1869, For. Pol. A Progs., March 1869, no. 263.

138. Meade to Lytton, 26 Sept. 1877, Lytton Papers, reel 13.

139. *London Statesman*, Oct. 1880, no. 5; *The Friend of India and Statesman*, 20 & 27 Aug. 1878.

140. Bayley to Ripon, 26 April 1881, Ripon Papers, Add. MSS. 43612.

141. For. Secy. to Res., 23 Oct. 1877, For. Sec. Progs. Dec. 1879, no. 377.

142. Lytton to John Strachey, 7 Oct. 1877, Lytton Papers, reel 7.

143. Meade to Lytton, 18 Dec. 1877 & Meade's Confidential memo, 26 Jan. 1878, ibid., reel 14.

144. Lytton to Salisbury, 11 Oct. 1877; to Meade, 21 Oct. 1877, ibid., reel 7. Oliphant's appointment had been sanctioned by the Govt. of India on the Minister's application. For. Secy. to Res., 3 Feb. 1876, For. Pol. B Progs., April 1876, no. 25.

145. Lytton to Salisbury, 23 Nov. 1877; to Meade, 11 Dec. 1877; to Queen, 18 Jan. 1878; & to Lord George Hamilton, 7 Feb. 1878, Lytton Papers, reel 7.

146. For. Secy. to Res., 23 Oct. 1877, For. Sec. Progs., Dec. 1879, no. 379.

147. Meade to Lytton, 21 Feb. 1878, Lytton Papers, reel 14.

148. Lytton to Disraeli, 20 Dec. 1877, ibid., reel 7.

149. Salisbury to Lytton, 29 Nov. & 5 Dec. 1877, ibid., reel 2.

150. Salisbury to Lytton, 19 Dec. 1877, ibid.

151. Questions by Chaplin in the Commons, 28 Jan. 1878 & by Halifax in the Lords, 25 March 1878, *Hansard*, vol. 237, p. 530; & vol. 238, p. 1924.

152. Speeches by Hamilton in the Commons, 28 Jan. 1878; & by Salisbury in the Lords, 25 March 1878, *Hansard*, vol. 237, p. 530; & vol. 238, p. 1924. See *The Friend of India and Statesman*, 1 March 1878, for strong criticism of Salisbury's action.

153. Northbrook to Saunders, 10 Sept. 1874; to Salisbury, 2 Oct. 1874, Northbrook Papers, reels 4 & 6; Salisbury to Northbrook, 30 Oct. & 18 Nov. 1874, Salisbury Papers, reel 7.

154. Salisbury to Lytton, 7 April 1876, Lytton Papers, reel 3.

155. Lytton to Queen, 20 Aug. 1876, ibid., reel 6.

156. Lytton to Salisbury, 20 Aug. 1876, ibid.

157. Meade to Lyall, Confidential, 11 March 1880, ibid., reel 19.

158. Salisbury to Lytton, 18 Sept. 1876 ibid., reel 3.

159. Sec. Desp. S.S. to G.G., no. 34, 20 July 1876; For. Under Secy. to Res., 1 Nov. 1876; Res. to Offg. For. Secy., 6 Dec. 1876, For. Sec. Progs., Dec. 1879, nos. 479, 480 & 484.

160. Meade to Northbrook, 12 Aug., 1877, Northbrook Papers, reel 8.

161. Meade to Lytton, 23 June, 10 & 21 July 1877, Lytton Papers, reel 12.

162. Lytton to Salisbury, 18 Oct. 1877, ibid., reel 6.

163. Lytton to Salisbury, 25 May 1876, ibid., reel 5.

164. Report of the Native States' Armament Committee, 27 Oct. 1877, For. Sec. Sup., Dec. 1879, no. 333. The members of the Committee were E.B. Johnson, H.D. Daly, A.C. Lyall, P.S. Lumsden, F. Roberts, J. Watson and E.R.C. Bradford.
165. For. Secy. to Res., 15 Jan. 1878, For. Sec. Sup., Dec. 1879, no. 338.
166. Res. to Salar Jung, 21 Feb. & to For. Secy., 21 June 1878, ibid., nos. 358 & 359.
167. A return submitted by the Minister in 1880 showed a reduction in the number and cost of the army over 25 years, as follows:

	1262 *Fasli*	1270 *Fasli*	1284 *Fasli*	1288 *Fasli*
Men	33,816	32,704	31,350	30,701
Horse	5,631	5,176	5,235	5,031
Cost	Rs 78,70,629	Rs 67,64,736	Rs 66,88,308	Rs 66,06,812

Fin. Statement for 1288 *Fasli*, For. Pol. A Progs., Sept. 1881, no. 28.
168. Meade to Lytton, 8 Sept. 1877, Lytton Papers, reel 13.
169. Meade often intervened with Clerk's work. See Meade to Clerk, 9 March & 19 Oct. 1877, 15 Jan. & 22 April 1878, & 11 Feb. 1879, Claude Clerk Papers (India Office Library, London), MSS. EUR. D 538/14.
170. Lytton to Salisbury, 28 May 1877, Lytton Papers, reel 6.
171. Lytton to Salisbury, 24 Sept. 1877, ibid., reel 7.
172. For. Secy. to Res., 6 Aug. 1879, For. Pol. A Progs., Sept. 1879, no. 14; Res. to For. Secy., tel., 10 April 1880, For. Pol. A Progs., June 1880, no. 125.
173. Res. to For. Secy., D.O., 28 Jan. & 12 March 1880, ibid., K.W. Nos. 117-35.
174. Dowding's report, 30 June 1880, For. Pol. A Progs., Aug. 1881, no. 107; & Clerk's memorandum, 3 May 1881, For. Pol. A Progs., Feb. 1882, no. 462.
175. Salisbury to Lytton, 15 April 1878, Lytton Papers, reel 4.
176. Lytton to Queen, 4 May 1880, ibid., reel 9.
177. Lytton to Cranbrook, 15 July 1878, ibid., reel 7.
178. Lytton to Ripon, 8 June 1880, ibid., reel 9.
179. *The Friend of India and Statesman*, 27 Oct. 1880.
180. Ripon to Gladstone, 2 Oct. 1880 & 22 Oct. 1881, Gladstone Papers, Add. MSS, 44286.
181. Ripon to Hartington, 25 March & 17 Dec. 1881, Ripon Papers, BP 7/3, vol. 2.
182. Ripon to Northbrook, 11 July 1881, & 21 Jan. 1882, Northbrook Papers, reel 1.
183. Res. to For. Secy., 20 Aug. 1881; & For. Secy. to Res., 9 Jan. 1882, For. Pol. A Progs., Feb. 1882, nos. 460, 464; S.S. to G.G., 23 Feb. 1882, For. Pol. A Progs., May 1882, no. 224.
184. For a discussion of the opium policy of the British, see M. Greenberg, *British Trade and the Opening of China, 1800-1842* (Cambridge, 1951), D.E. Owen, *British Opium Policy in China and India* (New Haven, 1934), K.N. Chaudhuri (ed.), *The Economic Development of India under the East India Company, 1814-58* (Cambridge, 1971), & John Strachey & Richard Strachey, op. cit., ch. 14.
185. Resolution by Fin. & Com. Dept., 19 July 1879, For. Pol. A Progs., March 1880, no. 579.
186. For. Secy. to Res., 20 Nov. 1879, ibid., no. 581.
187. Res. to For. Secy., 11 Feb. 1881; Offg. Fin. & Com. Under Secy. to Res., 27 May 1881, For. Pol. A Progs., Jan. 1882, nos. 147 & 153; Opium Rules issued by the Nizam's Govt., For. Pol. B Progs., July 1882, no. 82. A formal agreement between the two Governments was concluded after Salar Jung's death. See C.U. Aitchison, op. cit., pp. 131-2.

188. Bayley to Ripon, 26 April & 2 & 24 Sept. 1881, Ripon Papers, Add. MSS. 43612.
189. Ripon to Bayley, 13 Dec. 1881, ibid., BP 7/6, vol. 2.
190. Ripon to Hartington 17 & 21 Dec. 1881 & 7 Jan. 1882, ibid., BP 7/3, vols. 2 & 3.
191. Ripon to Northbrook, 9 & 21 Jan. 1882, Northbrook Papers, reel 1.
192. Bayley to Ripon, 24 Sept. 1881, Ripon Papers, Add. MSS. 43612,
193. For details, see For. Sec. Progs., May 1883, nos. 23-100. See also Claude Clerk Papers, for details of the politics concerning the visit. It appears that Clerk did not want Salar Jung to accompany the young Nizam and felt that the Minister was unwilling to let anyone else come in close contact with him.
194. Res. to For. Secy., 9 Feb. 1883, For. A Pol. I Progs., April 1883, no. 95. For touching details of Salar Jung's death, see Syed Hossain Bilgrami & C. Willmott, op. cit., vol. I, pp. 179-81.
195. Hyderabad Govt. Gazette Extraordinary, ibid., p. 185.
196. Res. to Grant, cipher tel., 10 Feb. 1883, encl. to Grant to Ripon, 11 Feb. 1883, Ripon Papers, Add. MSS. 43604.
197. Bayley to Grant, 11 Feb. 1883, ibid.
198. Karen Leonard, 'Hyderabad : The Mulki—Non-Mulki Conflict', p. 73. For contemporary account of the political situation, see Dinshah Ardeshir Taleyarkhan, *The Jubilee Dawn in Nizam's Hyderabad, 1887* (Bombay, 1887), pp. 1-9.
199. Nawab Mir Laik Ali Khan, Munir-ud-Daula (1862-89), son of Sir Salar Jung; became Nawab Salar Jung II on his father's death; Secretary, Council of Regency, 1883; Dewan, 1884-7.
200. Grant to Ripon, 11 Feb. 1883, Ripon Papers, Add. MSS. 43604.
201. Bayley to Grant, 11 Feb. 1883, & Grant to Ripon, 11 Feb. 1883, ibid.
202. Bayley to For. Secy., 22 Feb. 1883, For. Sec. I Progs., April 1883, no. 29. In this official letter Bayley seems to have changed his view, presumably to make an arrangement acceptable to all. He advised against the immediate appointment of Laik Ali as the Dewan.
203. Ripon to Kimberley, 5 March 1883, Ripon Papers, BP 7/3, vol. 4.
204. Kimberley to Ripon, 9 March & 20 April, 1883, ibid., Add. MSS. 43523.
205. W.S. Blunt, *India Under Ripon. A Private Diary* (London, 1909), p. 72.
206. Bayley to Ripon, 11 Dec. 1883, Ripon Papers, Add. MSS. 43612.
207. Cordery to Ripon, 2 Dec. 1883, ibid., Add. MSS. 43613.
208. Cordery to Ripon, 19 Jan. 1884, ibid.
209. Ripon to Kimberley, 15 Jan. 1884, ibid., BP 7/3, vol. 5.
210. Bayley to Ripon, 25 Dec. 1883, ibid., Add. MSS. 43612. The Nizam had also asked Clerk to inform the Govt. of India that Salar Jung 'ought to be' appointed as the Dewan. Clerk to Cordery, 5 Jan. 1884, ibid., Add. MSS 43613.
211. Ripon to Kimberley, 15 Jan. 1884, ibid., BP 7/3, vol. 5.
212. Kimberley to Ripon, 15 & 16 Nov. 1883 & Feb. 1884, ibid., Add. MSS. 43524. Unfortunately, Salar Jung II soon fell out with the Nizam, probably because he was excessively influenced by the non-Mulki and Residency officials, thereby offending the conservative opposition and the Nizam himself. A contemporary remarked that his friendship with the Nizam had been 'too youthful and too warm' to be lasting. He resigned in 1887. See Dinshah Ardeshir Taleyarkhan, op.cit., pp. 10-13, 20-30; & Karen Leonard, 'Hyderabad:the Mulki-Non-Mulki Conflict', p. 75.
213. S. Gopal, *Viceroyalty of Lord Ripon, 1880-4* (Oxford, 1953), p. 212.

Chapter IV THE QUESTION OF BERAR

1. For details, see Prologue.
2. 7,53,571 acres of land were under cotton in 1861-2, 16,66,014 acres in 1872-3. The end of the American Civil War deflated the demand for cotton from Lancashire, so surplus cotton was sent to Bombay in increasing quantities—from 38,150 tons in 1867-8 to 45,597 tons in 1874. Berar Report by O.T. Burne, For. Sec. Progs., Oct. 1874, K.W.2, nos. 33-43; & Office-memo of the A.R.& C. Dept. to For. Secy., 24 June 1874, For. Genl. B Progs., Sept. 1874, no. 6. For Berar cotton fabrics, see R. V. Garrett, *Monograph On Cotton Fabrics in the Hyderabad Assigned Districts* (Hyderabad, 1897).
3. *The Imperial Gazetteer of India* (Oxford, 1908), vol. 7, p. 404.
4. Salar Jung complained that these railways were built out of the surplus revenues of Berar without the permission of his Govt. Draft of letter, Salar Jung to J. Oliphant, 16/6 (year not mentioned), Salar Jung Papers, file 314.
5. First Asst. Res. to For. Secy., 19 Dec. 1867, For. Fin. A Progs., June 1868, no. 4.
6. J.D.B. Gribble, *A History of the Deccan* (London, 1924), vol. 2, p. 231.
7. Draft of letter, Salar Jung to H. Russell, 17 Feb. 1877, Salar Jung Papers, file no. 299/4.
8. Salar Jung to Res., 19 Sept. 1872, For. Sec. Progs., Jan. 1874, no. 60.
9. Yule to Lawrence, 20 Aug. 1866, Lawrence Papers, reel 11.
10. Temple to Northbrook, 25 Jan. 1875, Northbrook Papers, reel 7.
11. Salar Jung to Northbrook, 27 April 1877, ibid., reel 8.
12. See my article, 'Salar Jung, Berar and the British', *The Calcutta Historical Journal*, vol. 2, no. 1, July-Dec. 1977, pp 105-6.
13. Wood to Denison, 9 Sept. 1863, Wood Papers (IO), LB 14. Wood expressed similar views to Canning and Elgin. Wood to Canning, 18 Aug. & 25 Dec. 1861; to Elgin, 24 Sept. 1862, ibid., LB 8, 9 & 11.
14. *Khureeta* from Maharajah of Mysore to Lawrence, 25 Jan. 1865, *PP. 29 of 1867-8*, pp. 66-7.
15. G.G. to S.S., 5 May 1865, ibid., pp 54-6.
16. C.U. Aitchison, op.cit., p. 59.
17. For debates in Parliament on Mysore on 19 July 1866, 22 Feb. & 24 May 1867, see *Hansard*, vol. 184, p. 1107, vol. 185, pp 828-41, & vol. 187, pp 1027-75.
18. Yule to Lawrence, 20 Aug. 1866, Lawrence Papers, reel 11.
19. Yule to Lawrence, 25 Oct. 1866, ibid.
20.

Revenue of Kurnool less *peshkush*	Rs 17,00,000
½ of the revenue from Goomsoor	Rs 1,50,000
½ of the revenue from Mysore	Rs 41,50,000
Total	Rs 60,00,000

21. Salar Jung to Res., 29 Oct. 1866, For. Pol. A Consult., Feb. 1867, no. 82.
22. Res. to For. Secy., *PP. 29 of 1867-8*, p. 317.
23. Yule to Lawrence, 20 Aug. 1866, Lawrence Papers, reel 11.
24. Lawrence to Cranborne, 20 Sept. 1866; to Northcote, 2 May 1867, ibid., reels 3 & 7
25. Lawrence to Cranborne, 19 Dec. 1866, ibid., reel 7.
26. Offg. Secy. Govt. of India to Res., 13 Feb. 1867, For. Pol. A Consult., Feb. 1867, no. 83.

27. Lawrence to Cranborne, 19 Dec. 1866, Lawrence Papers, reel 7.
28. Cranborne to Lawrence, 4 Feb. 1867, ibid., reel 4.
29. Offg. Secy. Govt. of India to Res., 13 Feb. 1867, For. Pol. A Consult., Feb. 1867, no. 83.
30. Northcote to Lawrence, 26 May 1867, Lawrence Papers, reel 4.
31. Yule to Lawrence, 1 Dec. 1866, ibid., reel 11.
32. Northcote to Lawrence, 26 March, 3 & 20 April 1867; Lawrence to Northcote, 2 & 16 May 1867, ibid., reels 1 & 3.
33. Lawrence to Cranborne, 19 Dec. 1866, ibid., reel 7.
34. Extract from Fin. Progs., Govt. of India, 12 Sept. 1867, For. Genl. Progs., Sept. 1867, no. 42.
35. Report of Hyderabad Commission on expenditure, civil, military & political, 10 Aug. 1861, For. Fin. A Progs., April 1862, no. 18. Col. Davidson, R. Temple & Col. Browne were the members of the Commission.
36. For. Sec. Progs. May 1874, K. W. 2, nos. 103–12.
37. Northcote to Lawrence, 2 Dec. 1867, Lawrence Papers, reel 4.
38. Pol. Desp., S.S. to G.G., 4 March 1869, For. Genl. A Progs., April 1869, no. 41.
39. 1st Asst. Res. to For. Secy., 18 Dec. 1867, For. Genl. A Progs., Jan. 1868, no. 27; Res. to Salar Jung, 3 Nov. 1871, For. Pol. A Consult., Jan. 1872, no. 228; C.U. Aitchison, op.cit., pp 116-21
40. Moulavi Cherag Ali, op. cit., vol. 1, p. 23.
41. Salar Jung's reasons for building up the Reformed Troops were neatly summarized in his letter to Capt. John Clerk. Draft of the letter, 5 Dec. 1881, Salar Jung Papers.
42. Drafts of letters, Salar Jung to T.G.A. Palmer, 30 Aug. 1871, ibid., file no. 298/3-2; see also drafts of letters, Salar Jung & Bowen to Palmer, 1 3 & 12 June, 7 Aug., 26 Sept., 1 Nov. & 20 & 28 Dec. 1871, instructing Palmer to negotiate with the Oriental Bank in order to raise money for the restoration of Berar, ibid., file no. 299/1.
43. Palmer to Salar Jung, 30 Aug. 1871, 19 Jan. & 21 April 1872, ibid., packets 18A & 285.
44. Chief Manager, Oriental Bank to Salar Jung (n.d.); Remington & Co. to Salar Jung, 16 May 1872; Palmer to Salar Jung, 9 Feb. 1872, ibid., packet 285. The Oriental Bank's terms were mentioned in their letter to Palmer, 24 May 1872, ibid., packet 18A.
45. Palmer to Salar Jung, 2 April & 24 May 1872, ibid., packet 285.
46. For these paragraphs in Dalhousie's minute & Low's letter, see *P.P. 418 of 1854*, pp 109, 114 & 122.
47. Salar Jung to Res., 19 Sept. 1872, For. Sec. Progs., Jan. 1874, no. 60. Act 37, Geo III, Chap. 142 (Sec. 28) prohibited borrowing from British subjects by Indian states and princes. The Secy. of State's permission was thus necessary to borrow money in England.
48. Northbrook to Argyll, 3 Oct. & 14 Nov. 1872, Argyll Papers, reel 7.
49. For. Secy. to Res., 24 Sept. 1873, For. Sec. Progs., Jan. 1874, no. 61.
50. To prove that Dalhousie was determined to use force if necessary, Salar Jung referred to paras 46-9 of the G.G.'s minute of 30 March 1853. See *P.P. 418 of 1854*, p. 113.
51. Here the reference is to Low's minute on a private conference with the Nizam, 12

March 1853, ibid., p. 95. See also 'Hyderabad—the Nizam's Contingent', *Calcutta Review*, vol. XI, 1849, p. 146.

52.   On 28 Nov. 1853 the Govt. of India ordered that from 1 Jan. 1854 the Contingent would be re-organized, the number of Europeans decreased and its cost reduced, For. Sec. Progs., Jan. 1874, K.W.I., nos. 59-62. The following table gives a rough idea of the changes made :

	European officers	Non-commissioned officers	Indians			Camp followers
			Cavalry	Infantry	Artillery	
1853-4	76	82	2910	6731	37	881
1854-5	49	56	2300	6282	24	644

Return of Hyderabad Contingent, Part II, For. Sec. I. Progs., July 1883, no. 15;

53.   See dissent of Moore, *P.P. 234 of 1859*, p. 4 & Res. to For. Secy., 12 Oct. 1860, *P.P. (The Deccan) 338 of 1867*, p. 27.

54.   The Co-Regents to Res., 24 Nov. 1873, For. Sec. Progs., May 1874, no. 103A.

55.   Northbrook to Salisbury, 27 March & 2 Oct. 1874, Northbrook Papers, reel 4.

56.   Northbrook to Salisbury, 3 April, 26 May & 16 June 1874, ibid. These letters disprove Moulton's view that Northbrook was sympathetic to Hyderabad's claims. See E.C. Moulton, op.cit., p. 127. Northbrook had merely admitted that the treaties might be revised, but certainly wanted to make the revision difficult, if not impossible, from Hyderabad's point of view. Salar Jung later complained that Northbrook had closed the prospect of revision. Draft of letter, Salar Jung to Fleming (n.d.), Salar Jung Papers.

57.   Salisbury to Northbrook, 24 April, 1 & 28 May & 2 Sept. 1874, Salisbury Papers, reel 7.

58.   Pol. Desp., S.S. to G.G., 17 July 1874, For. Sec. Progs., Oct. 1874, no. 36.

59.   Res. to For. Secy., 22 Aug. 1874, ibid., no. 39. Ibid., no. 40A for English version of the Resident's speech on 21 Aug. 1874.

60.   Northbrook to Saunders, 10 Sept. 1874; to Salisbury, 27 Nov. 1874, Northbrook Papers, reels 4 & 6.

61.   Salisbury to Northbrook, 30 Oct. 1874, Salisbury Papers, reel 7.

62.   *The Friend of India and Statesman*, 30 Nov. 1877. See also Keay's interesting letters to Bowen, 24, 26 & 28 Aug. 1874, Salar Jung Papers, packet 18A.

63.   Salar Jung to Richard Temple, 9 Feb. 1875, Temple Collection, vol. 77; draft of letter, Salar Jung to Yule, 7 July 1875; memo on reasons why Amir-i-Kabir should sign the next letter to the Res. (n.d.), Salar Jung Papers, files 314 & 293.

64.   Co-Regents to Res., 6 July 1874, For. Sec. Progs., Oct. 1874, no. 34.

65.   Northbrook to Queen, 8 Jan. 1875, Northbrook Papers, reel 3.

66.   Pol. Desp., G.G. to S.S., 2 Oct. 1874, For. Sec. Progs., Oct. 1874, no. 42 & Sec. Desp., G.G. to S.S., 1 Jan. 1875, For. Sec. Progs., Dec. 1879, no. 404.

67.   Salisbury to Northbrook, 30 Oct. 1874 & 25 Aug. 1875, Salisbury Papers, reel 7.

68.   Northbrook to Salisbury, 30 Sept. 1875, Northbrook Papers, reel 4.

69.   Salisbury to Northbrook, 24 April 1874, & 25 Aug. & 19 Nov. 1875, Salisbury Papers, reel 7.

70.   Salisbury to Northbrook, 25 Aug. 1875. ibid.

71.   Northbrook to Salisbury, 26 July 1875, Northbrook Papers, reel 4.

72. Northbrook to Salisbury, 8 Jan. & 26 July 1875, ibid.
73. Salisbury to Northbrook, 25 Aug. 1875, Salisbury Papers, reel 7.
74. Northbrook to Salisbury, 30 Sept. 1875, Northbrook Papers, reel 4; & Salisbury to Northbrook, 19 Nov. 1875, Salisbury Papers, reel 7.
75. Aitchison to Northbrook, 23 Sept. 1875, Northbrook Papers, reel 7.
76. Meade to Northbrook, 30 Dec. 1875, ibid ; draft of letter, Salar Jung to Col. J. Oliphant, 16/6 (year not mentioned), Salar Jung Papers, file no. 314.
77. Draft of letter, Salar Jung to Fleming, 30 July 1878, ibid.
78. Drafts of letters, Salar Jung to Bowen, 21 June 1870; to Palmer, 30 Aug. 1871, ibid., file nos. 299/1 & 298/3-2.
79. Drafts of letters, Salar Jung to Agent, Oriental Bank Corporation, Bombay, 20 May 1875; to Yule, 7 July 1875, ibid., file no. 314. Several letters in the State Archives, Andhra Pradesh, throw interesting light on the subject. Of particular interest are the Salar Jung - Palmer correspondence, 1872-6; Keay to Bowen, 31 July, 20 Aug. & 18 Sept. 1874, & Oliphant to Salar Jung, 11 July 1876, ibid., file no. 298/3-2.
80. Palmer to Salar Jung, 19 Jan. 1872, ibid., packet 285.
81. Salisbury to Northbrook, 28 May, 24 July & 20 Nov. 1874; to B. Ellis, 12 Sept. 1874, Salisbury Papers, reel 7.
82. Northbrook to Salisbury, 26 May, 20 Aug. & 2 Oct. 1874, Northbrook Papers, reel 4.
83. Salisbury to Northbrook, 18 Nov. 1874, 27 Jan. & 5 Feb. 1875, Salisbury Papers, reel 7.
84. Draft of letter, Salar Jung to Palmer, 8 Jan., 26 Feb., 18 March & 1 April 1876, Salar Jung Papers, file no. 299/4. 'If you ever visit England', Oliphant wrote to Salar Jung as early as 14 Nov. 1872, 'you will see, the Prince will be your friend'. Ibid., packet 188.
85. Palmer to Salar Jung, 3 March 1876, ibid., packet 18C.
86. Salisbury to Lytton, 16 June & 28 July 1876, Lytton Papers, reel 3.
87. K. Sajun Lal, 'Sir Salar Jung's visit to England and the Berar Question', *Journal of Osmania University*, Golden Jubilee Volume, 1968, pp. 138-9.
88. Draft of letter, Salar Jung to Fitzgerald, 29 March 1877, Salar Jung Papers; Meade to Northbrook, 13 Jan. 1877, Northbrook Papers reel 6.
89. For details, see Chap. III.
90. Note of communication between Salar Jung and Meade, 24-27 Dec. 1876, & note of private interview between Salar Jung and Lytton, 2 Jan. 1877, For. Sec. Progs., Dec. 1879, nos. 429 & 423.
91. Lytton to Salisbury, 16 March 1877, Lytton Papers, reel 6.
92. Co-Regents to Res., 7 Feb.; & Salar Jung to Res. 10 April, 1877, For. Sec. Progs., Dec. 1879, nos. 415 & 417.
93. Lytton to Salisbury, 25 April 1877, Lytton Papers, reel 6.
94. Pol. Desp., G.G. to S.S., 11 June 1877, For. Sec. Progs., Dec. 1879, no. 419.
95. Salisbury to Lytton, 27 Oct. 1876 & 15 March 1877, Lytton Papers, reel 4; Sec. Desp., S.S. to G.G., 28 March 1878, For. Sec. Progs., Dec. 1879, no. 441.
96. Meade to Northbrook, 13 Aug. 1878, Northbrook Papers, reel 8.
97. Lytton to O.T. Burne, 16 June 1878, Lytton Papers, reel 7.
98. *The Friend of India and Statesman*, 30 Nov. 1877, 25 June & 2 July 1878.
99. *The Times of India*, 24 July 1876.
100. Drafts of letters, Salar Jung to Fleming, 23 July (year not mentioned) & 30 July

1878, Salar Jung Papers. Fleming had complained that the pledge given by Salar Jung was 'embarrassing' for his friends and restricted their action in Parliament. Fleming to Salar Jung, 24 June 1878, ibid., file no. 314.

101.   Draft of letter, Salar Jung to Yule, 6 Dec. 1881, ibid. Yule had earlier informed Salar Jung that the Liberal Party was sympathetic to his cause. Yule to Salar Jung, 10 Oct. 1881, ibid., file no. 291/2.

102.   Speeches by Balfour and Hartington, 11 & 25 Aug. 1881, *Hansard*, vol. 264, p. 1528 & vol. 265, p. 875.

103.   Bayley to Ripon, 24 Sept. 1881, Ripon Papers, Add. MSS. 43,612.

104.   Hartington to Ripon, 7 Sept. 1882, Ripon Papers, Add. MSS. 43,569.

105.   Bayley to Ripon, 28 Dec. 1882 & 7 Feb. 1883, ibid., Add. MSS. 43612.

106.   Jones to Grant, 18 Jan. 1883, encl. to Grant to Ripon, 23 Jan. 1883, ibid., Add. MSS. 43,604.

107.   Ripon to Hartington, 24 Feb., 19 May, 7 June 1882, ibid., BP 7/3, vol. 3.

108.   Ripon to Kimberley, 10 Feb. 1883, ibid., vol. 4.

109.   Hamilton to Curzon, 17 Aug. 1899, & 16 May & 17 Oct. 1901, Curzon Papers (microfilm, National Archives of India), reels 1 & 2.

110.   Salisbury to Lytton, 16 Feb. 1877, Lytton Papers, reel 4.

111.   Salisbury to Lytton, 7 April 1876, ibid., reel 3.

112.   Steeped in conservatism since his Eton and Oxford days, this Derbyshire noble-man was the choice of Prime Minister Salisbury, under whom he had served as Under Secretary of State for India and Under Secretary for Foreign Affairs. He was naturally deeply influenced by Salisbury's views.

113.   Curzon to Hamilton, 22 April, 18 & 25 Sept. & 26 Dec. 1901, Curzon Papers reel 2.

114.   Hamilton to Curzon, 17 Oct., 12 & 26 Dec. 1901, & 25 March 1902; Ritchie to Curzon, 11 Feb. 1902, ibid.

115.   Curzon to Hamilton, 20 & 27 March & 2 April 1902, ibid., reel 3. Hamilton was emphatic in his opposition to the Viceroy visiting Hyderabad. 'I should be most reluctant', he wrote, 'that you should in any way be associated or connected with negotiations which either failed, or, which were brought to a conclusion by your exercising personally upon the Nizam the authority and coercion of a Viceroy.' Hamilton to Curzon, 13, 20 & 25 March, ibid., reel 2.

116.   Curzon to Hamilton, 2 & 9 April 1902, ibid., reel 2. For the official version of the story see G.G. to S.S., 13 Nov. 1902, *P.P.C. 1321 of 1902*, pp. 6-8. The state of Hyderabad was allegedly 'a substantial gainer' from the transaction. Ronaldshay, *The Life of Lord Curzon* (London, 1928), vol. II, gives an even more glorified picture of Curzon's achievements regarding Berar.

117.   W.S. Blunt, op. cit., p. 207.

118.   For the terms of the treaty, see. C.U. Aitchison, op. cit., p. 175.

Chapter V THE INTRODUCTION OF RAILWAYS

1.   For an analysis of the motives of the three main groups interested in the enterprise, viz., the Govt of India, the investors and promoters, and the business groups in U.K., see W.J. Macpherson, 'Investment in Indian Railways, 1845-73', *The Economic History Review*, vol. 8, second series (1955). For a contemporary

analysis of the reasons for building of railways in India, see John Dickinson, *Remarks on the Indian Railway Reports Published by the Government and Reasons for a change of Policy in India* (London, 1862), pp 21–2.

2. Arthur Silver, op. cit., gives a good account of the impact of this pressure on the British Government.
3. With the Industrial Revolution, the production of factory-made cotton goods had expanded very rapidly in Britain. But it was said that the vast population of India consumed less cloth than a few thousand in Australia or Brazil.
4. For the negotiations which preceded the contracts and for their terms, see Daniel Thorner, *Investment in Empire* (Philadelphia, 1950), pp. 119-60, 169-72. Thorner points out that manufacturers and businessmen from Manchester, 'the heart of *laissez faire*', continually clamoured in Parliament and campaigned outside Parliament, urging governmental intervention for the speedy construction of India's railways.
5. Wood to Dalhousie, 8 & 24 March 1853, Wood Papers (IB), LB 3. One can question West's statement that Wood put the wider interests of India before the selfish motives of Cottonpolis. See A. West, *Sir Charles Wood's Indian Administration* (London, 1867), p. 116.
6. Wood considered Dalhousie 'a great authority' on the subject, presumably because Dalhousie had acquired much experience in railway administration as President of the Board of Trade.
7. Wood to Dalhousie, 22 Jan. 1853, Wood Papers (IB), LB 3. Wood was in favour of private companies building these railways under governmental control. 'I should like to send private capital to India', observed Wood.
8. Minute by Dalhousie, 20 April 1853, *P.P. 787 of 1852-3*, pp. 113-42.
9. Wood to Dalhousie, 25 July & 20 Oct. 1853, Wood Papers (IB), LB 3.
10. In 1859 the construction of 5000 miles of railroad by eight companies was sanctioned. The Govt.of India was to guarantee interest at rates varying between 4½% to 5% per annum. Vera Anstey, *The Economic Development of India* (London, 1949), p. 101.
11. Salar Jung to Res., 13 Aug. 1860; C.U. Aitchison, op. cit., p. 107; Salar Jung to Res., 26 Jan. 1861, Hyderabad Residency Records, vol. 106, p. 135.
12. Frere to Wood, 25 July & 4 Oct. 1862, Wood Papers, 88/3 & 88/4.
13. Wood to Frere, 29 Aug. & 16 Nov. 1862, ibid., (IO) LB 11.
14. Wood to Denison, 10 & 26 Nov. & 27 Dec. 1862, ibid.
15. Denison to Wood, 25 Dec. 1861, Wood Papers, 87/1.
16. Denison to Wood, 4 Dec. 1862, 7 Jan. & 4 Feb. 1863, ibid. 87/2 & 87/3.
17. Wood to Elgin, 3 March 1863; to Denison, 10 March 1863, ibid. (IO) LB 12.
18. Wood to Trevelyan, 18 March 1863, ibid.
19. Yule to Elgin, 18 May 1863, Elgin Papers, vol. 17.
20. Ibid. As early as 1861 Salar Jung had contributed Rs 5,000 from his private purse to the G.I.P. Co. for the survey of a line from Sholapur to Hyderabad. The Company had not proceeded with the work and reimbursed the money. Res. to For. Secy., 26 June 1861, For. Part A Prog., Aug. 1861, no. 100.
21. Elgin to Yule, 11 July 1863, Elgin Papers, vol. 17.
22. Yule to P.W.D. Secy., Govt of India, 17 Nov. 1863, For. Genl. A Prog., Dec. 1863, no. 58.
23. Lawrence to Wood, 3 April 1864, Wood Papers, 113(2).

24. Wood to Denison, 10 March 1863, ibid. (IO) LB 12.
25. Wood to Elgin, 3 March 1863, ibid.
26. Wood to Lawrence, 15 Oct. 1864, ibid., LB 18.
27. Temple to Salar Jung, D.O., 10 Dec. 1867 & the heads of arguments encl. with the letter, Temple Collection, vol. 76.
28. Salar Jung to Temple, 13 Dec. 1867, ibid., vol. 77.
29. Temple to Salar Jung, D.O., 17 Dec. 1867, ibid., vol. 76.
30. Salar Jung to Temple 13 & 26 Dec. 1867, ibid., vol. 77.
31. Pol. diary of Temple, 27 Dec. 1867, ibid., vol. 81.
32. Salar Jung to Temple, 17, 21 Dec. 1867, ibid., vol. 77.
33. Pol. diary of Temple, 27 Dec. 1867, ibid., vol. 81.
34. Ibid., 30 Dec. 1867; Min. to Res., 31 Dec. 1867, For. Genl. A Prog., Feb. 1868, no. 14.
35. For. Secy. to Res., 16 April 1868, For. Genl. A Prog., April 1868, no. 88.
36. W.W. Hunter, op. cit., p. 169.
37. Mayo to Frere, 21 Aug. 1869, Mayo Papers, reel 1.
38. Argyll agreed whole-heartedly with Mayo's railway policy. Argyll to Mayo, 23 April 1869, ibid., reel 7; speech by Argyll, 23 July 1869, *Hansard*, vol. 198, p. 533.
39. Report of the Select Committee on East India Finance, 28 July 1874, *P.P. 329 of 1874*. See also N. Sanyal, *Development of Indian Railways* (Calcutta, 1930). pp. 63-8, 70-8.
40. P.W.D. Railway Desp., G.G. to S.S., 6 Jan. 1870. This decision was approved by Argyll. Railway Desp., S.S. to G.G., 13 April & 26 Oct. 1870, *P.P. 156 of 1871*, pp. 19 & 30-3.
41. Mayo to Argyll, 29 Oct. 1869, Argyll Papers, reel 2; Mayo to Fitzgerald, 2 Oct. 1869, Mayo Papers, reel 2.
42. Mayo to Saunders, 18 Oct. 1869, Mayo papers, reel 2. Later, Mayo refused to set aside any stipulated amount from the Berar revenues for payment of the guaranteed interest on the grounds that it would be embarrassing to provide for a given surplus at any given moment. Whatever actual surplus accrued, however, would go to the Nizam. For. Secy. to Res., D.O., 4 March 1870, For. Genl. A Prog., Sept. 1870, no. 5.
43. Mayo to Saunders, 29 Nov. 1869, Mayo Papers, reel 2.
44. Mayo to Saunders, 18 Oct. 1869, ibid.
45. Mayo to Argyll, 22 Feb. 1870, Argyll Papers, reel 2. Bawa is wrong in arguing that the railway negotiations were characterized by close co-operation between Salar Jung, the Res. and the Viceroy. See V.K. Bawa, 'Salar Jung and the Nizam's State Railway, 1860-1883', *The Indian Economic and Social History Review* (1965), vol. 2, no. 4, pp. 312-13. The Hyderabad Minister did not co-operate, he merely yielded.
46. Salar Jung to Res., 9 Jan. & 2 Feb. 1870, & translation of his scheme, For. Genl. A Prog., Sept. 1870, encl no. 4.
47. G.B. Mullick, op. cit., pp. 69-70.
48. Mayo to Argyll, 22 March 1870, Argyll Papers, reel 2.
49. C.U. Aitchison, op. cit., pp. 110-13.
50. Mayo to Argyll, 22 Feb., 29 March, 30 April, 20 May 1870, Argyll Papers, reel 2. Mayo had previously advised Argyll not to offer Salar Jung this reward until the railway question was settled. Mayo to Argyll, 29 Oct. 1869, ibid.

51. Draft of letter, Salar Jung to Oliphant, 16/6 (year not mentioned), Salar Jung Papers.
52. A.C. Campbell, *Glimpses of the Nizam's Dominions* (Bombay, 1898), p. 145.
53. *Hyderabad Affairs*, vol. 4, p. 178.
54. W.S. Blunt, op. cit., p. 191.
55. *Hyderabad Affairs*, vol. 4, p. 178.
56. See map facing page 143.
57. For comparative costs of construction and maintenance of broad-gauge and narrow-gauge railways, see Danvers's Railway Report for 1870-1, *P.P.C. 418 of 1871*, para 12. A committee appointed by the Govt of India decided in favour of the narrow gauge in India. Report of the committee, 26 Sept. 1870, *P.P. 156 of 1871*, pp. 33-8. For Mayo's view regarding narrow gauge and his recommendation for its adoption, see P.W.D. Railway Desp., G.G. to S.S., 17 May 1870, ibid., pp. 25-7.
58. Speech by Argyll, 23 July 1869, *Hansard*, vol. 198, pp 527-36. Macpherson points out that no purely military railway was built until the 1870's, although later military considerations became very important. W.M. Macpherson, op. cit., p. 178.
59. P.W.D. Secy., Govt of India to Res., 15 July 1871, For. Genl. A Progs., July 1871, no. 56.
60. Mayo to Saunders, 13 Sept. 1871, Mayo Papers, reel 6.
61. Res. to For. Secy., tel., 16 Oct. 1871, For. Genl. A Progs., Oct. 1871, no. 42. 'Had the Nizam's Govt used the narrow gauge instead of the broad, as originally intended, the railway might have been completed at one-third of its present cost.' *Times of India*, 1 July 1872.
62. Mayo to Saunders, 28 Oct. 1871, Mayo Papers, reel 6.
63. For a more detailed account, see Bawa, 'Salar Jung and the Nizam's State Railway', pp. 316-23.
64. Res. to For. Secy., 12 April & 18 May 1872, For. Genl. A Consult., Sept. 1875, encl. no. 56.
65. Northbrook to Argyll, 17, 24 June 1872, Argyll Papers, reel 7.
66. Ibid.
67. Salar Jung to Res., & Keay, 20 July 1872, For. Genl. A Consult., Sept 1875, encl. no. 56. Lumsden told Salar Jung that the Govt of India was prepared to advance the money, but Salar Jung declined the offer. Draft of letter, Salar Jung to Palmer (n.d.), Salar Jung Papers, file no. 299/1.
68. Northbrook to Argyll, 29 July 1872, Argyll Papers, reel 7.
69. Salar Jung to Res., 7 April, 1872, For. Genl. A Consult., Sept. 1875, encl. no. 56.
70. Keay to Salar Jung, 26 July 1872, Salar Jung Papers, packet 18 B.
71 Report of W.T. Blanford on Madhavaram field, 6 July 1871, For. Genl. A Progs., Sept. 1871, no. 8; W. King's note on the Singareni coalfield, For. Genl. B. Progs., Sept. 1874, K.W. nos. 202-4; Heenam to P.W.D. Secy., Hyderabad Govt., 6 Oct. 1875, For Pol. A progs., Feb. 1882, no. 277. See also A.I. Quershi, *The Economic Development of Hyderabad* (Bombay, 1947), vol. I, pp. 17-18.
72. Memorandum by Salar Jung, 27 Sept. 1876, For. Genl. A Progs., Sept. 1878, no. 1 A.
73. For. Secy. to Res., 12 Oct. 1871; & Res. to For. Secy., tel., 16 Oct. 1871, For Genl. A Progs., Oct. 1871, nos. 41 & 42.
74. Keay to Bowen, 29 Oct. 1871, Salar Jung Papers, packet 18 A.

75. Res. to Offg. For. Secy., 24 July & 2 Dec. 1876, For. Genl. A Progs., Sept. 1876, no. 9 & For. Genl. A Progs., Sept. 1878, no. 1.

76. Office-note of Dickens, 22 April 1875, For. Genl. A Consult., Sept. 1875, K.W. Nos. 54-68.

77. English trans. of the Nizam's edict, *Daftar-i-Motamad-tameera* Records, file no. 4, 1292 *H*. (State Archives, Andhra Pradesh). It seems that Keay helped Salar Jung make the arrangements specifically designed to give the railway an 'indisputable legal status', without which no British subject would be interested in holding its shares. See Keay to Salar Jung, 11 Oct. 1872, Salar Jung Papers, packet 18 A.

78. Draft of letter, Salar Jung to the Directors of the Nizam's State Railway Company, 15 May, 1874, ibid.

79. V.K. Bawa, 'Salar Jung and the Nizam's State Railway 1860-1883', p. 324.

80. Draft of letter, Salar Jung to Seth Lakhmidas Lachmondas, May 1874, & memorandum by Salar Jung encl. this letter, Salar Jung Papers.

81. Smith, Fleming & Co., to W. Nicol & Co., 14 May 1875, ibid., packet 18 B.

82. Salisbury to Northbrook, 4 June 1875, Salisbury Papers, reel 7.

83. S.S. to Viceroy., tel., 6 April 1875, & Viceroy to S.S., tel., 26 April 1875, For. Genl. A Consult., Sept., 1875, nos. 54 & 55.

84. Salisbury to Northbrook, 4 June 1875, Salisbury Papers, reel 7.

85. Maxwell of W. Nicol & Co., to Bowen, 24 May, 10, 17 & 19 June 1875, Salar Jung Papers, packet 18 B. In a letter to Salar Jung, Keay enclosed a rough statement of the net proceeds of the Railway Company's shares issued in London and paid over to the Hyderabad Govt.

Issue made in London	Rs 50,00,000
Less Investment with trustees	Rs 15,00,000
	Rs 35,00,000
Deduct commission at 3%	Rs 1,05,000
Net proceeds of the share issue	Rs 33,95,000

   Keay to Salar Jung, 27 Jan. 1876, Ibid.

86. Northbrook to Salisbury, 28 Sept. & 13 Nov. 1875, Northbrook Papers, reel 14.

87. Salisbury to Northbrook, 15 Oct., & 10 Dec. 1875, Salisbury Papers, reel 7.

88. Pol Desp., S.S. to G.G., 21 Oct. 1875, For. Genl. A Progs., March 1876, no. 9.

89. Speech by Hamilton, 10 June 1875, *Hansard*, vol. 224, p. 1626.

90. Draft of letter, Salar Jung to Sutherland, 24 July 1877, Salar Jung Papers, file no. 297.

91. Keay believed that all the capital for the railway could be raised in England. Keay to Bowen, 3 March 1876, ibid., packet 18 B.

92. Salisbury to Lytton, 16 June 1876, Lytton Papers, reel 3. Fleming to S.S., 11 May 1876; & Managing Director, G.I.P. Co., to Fleming, 5 May 1876, For. Genl. A Progs., Sept. 1876, no. 8 & encl.

93. In the mid-1870's England was deep in a depression. There was a general rise in prices and those of iron and coal remained very high. See J.H. Clapham, *Economic History of Modern Britain* (Cambridge, 1932).

94. Speech by Hamilton, 10 Aug 1876, *Hansard*, vol. 231, p. 990.

95. Danvers's Railway Report for 1875-6, *P.P.C. 1585 of 1876*, p. 36.

96. Salisbury to Lytton, 16 June 1876, Lytton Papers, reel 3.

97. Maxwell to Oliphant, 26 July 1877, Salar Jung Papers, file no. 2007; Fleming to S.S., 15 Feb 1877, For. Genl. A Progs., Sept. 1878, no. 3.
98. Salisbury to Lytton, 16 Feb & 11 May 1877, Lytton Papers, reel 4.
99. Lytton to Salisbury, 16 March 1877, ibid., reel 6.
100. Meade to Lytton, 27 Feb. 1877, ibid., reel 11.
101. Lytton to Meade, 2 April 1877, ibid., reel 6.
102. Meade to Lytton, 13 April 1877, ibid., reel 11.
103. Lytton to Salisbury, 4, 10, & 18 June 1877, ibid., reel 6; Viceroy to S.S., tel., 17 May 1877, For. Genl. A Progs., Sept. 1878, no. 5. This official telegram was based on the views expressed by Meade.
104. Salisbury to Lytton, 18 & 25 May, 22 June 1877, Lytton Papers, reel 4. In his letter of 18 May, Salisbury criticized every argument put forward in the Viceroy's telegram against the loan.
105. Salisbury to Lytton, 1 & 22 June 1877, ibid.
106. For. Secy. to Res., tel., 20 July 1877; Salar Jung to Res., 7 Aug. 1877, For. Genl. A Progs., Sept. 1878, nos. 7 & 10. Smith, Fleming & Co., also advised Salar Jung to decline pecuniary assistance from the Govt of India. Maxwell to Oliphant, 29 Aug. 1877, Salar Jung Papers, file no. 2007.
107. John Bright (1811-89), orator and statesman; began the agitation in England against the Corn Law, 1842; President, Board of Trade, 1868-70; Chancellor of Duchy of Lancaster and Cabinet Member, 1880; resigned, 1882.
108. Speech by Bright, 22 Jan. 1878, *Hansard*, vol. 237, p. 346.
109. Memorandum by Salar Jung, 1288 *Fasli*, For. Pol. A Prog., Sept. 1881, no. 275.
110. Abdul Hak, Sirdar Diler Jung (1853-96), head of the P.W. & Mines Dept., Hyderabad Govt.
111. Abdul Hak's report to Salar Jung, 7 Nov. 1881, For. Pol. A Progs., Feb. 1882, no. 250. Charles Hawes was the agent of the syndicate. Hawes, E.W. Barnett, C.B. Forbes (a Bombay merchant) and C.A. Winter (a Bombay lawyer and Salar Jung's solicitor) signed the memorandum on behalf of the promoters. Ibid., no. 251.
112. The mining proposal was mooted by Winter. Winter to Salar Jung, 1 Nov. 1881, ibid., no. 254. Abdul Hak had arranged with the syndicate that he should get £120,000 for the railway and one-fourth of the interest in the mining concession. Evidence by Winter before the Select Committee, *P.P. 327 of 1888*, p. 69.
113. Salar Jung to First Asst. Res., 14 Nov. 1881; to Res., 4 Dec. 1881, For. Pol. A Progs., Feb. 1882, nos. 249, 257.
114. Offg. Res. to Offg. For. Secy., 3 Dec. 1881, memorandum by Jones; & Res. to For. Secy., tel., 9 Dec. 1881, ibid., nos. 248, 255 & 259.
115. Notes by Bayley, 26 Dec. 1881; & by Grant, 9 Jan. 1882, ibid., K.W. Nos. 248-81.
116. Confidential notes of Evelyn Baring, 18 & 22 Jan. 1882, ibid.
117. Ripon to Hartington, 27 Jan. & 7 June 1882, Ripon Papers, BP 7/3, vol. 3.
118. For. Secy. to Res., 7 Feb. 1882, For. Pol. A Progs., Feb. 1882, no. 279.
119. Confidential memorandum by Abdul Hak, 1 Oct. 1882; & memorandum by Salar Jung, 10 Jan. 1883, For. Sec. I Progs., May 1883, no. 1 & encl.
120. S.S. to Govt of India, 9 Nov. 1882; & confidential memorandum by Abdul Hak to S.S. (n.d.), For. Sec. I Progs., Jan. 1883, nos. 1, 2; Memorandum by Abdul Hak, 1 Jan. 1883, For. Sec. I Progs., May 1883, encl. no. 1.
121. Proposal of Morton, Rose & Co., 10 Nov. 1882, ibid.

122. Stewart was a director of the National Provicial Bank and the Ottoman Bank. Watson was the brother-in-law of Winter and belonged to the firm of Godban, Watson & Co.

123. The mining proposal, 7 Nov. 1882, For. Sec. I Progs., May 1883, encl. no. 1.

124. Memorandum by Salar Jung, 10 Jan. 1883, ibid.

125. Bayley to Ripon, 10 Oct. 1882, Ripon Papers, Add. MSS. 43 612.

126. Memorandum by Salar Jung, 10 Jan. 1883, For. Sec. I Progs., May 1883, encl. no. 1.

127. Col. Hastings Fraser, Military Secretary of the Residency, was reported to be ready to confirm that Salar Jung had yielded only to the pressure that was put upon him by Trevor and Abdul Hak. Keay thought that Salar Jung's approval was due partly to real or fancied pressure and partly to his having been completely deceived about the commercial success of the undertaking. *Hyderabad Affairs*, Sup. vol., p. 503. In an interesting letter to the House of Commons Knight wrote that Abdul Hak had been 'imported' from a subordinate position in British Indian service into Hyderabad by Meade 'as the instrument that was required for outraging Sir Salar Jung into retirement'. His Sirdarship and titles were the rewards for his service. One of Hak's brothers was the head of the Hyderabad police, another the head of the cantonment police, and his nephew was at the Residency itself. He had long had the whole Residency in his hands. R. Knight to House of Commons, 29 Jan. 1884, ibid., p. 500.

128. Hartington to Ripon, 12 Oct. 1882, Ripon Papers, Add. MSS. 43569. Hartington had advocated Baring's appointment to the Viceroy's Council. Hartington to Gladstone, 7 & 16 June 1880, Gladstone Papers, Add. MSS. 44145.

129. Ripon to Hartington, 3 Nov. 1882, Ripon Papers, BP 7/3, vol. 3.

130. Hartington to Ripon, 27 Oct. 1882, ibid., Add. MSS. 43569.

131. Jenks says that in the mid-1870's England was almost at the end of her surplus capital for investment abroad. Nonetheless, even after 1875 the migration of British capital proceeded mainly to South America, the Dominions, the USA and the Far East. This investment came from the accruing profits from those that had already been made. L.H. Jenks, *The Migration of British Capital to 1875* (London, 1963), pp 326-36. Clapham also says that from 1881 England was able to keep the greater part of the earnings of its foreign investments abroad for fresh investment. J.H. Clapham, op. cit., vol. 2, p. 235.

132. L.H. Jenks, op. cit., p. 336.

133. D. Thorner, op. cit., p. 120.

134. Ripon to Hartington, 14 Sept. 1882, Ripon Papers, BP 7/3, vol. 3.

135. See Ripon's interesting letters to Gladstone, 22 Oct. 1881 & 6 Oct. 1882, Gladstone Papers, Add. MSS. 44 286.

136. Res. to For. Secy., 27 Feb. 1883; For. Secy. to Res., tel., 9 March & 15 March 1883; and note by Charles Grant, 17 Feb. 1883, For. Sec. I Progs., May 1883, nos. 7, 12, 14 & K.W.I.

137. Viceroy to Res., tel., 8 April 1883, For. Sec. I Progs., June 1883, no. 1.

138. Res. to For. Secy., 10 & 26 April 1883, ibid., nos. 3 & 9. All the members of the Council of Regency were reportedly against the scheme. *Hyderabad Affairs*, sup. vol., pp. 468, 470-1, 510.

139. Res. to For. Secy., tel. (n.d.), For. Sec. I Progs., June 1883, no. 10.

140. For. Secy. to Res., 24 May 1883 & Sec. Desp., G.G. to S.S., 15 June 1883, ibid, nos. 16, 17.
141. *Hyderabad Affairs*, Sup. vol., pp 470-6.
142. Speeches by O'Donnell and J.K. Cross, 2 & 9 July 1883, *Hansard*, vol. 281, pp. 49, & 788.
143. Abdul Hak to Res., 20 July 1883, For. Sec. I Progs., Jan. 1884, no. 3. See also *Hyderabad Affairs*, sup. vol., p. 481.
144. Cordery to Ripon, 2 & 4 Dec. 1883, Ripon Papers, Add. MSS. 43613.
145. *Hyderabad Affairs*, sup. vol., p. 500.
146. Desp. S.S. to G.G., 21 Feb. 1884, For. Sec. I Progs., Aug. 1884, no. 27.
147. C.U. Aitchison, op. cit., pp 132-50.
148. Yule to the Editor of *The Times*, 2 Jan. (pubd. 3 Jan.), 1884.
149. O.B. John to Ripon, 29 April 1884, Ripon Papers, Add. MSS. 43 613. John seems to have been quite surprised to see Abdul Hak's letters to Cordery marked 'strictly private.' In these Abdul Hak mentioned that he had induced Laik Ali to take £241,666 worth of debentures in part payment of the cash payable by the Nizam's Guaranteed State Railway Co. 'I do not like the look of it', John wrote. He again reported to Ripon that 'as regards the railway—the balance payable in cash has faded into empty air, or strictly speaking into £14000.' Of £341,666, £241,666 were accepted in debentures, £86,000 were spent by Abdul Hak in preliminary expenses. O.B. John to Ripon, 19 & 29 April 1884, ibid.
150. On 3 April 1886 the line up to Warangal was opened for traffic and in Feb. 1888 the extension upto Singareni was opened for coal traffic. *Census of India, 1891* (Bombay, 1893), vol. XXIII, p. 13. The old line, hitherto managed by the Govt of India, was transferred to the Nizam's Guaranteed State Railway Co. by an agreement between the Indian Govt and the Nizam in May 1885. C.U. Aitchison, op. cit., pp 150-3.
151. Ibid. App. I, pp. i-xiii.
152. I have borrowed these words from L.H. Jenks, op. cit., p. 223. He uses these words in connexion with the guaranteed interest railways in India.
153. Elgin to Wood, 17 Aug. 1862, Elgin Papers, vol. 2.
154. D. Thorner, 'Pattern of Railway Development in India', in *Far Eastern Quarterly* (1955), reprinted in *The Shaping of Modern India* (Bombay, 1980), p. 124. Knowles eulogizes the railways and their effect on India. L.C.A. Knowles, *The Economic Development of the British Overseas Empire* (London, 1928), pp. 320-7. Vera Anstey is inclined to take the same view. Anstey, op. cit., p. 148. Connell and Dutt, on the other hand, are highly critical of the Indian Govt's railway policy and the effect of the railways on India's economy. A.K. Connell, *The Economic Revolution of India* (London, 1883), Part II; Romesh Dutt, *The Economic History of India in the Victorian Age* (London, 1950), Book I, Ch. XI, Book II, Ch. IX, & Book III, Chaps X & XIV. For an analysis of the impact of the British railway policy on Hyderabad state, see my article, 'The Genesis of Railway Development in Hyderabad State: A Case Study in Nineteenth Century British Imperialism, in *The Indian Economic and Social History Review* (1984), vol. 21, no. 1.

CONCLUSION

1. Canning to Wood, 18 June 1860, Canning Papers, vol. 40.
2. T. Walrond (ed.), *Letters and Journals of James, Eighth Earl of Elgin* (London, 1872), p. 396.
3. Michael Edwardes, *High Noon of Empire—India Under Curzon (London, 1965)*, p. 8.
4. G.B. Mullick (ed.), *Speeches in England and India by Earl of Mayo*, pp. 76-7.
5. T.H. Thornton, op. cit., p. 349.
6. S. Sideri, *Trade and Power : Informal Colonialism in Anglo-Portuguese Relations*, quoted in Rudy Bauss, 'A Legacy of British Free Trade Policies : The End of the Trade and Commerce between India and the Portuguese Empire, 1780-1830', *The Calcutta Historical Journa*, Vol. 6, no. 2, p. 81.
7. S. Bhattacharya, *Financial Foundations of the British Raj* (Simla, 1971), p. 17. This book gives an excellent account of the nature of 'pressure groups' and the system of lobbying.by 'interest groups' in Britain and India. See pp. xviii-xxxiii.
8. Salar Jung to Res., 14 April 1874, For. Rev. A Progs., Aug. 1874, no. 34; Salar Jung to Res., 26 Feb. & 29 March 1875; & For. Under Secy. to Res., 19 May 1875, For. Pol. A Consult., July 1875, nos. 2, 4 & 5.
9. Ripon to Kimberley, 2 April 1883, Ripon Papers, BP 7/3, vol. 4.
10. *Hyderabad Affairs*, vol. 3, p. 180.
11. Temple to Salar Jung, 20 May & 10 July 1867, Temple Collection, vol. 76.
12. Temple to Salar Jung, 18 July 1867, ibid.; Res. to For. Secy., 10 Dec. 1867, For. Genl. A Progs., Jan. 1868, no. 50.
13. Temple to Salar Jung, 20 Aug. 1867, Temple Collection, vol. 76.
14. Res. to For. Secy., 6 March 1869, For. Pol. A Progs., March 1869, no. 279; & Res. to For. Secy., 15 Dec. 1869, For. Pol. A Consult., Feb. 1870, no. 1.
15. Memorandum by Salar Jung, 1288 *F.*, For. Pol. A Progs., Sept. 1881, no. 275, & Statement showing the actual Diwani Revenue Receipts from 1287 *F.*, to 1291 *F.*, For. A Pol. I Progs., April 1884, no. 284.
16. Temple to Salar Jung, 1 Oct. 1867, Temple Collection, vol. 76.
17. Syed Hossain Bilgrani, Nawab Imad-ul-Mulk Bahadur (1844-1926), Professor of Arabic, Canning College, Lucknow, 1866-73; Private Secy. to Salar Jung till 1883; Private Secy. to Nizam, 1884; Director of Public Instruction for Hyderabad up to 1907; member, India Council, 1907–9; published *A Memoir of Sir Salar Jung* & *Historical Sketches of His Highness the Nizam's Dominions.*
18. *Hyderabad Affairs*, vol. 3, p. 154.
19. Ibid., Sup. Vol., p. 474.
20. Northbrook to Gladstone, 9 Sept. 1872, Gladstone Papers, Add. MSS. 44,266.

Glossary

abadee	revenue
abkaree	excise
Dewan	the Chief Minister of an Indian prince
durbar	the executive government of a princely state, his court.
dustaband	ornament for hand
enam	gift
fasil year	harvest year
faujdar	military commander
feringhee	European
firman	royal mandate
guttidari	revenue-farming
Halli Sicca	currency of Hyderabad State
hukumat	order of a superior
hundi	bill of exchange
jagir	estate
khillut	robe of honour presented by the superior authority to an inferior as a mark of distinction
khutba	Friday prayer or discourse
khureeta	a letter
mahal	a small administrative unit
maulavi	Muslim man of learning; master of Muslim Law
musnud	throne
nuzzur	gift from an inferior to a superior
paigah	household troops or bodyguards
pergana	small administrative unit; collection of villages
peshkar	deputy to Dewan
peshkush	tribute
radharry	transit duty
sanad	grant
sahukar	banker or moneylender
sarkar	administrative division; district
simt	an administrative unit; a circle
sirpesh	head ornament
suba	province

subabadar	provincial governor
surf-i-khas	crown-land
taluk	estate
talukdar	collector of revenue; one who holds an estate
vakil	agent, advocate
Wazier	Chief Minister
zillabandi	Salar Jung's division of land into *taluks, zillas* and *simts*

Bibliography

I. UNPUBLISHED SOURCES

A. Private Papers
(arranged according to repository)

a) BRITISH MUSEUM AND LIBRARY, LONDON

Gladstone Papers

Add. MSS. 44100–3, Correspondence with Duke of Argyll, 1865–76; Add. MSS. 44145–6, Correspondence with Marquess of Hartington, 1879–83; Add. MSS. 44266–7, Correspondence with Earl of Northbrook, 1868–85; Add. MSS. 44286–7, Correspondence with Marquess of Ripon, 1853–97; Add. MSS. 44185–6, Correspondence with Sir Charles Wood, 1870–85.

Iddesleigh Papers

Add. MSS. 50016, Correspondence with Disraeli, 1868–74; Add. MSS. 50023–6, Correspondence with Sir John Lawrence, 1867–8.

Palmerston Papers

Add. MSS. 48580, Correspondence with the Chairman of the East India Company, the President of the Board of Control and the Governor-General, 1856–7.

Ripon Papers

Second Series. Add. MSS. 43565–9, Correspondence with Marquess of Hartington, 1880–1904; Add. MSS. 43523–5, Correspondence with Earl of Kimberley, 1883–4; Add. MSS. 43602–3, Correspondence with A. C. Lyall, 1880–1909; Add. MSS. 43604, Correspondence with C. G. Grant, 1880–4; Add. MSS. 43612, Correspondence with S. C. Bayley, 1881–4; Add. MSS. 43613, Correspondence with J. G. Cordery, 1883–4, and Correspondence with Sir O. B. Coventry St. John, 1881–4; Add. MSS. 43596–8, Correspondence with Major Evelyn Baring, 1880–3; Add. MSS. 43570–2, Correspondence with Earl of Northbrook, 1873–83; BP 7/3 Correspondence with the Secretary of State, 1880–4; BP 7/6, Correspondence with Persons in India.

b)   CENTRAL LIBRARY, LEEDS

Papers of Lord Canning

Vol. I, Letters from and to the Queen, 1856–61; Vol. 2, Letters from H. M.'s Ministers, 1856–62; Vol. 3, Letters from the Court of Directors, 1856–8; Vol. 4, Letters from the President of the Board of Control, 1856–8; Vols. 6, 8 & 11, Letters from the Secretary of State, 1858–62; Vol. 30, Letters to H. M.'s Ministers, 1856–62; Vol. 31, Letters to the Court of Directors, 1856–9; Vols. 32–4, Letters to the President of the Board of Control, 1857–8; Vols. 36, 38, 40 & 42, Letters to the Secretary of State, 1858–62; Vols. 61–3, Miscellaneous letters to persons in India, 1859–62; Vol. 64, Miscellaneous letters to persons in Europe, 1856–62.

c)   INDIA OFFICE LIBRARY, LONDON

Sir Charles Wood Papers (MSS.Eur.F.78)

India Board Letter Books, 1853–6, .Vols. 3–7; India Office Letter Books, 1859–66, Vols. 1–22.
India Office Correspondence. Letters from the Queen, 1858–64, Vol.60/1, Letters from Sir W. Dension, 1860–6, Vols. 87/1–87/6, Letters from Sir H. B. Frere, 1862, Vols. 88/3–88/4; Letters from Cecil Beadon, 1860–5, Vols. 89/1–89/3

Papers of the Eighth Earl of Elgin (MSS.Eur.F.83)

Section I, Part I. Vols. 1–5, Letters to Secretary of State, 1862–3.
Section I, Part II. Vol. 17, Letters to Miscellaneous, 1862–3; Vol. 24, Letters from Miscellaneous, 1861–3.
Section I, Part IV, Vol. 30, Letters to the Queen.

Claude Clerk Collection (MSS.Eur.D.538)

Bundle no. 13, Letters from Claude Clerk to his brother John Clerk and to his father Sir George Clerk, and miscellaneous letters to Clerk (1874–89); bundle no. 14, letters from Sir Richard Meade, 1877–81.

Richard Temple Collection (MSS.Eur.F.86)

Part I, Section D, Papers relating to Sir Richard Temple's period of office as Resident of Hyderabad in 1867.
Vol. 76, Demi-official Letters, Hyderabad Residency; Vol. 77, Letters from Salar Jung; Vol. 81, Political Diary: Hyderabad; Vol. 84, Manuscript of Journals kept in Hyderabad, Sikkim and Nepal.

d)   NATIONAL ARCHIVES OF INDIA, NEW DELHI (microfilm copies
     of private papers)

Argyll Papers

Reels 1–4, Letters from Mayo, 1868–72; Reel 6, Letters from Government of

Bombay 1872–4, Correspondence with Northbrook, 1872; Reels 7–8, Correspondence with Northbrook, 1873–5.

Curzon Papers

Reel 1, Correspondence with the Queen-Empress, 1898–1901, Correspondence with the King-Emperor, 1901–5, Correspondence with the Secretary of State, 1898–1900; Reels 2–3, Correspondence with the Secretary of State, 1900–3.

Dalhousie Papers

Reel 10, Letters from the Board of Control, 1850–4; Reels 21–2, Letters despatched, 1850–3.

Lawrence Papers

Reel 1, Letters from the Secretary of State, 1864–7; Reel 2, Letters from the Secretary of State, 1868, Letters to the Secretary of State, 1865–6; Reel 3, Letters to the Secretary of State, 1867–9; Reel 11, Letters to and from the Agents, Residents and Chief Commissioners, 1864–9.

Lytton Papers

Here the numbers on the reels do not always coincide with the numbers given in the index. I have mentioned the numbers marked on the reels.
Reel 3, Letters to and from the Queen, 1878–80, Letters from the Secretary of State, 1876; Reel 4, Letters from the Secretary of State, 1877–8; Reel 5, Letters from the Secretary of State, 1879–80, Letters despatched, 1876; Reels 6–8, Letters despatched, 1876–9; Reel 9, Letters despatched, 1880, Correspondence in India, 1876; Reels 10–18, Correspondence in India, 1876–80; Reel 19, Correspondence in India, 1880, Minutes and notes, 1876–7; Reel 20, Minutes and Notes, 1878–80.

Mayo Papers

Reels 1–6, Letters despatched, 1868–72; Reel 7, Letters from the Duke of Argyll, 1868–9.

Northbrook Papers

Reel 1, Correspondence with Ripon, 1881–3; Reel 3, Letters to the Queen, 1872–6; Reel 4, Correspondence with Duke of Argyll, 1872–4, Telegrams to and from Duke of Argyll, 1873–4, Correspondence with Marquess of Salisbury, 1874–6; Reels 5–8, Correspondence with persons in India, 1872–80.

Salisbury Papers

Reel 7, Letters to Northbrook and Lytton, 1874–7.

e) STATE ARCHIVES, ANDHRA PRADESH

Salar Jung Papers

There are innumerable letters, drafts of letters, files and despatches. The papers were consulted when the catalogue was still in the process of preparation. I have tried, as far as possible, to mention in the notes the numbers of files or packets in which I found them. These may now have been renumbered.

B.   Official Records
(arranged according to repository)

a) INDIA OFFICE LIBRARY

Letter Books from the Board of Control, 1857–8, F/2/20
Minutes of the Court of Director and Proprietors, 1856–8, B/233-B/236
General Correspondence
Correspondence with India, Letters received from India and Bengal, 1857–8, E/4/267–E/4/288
Letters from the Company to the Board of Control, 1856–8, E/2/24–E/2/27
Letters from the Board of Control to the Company, 1856–8, E/2/48–E/2/50.

b) NANATIONAL ARCHIVES OF INDIA, NEW DELHI

The Records of the Government of India in the Foreign Department, 1858–84.
Foreign Consultations, Foreign Finance Proceedings, Foreign General Consultations, Foreign General Proceedings, Foreign Part A and Part B Proceedings, Foreign Political Consultations, Foreign Political Proceedings, Foreign Judicial Proceedings, Foreign Military Proceedings, Foreign Revenue Proceedings, Foreign Secret Consultations, Foreign Secret Proceedings, Foreign Secret Supplementary Proceedings.

Despatches to and from the Court of Directors, 1858
Despatches to and from the Secretary of State, 1858–84

Hyderabad Residency Records
There are many volumes of these records. Of some use to me have been vols. 72, 79, 88, 91, 97, 102, 106, 107, 486, 514, 655, 670, 678, 825 & 830.

c) STATE ARCHIVES, ANDHRA PRADESH

Records in His Highness the Nizam's Government Private Secretary's Office. *Daftar-i-Motamad-tameerat* Records (only English records were consulted).
These records were not catalogued when I consulted them.

II. PUBLISHED SOURCES

A. Parliamentary Papers
(House of Commons)

Nizam's Territory, 418 of 1854, vol. 47; Annexation of Berar, 82 of 1856, vol. 45; Marquis of Dalhousie, 245 of 1856, vol. 45; Railways (India), 787 of 1852–3, vol. 76; The Nizam, 234 of session I, 1859, vol. 40; The Deccan, 338 of 1867, vol. 30; Cession of Berar, 29 of 1867–68, vol. 49; Railway Extensions, 156 of 1871, vol. 51; Railway Reports by the Director of the Indian Railways Companies to the Secretary of State, C.418 of 1871, vol. 51, C.1854 of 1876, vol. 56; East India Finance, 329 of 1874, vol. 8; Famine Correspondence, 298 of 1878, vol. 59; Famine Commission, C.3086 of 1881, vol. 71; Statement showing the lengths opened and the general results of working of all Indian Railways for the five years from 1876 to 1880, C.3172 of 1882, vol. 49; Hyderabad Deccan Mining Company, 177 and 327 of 1888, vol. 11; Hyderabad, C.1321 of 1902, vol. 71.

B. Debates

Hansard's Parliamentary Debates, Third Series, especially vols. 148–9, 151–2, 154–6, 158–60, 162–3, 167–9, 172, 176–7, 180, 184, 186–7, 189, 198–9, 202, 204, 214, 222–4, 229, 231–2, 235–8, 240–1, 243, 255, 266, 268 and 281.

C. Official Reports and Publications

Administration Report of His Highness the Nizam's Dominions for 1294 F. (1884–85 A.D.) (Bombay, 1886)

Aitchison, C. U., *A Collection of Treaties, Engagements and Sanads* (Calcutta, 1909), vol. IX.

Beaumont, T., *Report on the Medical Department of His Highness the Nizam's Government for the year 1293 F. (1883–84)* (Hyderabad Residency, 1884).

Burton, Major R. G., *A History of the Hyderabad Contingent* (Calcutta, 1905).

Census of India, 1891, His Highness the Nizam's Dominions (Bombay, 1894), vol. 23, parts I–III.

Central Provinces and Berar District Gazetteers (Calcutta, 1906–12), vol. A.

Cotton Report of the Hyderabad Assigned Districts, 1877/8 – 1882/3 (Hyderabad, 1879–83).

Dunlop, A. J., *Inspection Report of the Customs Department of His Highness the Nizam's Government* (Hyderabad, 1885).

Garrett, Major R. V., *Monograph on Cotton Fabrics in the Hyderabad Assigned Districts* (Hyderabad, 1897).

Hunter, W. W., *Imperial Gazetteer of India* (London, 1881), vol. 3.

Hyderabad Papers (Hyderabad, 1819).

Imperial Gazetteer of India. Provincial Series. Hyderabad State (Calcutta, 1909)

Joshi, P. M. & M. A. Nayeem (eds.), *Studies in the Foreign Relations of India: Prof. H. K. Sherwani Felicitation Volume* (Hyderabad, 1975).

Malcolm, D. A., *Sketch of the History of the Asuphea Dynasty and its Political Connection with the Government of British India* (Hyderabad Residency, 1843).

Mirza Khurshid, *A Brief Outline of the Geological History of the State with Special Reference to its Mineral Resources* (Hyderabad, 1943).

Report on the Administration of His Highness the Nizam's Dominions for 1303 Fasli (1893–94) (Bombay, 1893).

Some Notes on the Hyderabad Residency (Hyderabad, n.d.).

The Chronology of Modern Hyderabad, 1720–1830 (Hyderabad, 1954).

The Freedom Struggle in Hyderabad (Hyderabad, 1956), 2 vols.

Wheeler, J. T., *Summary of Affairs of the Government of India in the Foreign Department from 1864–69* (Calcutta, 1868).

Wilson, H. H., *A Glossary of Judicial and Revenue Terms, and of Useful Words Occurring in Official Documents Relating to the Administration of the Government of British India, from the Arabic, Persian, Hindusthani, Sanskrit, Telegu, Karnataka, Tamil, Malayalam, and other Languages* (London, 1855).

D. Newspapers (National Library, Calcutta)

Bombay Telegraph and Courier
Englishman
Friend of India and Statesman
Pioneer
The Statesman
Times
Times of India

E. Books and Tracts

Aitchison, C. U., *Lord Lawrence and the Reconstruction of India under the Crown* (Oxford, 1899).

Anstey, Vera Powel, *The Economic Development of India* (London, 1949).

Argyll, 8th Duke of, *India under Dalhousie and Canning* (London, 1865).

Ali, Moulavi Cherag, *Hyderabad (Deccan) under Sir Salar Jung* (Bombay, 1886), 4 vols.

Ali, Moulavi Syed Mahdi (compiled), *Hyderabad Affairs* (Bombay, 1883–86 & 1889), 10 vols. & Supplementary vol.

Arnold, E., *The Marquis of Dalhousie's Administration of British India* (London, 1862), 2 vols.

Ashton, S. R., *British Policy Towards the Indian States, 1905–1939* (London, 1982)

Baird, J. G. A. (ed.), *Private Letters of the Marquess of Dalhousie* (Edinburgh, 1911).

Balfour, Lady Betty, *The History of Lord Lytton's Indian Administration, 1876 to 1880* (London, 1899).

—— (ed.), *Personal and Literary Letters of Robert, First Earl of Lytton* (London, 1906), 2 vols.

Bell, Major Evans, *Retrospects and Prospects of Indian Policy* (London, 1868).

—— *Our Great Vassal Empire* (London, 1870).

Bhattacharya, Sabyasachi, *Financial Foundations of the British Raj* (Simla, 1971).

Bilgrami, Syed Hossain, *A Memoir of Sir Salar Jung, G.C.S.I.* (Bombay, 1883).

—— & C. Willmott, *Historical and Descriptive Sketch of His Highness the Nizam's Dominions* (Bombay, 1883–84), 2 vols.

Blunt, W. S., *India under Ripon. A Private Diary* (London, 1909).

Briggs, H. G., *The Nizam. His History and Relations with the British Government* (London, 1861), 2 vols.

Buckland, C. E., *Dictionary of Indian Biography* (London, 1906).

Burne, General Sir O. T., *Memoirs* (London, 1907).

Campbell, A. C., *Glimpses of the Nizam's Dominions* (Bombay, 1898).

Chapman, J., *The Cotton and Commerce of India, considered in relation to the interests of Great Britain* (London, 1851).

Chatterji, P. K., *The Making of India Policy* (Burdwan, 1975).

Chaudhuri, K. N., *The Economic Development of India under the East India Company 1814–58; a Selection of Contemporary Writings* (Cambridge, 1971).

Chaudhury, N. G., *British Relations with Hyderabad, 1798–1843* (Calcutta, 1964).

Chaudhury, S. B., *Civil Rebellion in the Indian Mutinies 1857–59* (Calcutta, 1957).

Chudgar, P. L., *Indian Princes under British Protection* (London, 1929).

Clapham, Sir J. H., *An Economic History of Modern Britain* (Cambridge, 1928–38), 3 vols.

Coen, T. C., *The Indian Political Services: A Study in Indirect Rule* (London, 1971).

Connell, A. K., *Economic Revolution of India* (London, 1883).

Copland, Ian, *The British Raj and the Indian Princes: Paramountcy in Western India, 1857–1930* (Bombay, 1982).

Cotton, A., *Public Works in India: their importance. With suggestions for their Extension and Improvement* (Madras, 1885).

Dickinson, John, *Remarks on the Indian Railway Reports Published by the Government and Reasons for a Change of Policy in India* (London, 1862).

—— *Last Counsels of an Unknown Councillor* (London, 1877).

—— *A Letter to Lord Stanley on the Policy of the Secretary of State for India* (London, 1863).

Dutt, Romesh, *The Economic History of India in the Victorian Age* (London. 1950).

Edwardes, Michael, *High Noon of Empire: India under Curzon* (London. 1965).

Forrest, G. W., *A History of the Indian Mutiny* (London, 1904–12), 3 vols.

Fraser, Hastings, *Our Faithful Ally, the Nizam* (London, 1865).

——, *Memoir and Correspondence of General James Stuart Fraser* (London. 1885).

Furber, Holden (ed.), *The Private Record of an Indian Governor Generalship* (Cambridge, 1955).

——, *John Company at Work. A Study of European Expansion in India in the Late Eighteenth Century* (London, 1951).

Gallagher, J. A., Gordon Johnson and Anil Seal (eds.), *Locality, Province and Nation: Essays on Indian Politics, 1870 to 1940* (Cambridge, 1973).

Gopal, S., *The Viceroyalty of Lord Ripon, 1880–1884* (London, 1953).

——, *British Policy in India, 1858–1905* (Cambridge, 1965).

Greenberg, M., *British Trade and the Opening of China, 1800–1842* (Cambridge, 1951).

Gribble, J. D. B., *A History of the Deccan* (London, 1896 & 1924), 2 vols.

——, *Two Native States, Hyderabad and Mysore* (Madras, 1886).

Guha, R., *Subaltern Studies I: Writings on South Asian History and Society* (Delhi, 1982).

Habib, I., *The Agrarian System of Mughal India* (Bombay, 1964).

Hunter, W. W., *A Life of the Earl of Mayo, 4th Viceroy of India* (London, 1876). 2 vols.

Hutchins, Francis G., *The Illusion of Permanence: British Imperialism in India* (Princeton, 1967).

Hyderabad in 1890 and 1891. Letters Written to Madras Hindu by its Hyderabad Correspondent (Bangalore, 1892).

Jackson, Sir Charles, *A Vindication of the Marquess of Dalhousie's Indian Administration* (London, 1865).

Jeffrey, Robin (ed.), *People, Princes and Paramount Power* (Delhi, 1978).

Jenks, Leland H., *Migration of British Capital to 1875* (London, 1963).

Kaye, J. W., *The Life and Correspondence of Charles, Lord Metcalfe* (London, 1858), 2 vols.

—— & Malleson, G. B., *History of the Indian Mutiny* (London, 1878–80), 3 vols.

Kennedy, A. L., *Salisbury (1830–1903): Portrait of a Statesman* (London, 1953).

Khan, Fathulla M., *A History of Administrative Reforms in Hyderabad State* (Secunderabad, 1935).

Khan, Yusuf Husain, *The First Nizam; The Life and Times of Nizamu'l Mulk Asaf Jah I* (Bombay, 1963).

Knowles, L. C. A., *The Economic Development of the British Overseas Empire* (London, 1928).

Krishnaswamy Mudiraj, K. (compiled), *Pictoral Hyderabad* (Hyderabad, 1929–34), 2 vols.

Law, John, *Modern Hyderabad* (Calcutta, 1914).

Lee-Warner, Sir William, *The Life of the Marquis of Dalhousie* (London, 1904), 2 vols.

——, *The Native States of India* (London, 1910).

Lethbridge, Sir Roper, *The Golden Book of India* (London, 1893).

Low, Sir Sidney, *The Indian States and the Ruling Princes* (London, 1929).

Maclagan, Michael, *Clemency Canning* (London, 1962).

Majumdar, R. C., *The Sepoy Mutiny and the Revolt of 1857* (Calcutta, 1957).

——, (ed.), *British Paramountcy and Indian Renaissance. The History and Culture of the Indian People* (Bombay, 1963).

Malleson, Col. G. B., *An Historical Sketch of the Native States of India in Subsidiary Alliance with the British Government* (London, 1875).

Mallet, B., *Thomas George, Earl of Northbrook* (London, 1908).

Maltby, F. N., *Memorial to the Governor-General* (London, 1858).

Martin, R. M., *The Despatches, Minutes and Correspondence of the Marquess Wellesley* (London, 1936–37), 5 vols.

Marx, Karl and Engels, F., *The First Indian War of Independence* (Moscow, 1960).

Metcalfe, T. R., *The Aftermath of Revolt: India, 1857–1870* (Princeton, 1964).

Moneypenny, W. F. and Buckle, G. E., *The Life of Benjamin Disraeli, Earl Beaconsfied* (London, 1919–20), 6 vols.

Moore, R. J., *Sir Charles Wood's Indian Policy, 1853–66* (Manchester, 1966).

Morley, John, *The Life of William Ewart Gladstone* (London, 1903), 3 vols.

Morrison, J. L., *The Eighth Earl of Elgin. A Chapter in Nineteenth-Century Imperial History* (London, 1928).

Moulton, E. C., *Lord Northbrook's Indian Administration, 1872–1876* (Bombay, 1968).

Mullick, G. B., *Lord Northbrook and His Mission in India* (Calcutta, 1873).

—— (ed.), *Speeches in England and India by Earl of Mayo* (Calcutta, 1873).

Nayeem, M. A., *History of Postal Administration in Hyderabad* (Hyderabad, 1970).

Nicholson, A. P., *Scraps of Paper: India's Broken Treaties, Her Princes and the Problem* (London, 1930).

Pal, Dharm, *Administration of Sir John Lawrence in India* (Simla, 1952).

Palmer, J., *Sovereignty and Paramountcy in India* (London, 1930).

Panikkar, K. N., *An Introduction to the Study of the Relations of Indian States with the Government of India* (London, 1927).

——, *The Evolution of British Policy Towards Indian States, 1774–1858* (Calcutta, 1929).

——, *Indian States* (London, 1942).

Phadnis, Urmila, *Toward the Integration of Indian States, 1919–1947* (London, 1968).

Philips, C. H., *The East India Company, 1784–1834* (Manchester, 1940).

Prasad, Nandan, *Paramountcy under Dalhousie* (Delhi, 1964)

Qureshi, A. I., *The Economic Development of Hyderabad* (Bombay, 1947), 2 vols.

Ramusack, Barbara N., *The Princes of India in the Twilight of Empire* (Columbus, Ohio, 1978).

Regani, Sarojini, *Nizam–British Relations, 1724–1857* (Secunderabad, 1963).

Remarks on the Political Relations of the British Government with Hyderabad and Other Allied States of India by a Proprieter of East India Stock.

Ronaldshay, The Earl of, *The Life of Lord Curzon* (London, 1928), 3 vols.

Ross, C. (ed.), *Correspondence of Charles, First Marquis Cornwallis* (London, 1859), 3 vols.

Sanyal, N., *Development of Indian Railways* (Calcutta, 1930).

Sastry, K. R. R., *Indian States* (Allahabad, 1941).

Savarkar, V. D., *The Indian War of Independence*, 1857 (Bombay, 1947).

Sen, D. K. Sirdar, *The Indian States* (London, 1930).

Sen, S. N., *Eighteen Fifty-Seven* (New Delhi, 1957).

Sen, S. P., *The French in India* (Calcutta, 1958).

Server-ul-Mulk Bahadur, *My Life*. Translated by his son, Nawab Jiwan Yar Jung Bahadur (London, 1932).

Silver, Arthur, *Manchestermen and Indian Cotton, 1847–72* (Manchester, 1965).

Singh, Laxman, *Political and Constitutional Development in the Princely States of Rajasthan, 1920–1949* (New Delhi, 1970).

Singh, St. Nihal, *The Nizam and the British Empire* (privately printed for the author, 1923).

Smith, R. B., *The Life of Lord Lawrence* (London, 1883), 2 vols.

Stephen, Sir Leslie and Sir Sidney Lee (eds.), *The Dictionary of National Biography, from the Earliest Times to 1900* (London).

Stokes, Eric, *The English Utilitarians and India* (Oxford, 1959).

—— *The Peasant and the Raj: Studies in Agrarian Society and Peasant Rebellion in Colonial India* (Cambridge, 1978).

Strachey, Sir John, *India* (London, 1888).

—— and Lt. Gen. Richard, Strachey, *The Finances and Public Works of India from 1869 to 1881* (London, 1882).

Taleyerkhan, Dinshah Ardeshir, *The Jubilee Dawn in Nizam's Hyderabad, 1887* (Bombay, 1887).

Taylor, Col. Meadows, *The Story of My Life* (London, 1877), 2 vols.

Temple, Sir Richard, *Men and Events of My Time in India* (London, 1882).

——, *The Story of My Life* (London, 1896), 2 vols.

Thompson, Edward J., *The Making of the Indian Princes* (Oxford, 1943).

Thorner, Daniel, *Investment in Empire. British Railway and Steamshipping Enterprise in India, 1825–1849* (Philadelphia, 1950).

———, *The Shaping of Modern India* (New Delhi, 1980).

Thornton, H. T., *General Sir Richard Meade and the Feudatory States of Central and Southern India* (London, 1898).

Tripathi, Amales, *Trade and Finance in the Bengal Presidency, 1793–1883* (Calcutta, 1979).

Tupper, Sir Charles, *Our Indian Protectorate* (London, 1893).

Vadivelu, A., *The Ruling Chiefs, Nobles and Zemindars of India* (Madras, 1915).

Walrond, T. (ed.), *Letters and Journals of James, Eighth Earl of Elgin* (London, 1872).

Wedderburn, Sir D., *Protected Princes in India* (London, 1914).

West, A., *Sir Charles Wood's Administration of Indian Affairs from 1859 to 1866* (London, 1867).

——— *Recollections 1832 to 1886* (London, 1899).

Wheeler, J. T., *The History of the Imperial Assemblage at Delhi, held on the 1st January, 1877* (London, n.d.)

Wolf, Lucien, *Life of the First Marquess of Ripon* (London, 1921), 2 vols.

Wrong, G. M., *The Earl of Elgin* (London, 1905).

Yazdani, Zubaida, *Hyderabad during the Residency of Henry Russell, 1811–1820; A Case Study of the Subsidiary Alliance* (Oxford, 1976).

F. Articles

Anonymous, 'Hyderabad, the Nizam's Contingent', *Calcutta Review,* vol. 11 (1849).

Anonymous, 'The Nizam's Dominions', *Calcutta Review,* vol. 52 (1871).

Anonymous, 'In the Nizam's Country', *Calcutta Review,* vol. 63 (1876).

Bauss, Rudy, 'A Legacy of British Free Trade Policies: The End of the Trade and Commerce between India and the Portuguese Empire, 1780–1830', *The Calcutta Historical Journal* (1982), vol. 6, no. 2

Bawa, V. K., 'Salar Jang and the Nizam's State Railway 1860–1883', *The Indian Economic and Social History Review* (1965), vol. 2, no. 4

——— 'The French in India' in P. M. Joshi and M. A. Nayeem (eds.) *Studies in the Foreign Relations of India* (Hyderabad, 1975).

Bhattacharya, Sabyasachi, '*Laissez Faire* in India', *The Indian Economic and Social History Review* (1965), vol. 2, no. 1.

Brebner, J. Bartlet, '*Laissez Faire* and State Intervention in Nineteenth Century Britain', *The Journal of Economic History* (1948), vol. 8.

Cohn, Bernard S., 'Political System in Eighteenth Century India: The Banaras Region', *Journal of American Oriental Society* (1962), vol. 82.

———, 'Representing Authority in Victorian India' in Eric Hobsbawm and Terence Ranger (eds.), *The Invention of Tradition* (Cambridge, 1863).

D. W. K. B., 'The Indian Opium Revenue', *Calcutta Review*, vol. 63, (1876)

Elliott, Carolyn M., 'Decline of a Patrimonial Regime: The Telengana Rebellion in India, 1946–51', *Journal of Asian Studies* (1974), vol. 34, no. 1.

Gallagher, J. A. and Robinson, R., 'The Imperialism of Free Trade', *Economic History Review* (1953), vol. 6.

Hurd, John II, 'The Economic Consequences of Indirect Rule in India', and 'The Influence of British Policy on Industrial Development in the Princely States of India, 1890–1933', *The Indian Economic and Social History Review* (1975), vol. 12, nos. 2 & 4.

Lal, K. Sajun, 'Sir Salar Jung's Visit to England and the Berar Question, *Journal of Osmania University, Golden Jubilee Volume* (1968).

Leonard, Karen, 'The Hyderabad Political System and Its Participants', *Journal of Asian Studies* (1971), vol. 30.

——, 'British Impact on Hyderabad: Cultural Change and Bureaucratic Modernisation in the 19th Century Hyderabad: Mulkis, Non-Mulkis and the Ensligh', in P. M. Joshi and M. A. Nayeem (eds.), *Studies in the Foreign Relations of India: Prof. H. K. Sherwani Fellicitation Volume* (Hyderabad, 1975).

——, 'Hyderabad: The Mulki–Non-Mulki Conflict', Robin Jeffrey (ed.), *People, Princes and Paramount Power* (Delhi, 1978):

Macpherson, W. J., 'Investment in Indian Railways, 1845–1875', *The Economic History Review*, Second series (1955), vol. 8.

Manor, James, 'Princely Mysore before the Storm: The State-level Political System of India's Model State, 1920–1936', *Modern Asian Studies* (1975), vol. 9.

Qanungo, Bhupen, 'A Study of British Relations with the Native States of India, 1858–62', *Journal of Asian Studies* (1967), vol. 26.

Ray, Bharati, 'Salar Jung, Berar and the British', *The Calcutta Historical Journal*, vol. 2, no. 1 (1977).

—— 'The Politics of Imperialism: Lord Lytton and Sir Salar Jung', *Bengal Past and Present*, vol. C II, January–June, 1983.

—— 'The Genesis of Railway Development in Hyderabad: A Case Study of British Imperialism in India', *The Indian Economic and Social History Review*, vol. 21, no. 1, January–March, 1984.

—— 'A Reward That Was Not: An Examination of the Anglo-Nizam Treaty of 1860', *The Calcutta Historical Journal*, vol. 8, nos. 1–2, July 1983–June, 1984.

—— 'The Politics of Paramountcy: Lord Northbrook and Hyderabad State, 1872–1876', *The Quarterly Review of Historical Studies*, vol. 24, no. 1, 1984–85.

—— 'The Politics of Indirect Rule: Lord Ripon and Hyderabad State, 1880–1884', *India Past and Present*, vol. 2, no. 1, 1985.

Regani, Sarojini, 'An Unpublished Letter of the Resident Henry Russell, 1811–20', and 'The Appointment of *Diwan* in Hyderabad State (1803–87);, *Andhra Historical Research Society Journal* (1958–60), vol. 25.

Rudolf, L. I. and S. H., 'Rajputana under British Paramountcy; The Failure of Indirect Rule', *Journal of Modern History* (1966), vol. 38.
Tomlinson, B. R., 'India and the British Empire, 1880–1935', *The Indian Economic and Social History Review*, vol. 12, 1975.

Index

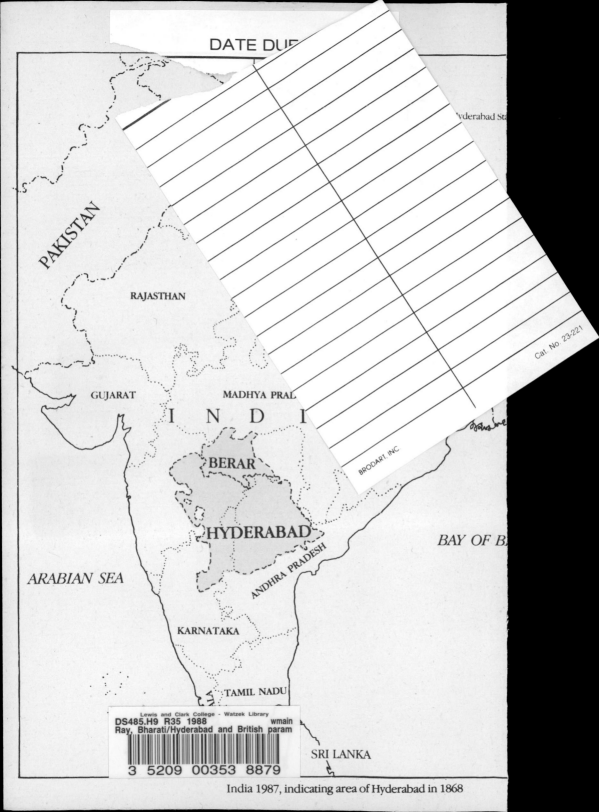

PAKISTAN

RAJASTHAN

GUJARAT

MADHYA PRAD

I N D I

BERAR

HYDERABAD

ANDHRA PRADESH

ARABIAN SEA

KARNATAKA

TAMIL NADU

BAY OF B

SRI LANKA

yderabad Sta

Cat. No. 23-221

BRODART, INC

India 1987, indicating area of Hyderabad in 1868